CONTEMPORARY PROBATION PRACTICE

For Jimmy, Judy and Jenni.

Contemporary Probation Practice

GWYNETH BOSWELL

MARTIN DAVIES

ANDREW WRIGHT

School of Social Work, University of East Anglia, Norwich

Avebury

Aldershot • Brookfield USA • Hong Kong • Singapore • Sydney

Published by
Avebury
Ashgate Publishing Limited
Gower House
Croft Road
Aldershot
Hants GU11 3HR
England

Ashgate Publishing Comp:
Old Post Road
Brookfield
Vermont 05036
USA

Typeset by
Neville Young
49 Muswell Avenue
London N10 2EH

British Library Cataloguing in Publication Data

Boswell, Gwyneth
    Contemporary Probation Practice
    I. Title
    364.6

    ISBN 1 85628 451 4

Printed and Bound in Great Britain by
Athenaeum Press Ltd, Newcastle upon Tyne.

1 Probation training: a consumer perspective

I   The survey

This survey is the first of four research studies carried out during 1987–89 at the University of East Anglia, Norwich under contract with the Home Office. The overall aim was to identify the kinds of skills, knowledge and qualities which probation officers use in their work, and to consider the implications of the findings for training, practice and management.

This study focuses its attention on a sample of newly qualified officers in order to seek their opinions about the training they received and their experience of the first year in post as probation officers. It is not assumed that they give wholly 'objective' evidence about either training or practice, but it is argued that their collective view constitutes a relevant and reliable perspective that ought not to be ignored. In particular, they are uniquely placed as the consumers of training and of the novitiate year to express a view about the relevance of both to the service's role as they interpret it.

The inescapable conclusion drawn by this survey of the experience of over 450 of these newly qualified officers is that CQSW courses have failed to meet the needs of probation students for a practice-relevant training.

II   The sample

Full methodological details are contained in Appendix 1 at the end of this chapter. The sample was drawn from the total population of those serving probation officers in England and Wales who had completed their training in 1985 and 1986. We had responses from 457 probation officers, a highly satisfactory response rate of 85%. Of these, 322 had been student probation officers in receipt of Home Office sponsorship; 62 had been unsponsored students on courses which attracted Home Office sponsorship; 14 had attended

1

other CQSW courses on which a probation option was available; and 59 had been on courses where there was no explicit commitment to cater for would-be probation officers.

Analyses based on tables 1.1–1.12 use a sub-sample of 398 respondents, with no account taken of the 59 ex-students who entered the probation service having been trained on CQSW courses ineligible for Home Office sponsorship and not claiming to offer a 'probation option'. This approach ensures that the findings can be said to apply unambiguously to those courses which explicitly claim to be providing a probation-relevant training facility.

After the sub-section containing table 1.12, the analysis is based on the full sample of 457, irrespective of whether they had attended probation-relevant courses.

46 per cent of the total sample had attended a graduate course; 46 per cent a non-graduate course; and 8 per cent had been on four-year first degree courses incorporating the award of the CQSW. A quarter of the graduates had completed their training in one year; the rest, and all the non-graduates, had taken two years.

99 per cent of all students in the sample had had at least one probation placement during training.

All the officers were currently in main-grade posts in the service; some were in specialist roles, but the majority were in field teams servicing the courts and supervising mainly adult offenders. 40 per cent of the sample were men; 60 per cent women. Their ages reflect the fact that the probation service recruits a mixture of generations: 36 per cent were in their twenties when we surveyed them; 40 per cent in their thirties; and 24 per cent forty or older.

The officers had attended, between them, a total of 49 different course-centres. Some courses provided only one officer in our sample; the most from any one course was 25. Assurances of personal confidentiality were given to officers and their managers.

III   The appropriateness of probation training

How well does probation training prepare students for the kind of work which newly-qualified officers are expected to do on appointment?

Our informants had all been in work for at least a year since qualifying, and, in some cases, for more than two years; they therefore all had a good idea of the nature of probation practice. We asked them to indicate how important various tasks were in their present job. The results are shown in rank order in Table 1.1. The preparation and writing of pre-sentence reports was widely agreed to be the most important task; the practice of family therapy was the least important from among those listed.

2

Table 1.1
The relative importance of different tasks in the work of the recently qualified probation officer (rank order)

MOST IMPORTANT
1 The preparation and writing of pre-sentence reports
2 Workload management
3 Counselling individuals
4 Court work
5 Keeping records
6 Dealing with/relating to other professionals
7 Groupwork
8 Family therapy.
LEAST IMPORTANT

All the tasks except family therapy were seen as being important by a majority of the sample: for example, 97 per cent thought pre-sentence report work important (91 per cent thought it very important), and 74 per cent thought groupwork important (although only 33 per cent thought it very important). The exception was family therapy: 8 per cent thought it very important; 33 per cent thought it important; 42 per cent thought it not very important; and 17 per cent thought it not at all important.

How did these ratings match up with the focus of probation training? We asked the respondents how well their courses had prepared them to undertake the same eight tasks, and we found that the rank order was quite different. (Table 1.2)

Table 1.2
The relative focus on different tasks in probation training (rank order)

GREATEST EMPHASIS
1 Counselling individuals
2 Dealing with/relating to other professionals
3 Groupwork
4 The preparation and writing of pre-sentence reports
5 Family therapy
6 Court work
7 Keeping records
8 Workload management.
LEAST EMPHASIS

To put it technically, there was no statistical relationship between the two rank orders shown in tables 1.1 and 1.2 [Spearman's Rho = 0.167]. In other words, the probation officers did not believe that the emphasis of the teaching on their courses bore a useful relationship to the demands made on them once they were in post. It was not that, in general, the courses concentrated on the very opposite of the tasks which the probation officers were going to have to perform (that would have led to a statistically significant negative correlation), but the rank orders were only randomly related to each other. The biggest discrepancies were in the teaching of groupwork (which courses emphasised disproportionately to its use in practice) and in the teaching of workload management (which 97 per cent thought important at work, but which was said to have been badly taught in 82 per cent of the students' experiences).

In fact, when we look in more detail at the precise distribution of opinions about how well the courses prepared them for practice, something more significant than the rank ordering emerges: that in five out of the eight task-areas a majority of the respondents thought themselves badly taught. (Table 1.3)

Table 1.3
How well do you think your course prepared you to undertake these ordinary probation tasks?

	Very well	Well	Badly	Very badly
Counselling individuals	21%	47%	21%	10%
Pre-sentence report work	17%	34%	26%	24%
Groupwork	13%	37%	32%	17%
Dealing with other professionals	9%	37%	37%	17%
Family therapy	9%	27%	32%	32%
Court work	9%	24%	25%	41%
Keeping records	8%	22%	32%	38%
Workload management	4%	14%	35%	47%

Even in respect of pre-sentence report work – described by our respondents as the most important of the jobs they were doing in practice – half of those who had attended probation-relevant courses said that they had been badly taught.

There were three major differences revealed between graduate and non-graduate courses so far as the quality of teaching was concerned. *Family therapy* was said to have been better taught to non-graduates: 45 per cent of them said it had been well-taught or very well-taught, compared with only 26 per cent of graduates (Chi-square = 14.209, p<.001). On the other hand, graduate courses prepared their students better in respect of pre-sentence reports and court work. 58 per cent of graduates viewed their courses' work on pre-sentence reports favourably, compared with only 43 per cent of non-graduates (Chi-square = 8.549, p<.01). And 40 per cent of graduates spoke well of their courses' teaching on courtwork, compared with only 27 per cent of non-graduates (Chi-square = 7.171, p<.01).

These figures would suggest that, as court work and pre-sentence report writing are said by the sample to be significantly more relevant to early practice than family therapy, then graduate courses have, to that extent, developed a more appropriate approach to practice learning than non-graduate courses.

IV   The probation focus

We explored in greater detail the extent to which those courses which claimed to provide a probation-specific training had adequately covered a variety of topics relevant to the work of the probation officer.

First of all, we asked the sub-sample of 398 recently qualified officers who had attended probation-relevant courses to review the teaching they had received in ten named subjects, and, in particular, to tell us whether, in their opinion, the amount of time devoted to each had been sufficient (Table 1.4).

Table 1.4
Probation course teaching: an assessment of quantity

	Dominant	Major	Minor	Marginal	Absent
Probation practice	0%	13%	50%	34%	3%
Probation law	1%	10%	37%	39%	13%
Penology/penal system	1%	15%	45%	32%	7%
Criminology	1%	20%	48%	24%	7%
Principles of sentencing	1%	8%	38%	32%	21%
Sociology	23%	56%	14%	5%	2%
Psychology	18%	61%	17%	3%	1%
Social policy	22%	63%	12%	2%	1%
Race awareness	4%	17%	27%	39%	13%
Sex and gender	6%	16%	26%	34%	18%

Five of these ten subject-areas might be thought of as being especially relevant to the job of the probation officer (as distinct from other social work jobs): probation practice and law, the principles of sentencing, penology and criminology. Of these, criminology was seen as having been a significant element in 21 per cent of the courses, penology in 16 per cent, probation practice in 13 per cent, probation law in 11 per cent and the principles of sentencing in only 9 per cent. It was far more likely that these subjects would be judged as having been either marginal to the course or absent altogether

(Table 1.5). An interesting contrast to this was to be found in four-year degree courses where 55 per cent of the students had received a significant amount of teaching in criminology.

Table 1.5
The marginality of five key probation subjects in social work training
(in rank order)

	Marginal or absent
Principles of sentencing	53%
Probation law	52%
Penology/penal system	39%
Probation practice	37%
Criminology	31%

It is manifestly unsatisfactory that key areas relevant to the work of the probation officer are given so little coverage in so many training outlets. Even if it is argued that the college course should concentrate on book learning and theory, leaving the teaching of practice to the fieldwork teacher on placement, the low coverage of criminology and penology and the very low coverage of law and the principles of sentencing must leave the new probation officer with some pretty big gaps in her/his armoury of knowledge. But, in any case, the pattern of teaching on probation practice – with 87 per cent of newly-qualified officers feeling that it was given at best only minor treatment on their course – cannot be seen as an appropriate approach given the increasingly specialised roles of probation officers.

A stark contrast in all courses can be seen in the heavy input of teaching in theoretical social science: the teaching of social policy was said to be a major or dominant component by 85 per cent of the students; sociology was seen as major or dominant by 79 per cent; and psychology as major or dominant by 79 per cent. This, of course, follows the traditional pattern of social work course content originally set down by the Privy Council and broadly reinforced in 1975 by the report of a CCETSW working group (CCETSW, 1975). Moreover, the emphasis in the syllabus often reflects the availability of teaching staff in a department and the commonly held view that social work is a form of applied social science. Government reports and training council papers have all tended to argue that the good social work practitioner needs to have a sound knowledge and understanding of the social sciences. The CCETSW working group in 1975 noted that 'sociology, developmental, social and general psychology, philosophy, political science, law, social anthropology and economics are disciplines which make vital contributions to the education of students for social work practice' – not to mention social policy and administration which was seen as 'an essential feature of social work education' (page 25).

We asked the respondents whether they thought the balance built into the syllabus was appropriate. Had there been too much or too little teaching on each of the ten named subjects, or was the amount provided just 'sufficient'? The responses are shown in Table 1.6.

Table 1.6
Student assessment of the sufficiency of course elements
in probation training

	Too much	Sufficient	Not enough
Probation practice	-	19%	81%
Probation law	-	17%	83%
Penology/penal system	-	29%	71%
Criminology	-	36%	64%
Principles of sentencing	-	18%	82%
Sociology	23%	72%	5%
Psychology	16%	73%	11%
Social policy	23%	73%	4%
Race awareness	4%	32%	64%
Sex and gender	5%	37%	58%

The opinions of these erstwhile probation students are surprisingly unambiguous. The vast majority wanted much more in the five areas of learning directly relevant to their work as probation officers: four-fifths of them were dissatisfied with the amount of teaching on probation practice and probation law and on the principles of sentencing; and around two-thirds had wished for more on criminology and penology.

There was no such criticism in respect of the mainstream social sciences. All course planners know that it is very unusual indeed for students to say that they would like to see less of *anything* in course syllabi. (Most people are able to suggest lots of things that they would like to see more of, without acknowledging that in a crowded time-table any additional input has to be at the expense of other existing topics.) So, for 16 per cent to say there was an excess of psychology, 23 per cent an excess of social policy, and 23 per cent an excess of sociology might be thought moderately important, and certainly suggests some scope for re-balancing the curriculum.

The non-graduate students said that sociology had been especially heavy in their settings: 93 per cent said it had played a major or dominant part in the course, compared with an equivalent 65 per cent among graduates. (Chi-square = 48.415, p<.001)

The message is reinforced by the answers we received to a general question concerning the amount of teaching time devoted to the work and interests of the probation service. Two per cent thought the subject was given generous time; 21 per cent thought it was sufficient; but 61 per cent thought it was inadequate and a further 16 per cent described it as negligible. If it is thought that the opinions of probation students should carry weight on a question of this kind, there is little doubt that one must conclude that there is a need for increased input on probation practice issues and related topics.

Two questions were asked about current areas of concern that have been felt to demand appropriate attention at the training level: race awareness and sex and gender. What appears to be happening is that some courses are giving sufficient (or even, in some students' eyes, 'too much') time to them, while others are ignoring them altogether. Twenty-two per cent of the officers said that their courses had accorded race awareness and sex and gender a dominant or major place in the curriculum, but 52 per cent said that they had been either absent altogether or present to only a marginal degree. Similarly, while a handful of officers felt that they had been over-emphasised, more than half saw them as learning-fields in need of increased attention.

V   The quality of college teaching

What about the quality of teaching? Table 1.7 shows the ex-students' assessment for ten named subjects.

Table 1.7
Consumers' assessment of the quality of teaching

	Good	Moderate	Bad
Social policy	53%	36%	11%
Psychology	42%	39%	19%
Sociology	39%	46%	15%
Criminology	34%	49%	17%
Probation practice	32%	48%	20%
Probation law	28%	45%	27%
Penology and the penal system	27%	50%	23%
Race awareness	20%	39%	41%
Principles of sentencing	20%	45%	35%
Sex and gender	16%	45%	39%

The traditional social sciences came out strongly, with criminology and probation practice also performing moderately well. The worst-taught courses were those covering sex and gender (39 per cent said it had been 'badly taught'), principles of sentencing (35 per cent said it had been 'bad') and race awareness (41 per cent 'bad'). Probation law and penology fell mid-way, with just over a quarter of the respondents saying that they had received 'good' teaching in each subject.

VI Fieldwork placements and practice

Almost all the respondents had had at least one placement in a probation office, and a minority had had more than one. It remained the norm, however, for students to have had experience of an agency other than the probation service, and there appeared to be no particular pattern about this: sometimes the probation placement came first, sometimes second. (Table 1.8).

Table 1.8
The type of placements experienced

Both main placements in a probation office	15%
One main placement in a probation office, the other in a related agency (e.g. a drug rehabilitation unit)	2%
One main placement in a probation office, the other in another social work agency (e.g. SSD, hospital, voluntary agency, etc.)	77%
No experience of the probation service on placement	1%

N = 398; no information = 24

Those who had done all penal system placements said that they felt better prepared to write reports, to maintain good records and to perform well in court; but there was no general sense of dissatisfaction among those who had had experience of other agencies.

It was surprising to discover that it is by no means the norm for probation students to have placement experience in a prison or other custodial establishment during their training course. 34 per cent did have such a placement, varying in length from one week to (exceptionally) seven months. The usual pattern was for the placement to be for two, three or four weeks; some students spent the time entirely in the prison probation office; others were attached to the prison training officer and were given experience of a number of departments. But 66 per cent of the sample did not appear to have had experience of working conditions in the prison system. 15 per cent of the sample had a placement in a probation or bail hostel, 12 per cent had experience in another residential setting (for example, with an intermediate treatment project or on a psychiatric hospital ward), but a surprising 39 per cent appeared to have had no institutional placement at all.

The students had a remarkably positive view of their placement experiences, with the vast majority entirely satisfied with the way they had worked out. Table 1.9 outlines the answers to five questions about the placements: those who said 'Yes' were understood to mean that the positive response applied to both (or all) their placements; those who said 'Mixed' were indicating that one placement was better than another or that the overall experience had been mixed; while the handful who said 'No' had had unusually negative experiences in both or all their placements.

Table 1.9
Consumers' assessments of the quality of fieldwork placements

	Yes	Mixed	No
The fieldwork placements provided a good foundation for probation practice	85%	13%	2%
The fieldwork teachers were conscientious in their provision of supervision	79%	20%	2%
Practice competence was properly assessed	78%	18%	4%
The fieldwork teachers were competent as teachers/trainers	69%	28%	3%
The placements were well organised by the college	59%	26%	15%

N = 398

The placements had provided a good foundation for probation practice; the fieldwork teachers (that is to say, the probation officers and social workers responsible for supervising the students' work in the agency placements) had been conscientious in fulfilling their duties and had generally been competent as teachers or trainers; and there was a sense of confidence in the process of assessment. The only criticisms – and even these were made by only a minority of the students – were of the colleges for their organisation of the placements. It must be said, with the advantage of inside knowledge, that while some of these criticisms may have been valid, they may also have reflected what are widely known to be great difficulties in the supply of placements, the responsibility for which may lie at least as much with the agencies as with the colleges. If a student is requesting a particular type of placement, and especially if s/he is restricted to a specific location, courses may well find this difficult to arrange, and the student will tend to be critical of the college as a result. Many do not realise how much colleges and the profession rely on the goodwill of agencies and their staff in providing placements; in view of the informality of this system, the generally positive vote of confidence in the placement arrangements is both surprising and reassuring.

VII Students evaluate their training

Social work training is a challenging and sometimes stressful experience for those who undertake it. Many are mature students who have invested heavily in their career choice and who therefore feel that they have a lot to lose if it goes wrong. The frequent switching between classroom learning and placement practice demands a flexibility of approach that is sometimes unsettling. Non-graduate students may find the demands of writing essays and studying for exams or other assessment systems unusually threatening; graduates may find that some of the teaching is covering familiar ground and hence they run the risk of underestimating the difficulties of becoming a social worker in practice. The lack of an agreed consensus in British social work theory means that most courses still incorporate conflicting teaching elements, including some lectures that seem to challenge the very raison d'être of social work under state auspices.

On top of all that, probation students can be in a minority on their CQSW course and have sometimes found that many lecturers know little or nothing about the penal system while some may be explicitly hostile towards it.

Such stresses are known to cause students a certain amount of anguish during their course, and sometimes even small problems can become magnified. It was for this reason that the present study chose to adopt a retrospective approach; it was felt that one or two years after qualifying, probation officers would be able to see the ups and downs of their training experience as a whole and so offer judgments which benefitted from a more reflective attitude and the experience of practice. This method had been used to good effect in an earlier study of social work training (Davies, 1984).

It is felt, therefore, that our respondents' comments, made, not in the heat of the moment but in the light of cool reflection, are sufficiently balanced for them to demand that they be taken seriously.

We asked the officers to judge their training experience in five ways, on a four-point plus–minus continuum. The results are shown in Table 1.10.

11

Table 1.10
Students' evaluation of probation training

++ + - --

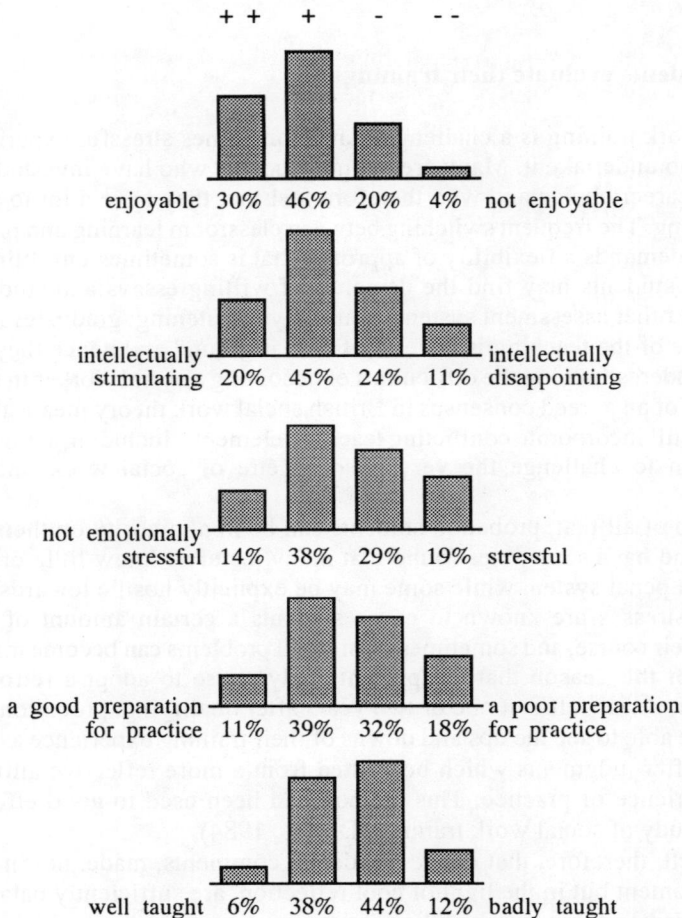

	++	+	-	--	
enjoyable	30%	46%	20%	4%	not enjoyable
intellectually stimulating	20%	45%	24%	11%	intellectually disappointing
not emotionally stressful	14%	38%	29%	19%	stressful
a good preparation for practice	11%	39%	32%	18%	a poor preparation for practice
well taught	6%	38%	44%	12%	badly taught

The figure of 76 per cent who say that they enjoyed their training course (including – as is the case with all five variables – both college and fieldwork elements) must be seen as a remarkably positive perspective. Many social work students have another career behind them (including the many women who have taken the major responsibility for child-rearing), and have often made great sacrifices to prepare for, get a place on and complete the programme. It must be a source of great satisfaction that it has at least proved enjoyable in three-quarters of the cases. And for only 4 per cent to have found it definitely lacking in any enjoyment is also reassuring.

Almost two-thirds of the respondents had found the course intellectually stimulating; the rest had been rather disappointed by it.

However, although enjoyment and the receipt of intellectual stimulus might be prerequisites for learning, one might also say that neither of them constitute the primary aim of a course of professional training; its raison d'être is to prepare people for employment in a stressful work setting. And here the indicators are less positive. The population split 50–50 when asked whether their course had provided them with a good preparation for practice; in other words, some of them had enjoyed their time on the course and others had been stimulated by it, but not all of these had found it very useful as far as their future career in the probation service was concerned.

Interestingly, there was a strong relationship between the plentiful teaching of law and the extent to which students judged their course to have given them a good preparation for practice (Table 1.11).

Table 1.11
The teaching of law and students' judgment on the course

The teaching of probation law was	Preparation for probation practice was	
	Good	Poor
Sufficient	51 = 74%	18 = 26%
Insufficient	147 = 45%	181 = 55%

N = 398; no information = 1

Chi-square = 18.158, df = 1, p<.001

It would perhaps be rash to deduce from this that a wholesale increase in the teaching of probation law would lead to a more positive perspective on probation training, but it is a hypothesis that cannot be dismissed out of hand. More modestly, perhaps, it might suggest that those courses which provided a 'sufficient' coverage of probation law were also the courses which in all sorts of ways were seen by students as offering a training appropriate to their practice needs; in other words, a 'sufficient' rating accorded to the teaching of law might be symptomatic of an approach to probation training that found favour with the students.

A small majority of the officers were critical of the quality of teaching: 44 per cent thought it had been well-taught (though very few gave it top marks), 56 per cent badly-taught. Although we have no means of knowing how this compares with vocational training elsewhere (for example in Schools of Education, Management or Medicine), we must certainly interpret the overall judgment as being: 'Could do better'. We shall see later on that most officers think that the quality of teaching would be improved if more use were made of people with one foot or both feet in the field of practice.

We asked the students to differentiate between the quality of their time in college and the quality of the time they spent on placement. How well did each setting prepare them for practice? The answers were unambiguous: the time spent in college was seen by the majority to have given them an inadequate or very inadequate preparation; that in the field was judged almost unanimously to have been worthwhile (Table 1.12).

Table 1.12
How well did the two course elements prepare you for practice?

	College	Fieldwork
Very well	4%	58%
Adequately	33%	36%
Inadequately	51%	5%
Very inadequately	12%	1%

N = 398

The starkness of the finding echoes that in earlier research studies; it can be interpreted in a variety of different ways but it certainly implies that, once the placements are organised, the students almost uniformly appreciate the opportunities for practice offered by the fieldwork teachers. This does not preclude the possibility of syllabus developments in fieldwork practice but it does indicate a high measure of confidence in the apprenticeship-model of learning. Conversely, for 63 per cent to be *critical overall* of the practice relevance of college teaching is a finding that will have to be taken into account in future course planning and organisation.

VIII Some possible developments

We put six possible developments to all the officers we contacted and we asked them to say which they thought would improve the quality and content of probation training as they had experienced it.

1) 96 per cent thought there should be more teaching input by practising probation officers.

For 96 per cent of any sample to agree on a single prescription is a very rare event in social research, but it reflects a widespread feeling among our respondents that there was too big a gap between the college setting and the 'real world' of professional practice.

2) 77 per cent thought there should be more influence exerted over course design by probation managers.

It was not altogether clear what effects the officers thought that this should or could have, but it appeared to be seen as one way of counteracting the tendency of many courses to under-resource specialist probation teaching.

3) 68 per cent thought there should be more use of role-play, audio-visual techniques and simulated practice.

As we shall see later in this report, many of the criticisms of probation officers concerned the felt inappropriateness of an over-academic approach on courses – especially in traditional subjects like psychology – and there was clearly a feeling that professional training requires different teaching styles from undergraduate education.

4) 62 per cent thought that standards of assessment should be tightened up.

Although it was not possible to replicate in this study an earlier finding to the effect that in social work training inadequate standards are maintained at the margins of competence, officers' opinions on this matter are reflected in their answers to this question. A majority of them felt a lack of confidence in the minimum standards required; it can be deduced from that that they had good reason to believe that some students had qualified who perhaps should have been failed.

5) 51 per cent thought that training should be more based in the field, with a system of day-release to college.

That this proposal secured majority support was surprising, given its radical nature, and it is possible that the concept of day-release was ambiguously understood. On the other hand, it again reflects the more positive impact of fieldwork practice and the unease with which many of the students had experienced their time in college. 51 per cent were looking for a more practice-based approach to learning than that which they were given.

6) Only 21 per cent thought that there should be an additional year of training before the award of the CQSW.

Given that the policy of a third year had, at the time of the survey, received massive coverage in the professional press (CCETSW, 1986), and that it had become the official policy of CCETSW and of the majority of social work pressure groups (though not of NAPO), it might be thought surprising that the students did not share this enthusiasm. On the other hand, given their criticisms of the *content* of social work training, it is perhaps a logical consequence for them to argue that 'more of the same' would simply mean an extra year of something which already left them feeling disgruntled.

IX Personal prescriptions for the improvement of training

We asked the full sample of probation officers to put forward their personal prescription for improving the quality of probation training. All but 21 (5 per cent of the sample) offered a suggestion, and the majority felt very strongly that their proposal, if acted on, would greatly improve the quality of the training as they had experienced it. (A handful of officers offered more than one suggestion, but, for the purposes of analysis, only the first-named was recorded.)

The suggestions were content-analysed and coded, and the following account seeks both to reflect the quantitative balance and to convey something of the qualitative nature of the officers' opinions.

Table 1.13
A summary of POs' recommendations
for improving probation training

Provide more and/or better teaching on matters directly related to probation practice	32%
Improve the quality of teaching, especially by involving more current probation officers	21%
Provide a better and more reality-based practice focus	17%
Improve placements	17%
Improve the teaching on social work	4%
Improve course planning and management	2%
Lengthen the course and/or provide extended training afterwards	3%
Improve teaching methods	2%
Make the system of assessment more rigorous	1%
Tighten the requirements for admission to training	1%
Provide more resources (cash)	1%
	100%

N=436

By examining each group of recommendations separately, we are able to review in detail the kinds of ideas which probation officers thought would lead to an improvement in the structure and content of training. We will consider the range of suggestions under each heading and give some specific examples of what the officers had in mind.

X   The recommendations in detail

1   Provide more and/or better teaching on matters directly related to probation practice   32%

Some suggestions referred specifically to aspects of probation practice that should have received more attention than they did; often, it was said, they had been ignored altogether: courtwork, the principles of sentencing, the writing of pre-sentence reports, civil work, law relating to probation practice or to criminal justice, the work of other penal system agencies – all were mentioned as having been inadequately covered in course teaching. But the majority in this group – 20 per cent of the total sample – said simply that their course had not done justice to its probation student minority: this must count as the strongest single message volunteered within the framework of our study.

Two per cent of the total sample wanted to go further than the rest and suggested that probation students would get a better preparation for practice if they were taught on courses designed solely for them.

Examples

There should be more specific probation training and a particular emphasis on probation core skills, especially as probation and SSD practice grow further apart.

More on the academic components of probation training (e.g. criminology, penology, probation law and practice) which, on my course, were rather hurriedly crammed.

More input on courtwork in general – presentation in court, speaking clearly and succinctly, how to prosecute a breach.

Colleges need to be made more aware that probation work is different to, and not just another branch of, generic social work.

Definitely more input on domestic work, on alcohol and drug abusers and on mentally disturbed offenders.

Adequate coverage of every aspect of a probation officer's job, and provision for practical learning within the University setting. Sounds a bit basic, but it never happened on my course.

Probation officers should be trained on their own; there was far too much time spent on SSD issues on my course.

At least *some* input on civil work – it was not mentioned on my course at all.

17

2 *Improve the quality of teaching, especially by involving more current probation officers* 21%

Most of these comments (making up 13 per cent of the total sample) made one clear recommendation: that serving probation officers should be used much more extensively in the college setting. Where this had been the pattern, it was always spoken of with warm appreciation, and was generally wanted in greater quantity.

A second significant element in this group (5 per cent of the whole) reflected some very disparaging remarks about the extent to which some of the college lecturers (in this case specifically those responsible for the probation teaching) were out of touch with contemporary practice.

A small number thought that the general standards of lecturing/teaching left something to be desired and recommended improvements. Rather more had been on courses where they felt that the academic input (either on criminology or social work theory) had been of a poor quality.

Examples

> Involve more practising fieldwork POs in the course – e.g. in seminars, discussion groups, etc.

> The teaching should be by practising probation officers or by university staff who work in probation part-time; the staff are *so* out of touch.

> Either increase the input of Student Units to CQSW courses, or re-establish a Probation Training College to work in conjunction with the CQSW courses.

> More input by practitioners with a greater emphasis on criminal justice, policy and practice.

> More interchange between probation staff and college staff.

> My mediocre experience of training was to do with the fact that the training staff were academics – not experienced probation officers.

> Using practising probation officers would allow a more detailed knowledge to be gained about the 'nuts and bolts' of the job, instead of just having discussions about the philosophical basis of practice.

3 *Provide a better and more reality-based practice focus* 17%

This group wanted a more far-reaching or more realistic approach to the teaching of practice: most spoke about it in general terms (sometimes indicating that they recognised the continuing importance of a theory-practice link); but some thought that its successful implementation would depend on a better relationship being developed between college and field; and others (4 per cent of the whole) pin-pointed the inadequate preparation which probation students receive for the task of workload management.

A small group thought that the only way to improve the teaching of practice would be to abandon a college-based approach altogether and teach students on an in-service basis.

Examples

More reality-based training – without losing the intellectual stimulus.

More practical input, partly from POs and longer placements, partly from more direct course experience.

More on coping with records and caseload management, meeting deadlines, etc.

Better preparation to meet the sheer volume of work when qualified.

Training should be more based in the field, with a system of day-release to college.

There should be a greater emphasis on how to deal with the client's practical problems like handling the DHSS or homelessness, etc.

A much more realistic approach to the pressures facing POs – workload management and work prioritisation; not being made to feel that you should be doing amazing work with every client.

4 Improve placements   *17%*

Most comments were general: give us longer and better placements, or, in a few cases, make them more like the real job which the probation officer will have to undertake on qualification. There were some more specific suggestions: concurrent placements should be abandoned; there should be more student units or more team-based placements. A small group (2 per cent of the whole) wanted better fieldwork teachers.

Examples

Ensure fieldwork teachers have some workload relief so that they can fulfil their role effectively.

Make placements as realistic as possible so that the students' perceptions of what the job will be like are more accurate.

Greater opportunity for observation of and co-working with skilled practitioners.

More fieldwork. Less college.

Longer placements to enable the acquisition of practice skills – e.g. report-writing, court work, work management and administration.

5 Improve the teaching on social work   4%

These suggestions mainly concerned the inadequacy of teaching in named areas: race awareness, family therapy, client perspectives, groupwork, self-awareness.

Example

More emphasis on the development of psychodynamic skills.

Encourage the students to use their intuition more and not to rely on the text-books.

More discussion on the ethics of probation social work.

6 Improve course planning and management   2%

These proposals were primarily aimed at introducing some consistency between the different probation courses in order to reduce what officers saw as widespread discrepancies in the experience of different students.

Example

The blanket introduction of a core curriculum designed by probation representatives relating to the probation officer's theory and practice.

7 Lengthen the course and/or provide extended training afterwards   3%

Apart from one recommendation that all one-year courses should be extended, all the comments referred, not to a college-based third year, but to the need to incorporate into the confirmation year either some clear training elements or improved supervision by the Senior Probation Officer.

Examples

Extend training to a three-year course and use the final year doing the job with a high level of protection, supervision and support. One day a week in college, half of it in lectures, half in discussion seminars.

Train SPOs to supervise first-year officers. Devise a proper training plan including protected caseloads.

8 Improve teaching methods   2%

Example

> Much more time spent on looking at approaches to specific cases, using
> role play, video, etc. – both before, during and after placements.

9 Make the system of assessment more rigorous   1%

Example

> Ensure that every probation student is observed and monitored with
> clients. Far too much assessment is based on supervision, discussion and
> records.

10 Tighten the requirements for admission to training   1%

Example

> Make sure that all new students have worked for a year as a probation
> trainee first.

11 Provide more resources (cash)   1%

Example

> Devote more money and resources to training. 'You get what you pay
> for.'

> Increase students' salaries. The financial pressures I experienced were
> very great.

XI Skills learnt

What had our probation officers learnt during their training?

Because this study was the first part of a four-stage enquiry into the skills,
knowledge and qualities used in probation practice, we gave our respondents
the opportunity to think about what their course had taught them. In an open-
ended question, we invited POs to name just one skill that they had learnt
during their training, either in the college or on placement – a skill that they
did not have before the course began.

21

The answers were content analysed, and table 1.14 summarises the results obtained. Nine per cent of the sample were unable to name a skill that they said they had learnt during their training.

Examples

> Whilst the course was of immense value in terms of the subjects taught and I personally found the content interesting, nevertheless I have to be honest and say that I did not learn any particular skill.

> I feel that the course teased out skills that already existed in me.

But the majority picked out areas of expertise in the mainstream of probation or social work practice which they said they had been able to develop in the course of their CQSW training. The process of content analysis posed some problems of interpretation (in particular the fact that interviewing skills are often inextricably tied up with the process of assessment and the writing of pre-sentence reports), but, for the most part, the phrasing used by the probation officers allowed us to categorise their responses without ambiguity.

Table 1.14
Skills learnt during training: a summary

Pre-sentence reports and assessment	31%
Court work	4%
Interviewing and counselling	22%
Confronting offending behaviour	2%
Specialist social work methods	13%
Using theory	2%
Self-awareness	1%
Workload management and reality-handling	6%
Welfare rights	1%
Working with colleagues and other agencies	1%
Self-confidence	4%
Study methods	2%
Miscellaneous	2%

None learnt/none identifiable	9%

	100%

The majority of these were explicitly to do with the business of preparing reports; indeed the fact that a quarter of all our respondents picked out pre-sentence report-writing as the chief identifiable skill they had developed in the course of training highlights just how central this role and task is perceived to be by the newly-qualified probation officer.

Examples

> Writing good quality, well thought out and strategically focused reports.
>
> The interviewing, information gathering, assessment and information presentation needed to prepare a report in a short period of time – plus knowledge of sentencing policy which enables you to make your recommendations and present your arguments in a clear and concise manner. I learnt this on placement.
>
> Making reports compatible with local practice as accepted by particular courts – (When in Rome ...) – otherwise the client can lose out.

A smaller number (5 per cent of the whole) said that they had developed skills in client assessment and in the organisation of relevant information for the purposes of social work intervention.

Examples

> The ability to identify problems more easily and to work on these throughout the course of a probation order.
>
> Learning that assessment must take account of my own skills, knowledge and experience and of the client's own wishes; i.e. seeing the client as an integral part of the assessment process.

Three respondents said they had gained writing skills on the course which had helped them not only in writing reports but in numerous other aspects of the probation officer's duties.

2   Court work   *4%*

Examples

> A general understanding of probation law.
>
> The importance of presentation in court.
>
> The succinct and confident representation of another in the formal and intimidating setting of a court. *[The question of whether the PO does 'represent' the client is taken for granted by this respondent.]*

3   Interviewing and counselling   22%

Most of the responses here cover a range of often quite specific skills but all to
do with the professional performance of the probation officer when in a one-
to-one relationship with a client – what to say, what not to say, how to react,
how to initiate client reactions. What is not usually made explicit is the nature
of the objectives to be pursued on such occasions; the emphasis is on the
process of relating, rather than on its purpose.

Examples

> Working at the client's pace.
>
> Awareness of non-verbal communication; learning to listen.
>
> Learning to read people's body language and being made aware of mine;
> the importance of the position of seating.
>
> Using open-ended questions to encourage people to talk in one-to-one
> interviews.
>
> Engaging with clients re sex and sexuality.
>
> How to counsel and how to listen.
>
> Asserting myself in interviews; i.e. keeping the focus, and not allowing
> the client to use the usual defensive ploys.

4   Confronting offending behaviour   2%

A recent trend in probation practice – though not one, it is apparent, that has
been universally accepted – involves not merely a focus on the client's
offending behaviour but a determination to invite her/him to face up to its
implications. A small number of our officers said that they had learnt how to
use these rather different counselling skills – different, that is, from those
employed in the largely non-directive tradition of social casework.

Examples

> Dealing effectively and specifically with offending behaviour.
>
> Interviewing in depth – in particular, challenging clients.
>
> Confronting an offender with her/his behaviour and encouraging him to
> discuss her/his reasons and alternatives.

5 Specialist social work methods   *13%*

It is noteworthy that these skills far outnumber those in the last section, though some of them, at least, might be mutually incompatible with them; groupwork, family therapy, behaviourism, transactional analysis and even massage – all are listed as skills learnt during training, most of them, almost certainly, under the tuition of an expert fieldwork teacher.

Examples

> Talking to children using the techniques of play therapy.

> Group work skills. I ran a motor bike group for nine weeks with a bikers' association and the police whilst on placement.

> Handling group dynamics; feeling confident(ish) about conflict; gaining an overview rather than being involved all the while with the minutiae.

6 *Using theory*   *2%*
and self-awareness   *1%*

These are both categories which tend to relate to the last group of social work methods but which each imply a particular form of skill-learning – one which indicates areas of knowledge which inform their practice (the theory of loss and knowledge about human growth and development, for example), the other which reflects the officer's realisation that much social work practice requires a degree of self-awareness which does not necessarily come naturally.

Examples

> *Theory*   Better understanding of the maintenance role of social work.

> *Self-awareness*   Perhaps I learnt a greater ability to assess myself – to see faults and be able to work on them.

7 *Workload management and reality-handling*   *6%*

This covers a wide range of learnt skills all to do with the nature of the probation officer's job – either as one requiring an orderly approach to daily tasks or as one which involves working with clients who pose problems of violence or complexity that cannot necessarily be dealt with on a 'common-sense' footing.

Examples

> How to manage a caseload. I still feel this is inadequately covered in CQSW courses, but at least a start was made.

> Coping with alcoholic duty callers.

8 Welfare rights   1%

This involves knowledge of the social security system and confidence in handling officials of the DSS on behalf of clients.

9 Working with colleagues and other agencies   1%

Example

> Ability to negotiate and to be assertive with other agencies in gaining help and resources for clients.

10 Self-confidence   4%

Examples

> Gaining the confidence to make contact with other professionals as equals.

> Having the confidence and skill to conduct myself competently in family interviews.

11 Study methods   2%

A small number indicated that the main skills they had learnt were more to do with doing the course than with the work of the probation service – how to read a book, write an essay, present a seminar; some generalised from this and indicated that the study methods learnt had also proved useful in tasks like the writing of pre-sentence reports. (Others, though, pointed out how different are the skills required to write reports and other professional papers from those needed to produce essays or dissertations in college.)

12 Miscellaneous   2%

These ranged from the serious (domestic conciliation skills; keeping records; race awareness skills) to the frivolous (escaping from college unnoticed) and the desperate (surviving on thirty-five pounds a week).

Summary

The skills identified by these probation officers present a clear profile of practice as they have experienced it during their first year in post.

Above all, they see their role in court as crucial to the job: one in which they have developed skills which set them apart from other professionals (including other social workers). They get close to the offender, assess her/his position, take full account of the offence and its place in the tariff, and prepare a pre-sentence report which they expect to have taken seriously. They are sensitive to the need to behave effectively in the court itself, not least because they recognise that their client's own future may depend on it.

Secondly, they operate still mainly in a one-to-one interviewing mode although they welcome the opportunity to develop skills in group work or in specialist forms of social work intervention. There is a strong undertone of therapeutic intent, though it sits (perhaps uneasily) alongside the view that clients are ultimately responsible for their own destiny. The probation officers' skills involve getting psychologically close to offenders and enabling them to see how to make the most of any opportunities that the officer is able to carve out for them.

Finally, the officers recognise that there are two main resources available to them: first, those offered by their agency which include the support they receive from their professional colleagues – they must learn to handle this adeptly (and they tend, we have already seen, to criticise courses for not adequately preparing them for this); second, their own self in whom they must develop both confidence and awareness – it is, for much of the time, and for most of their clients, the principal tool of their trade.

XII   The first year as a probation officer

Traditionally the probation service has laid particular emphasis on the officer's first year after training – the confirmation year or probationary year. At one time, the duty of inspecting new officers prior to confirmation was laid on the Home Office's shoulders, but this function is now carried out by a representative of the chief probation officer's office – usually an ACPO, sometimes a DCPO, and in a few areas still involving the CPOs themselves. The process is now inextricably linked with industrial relations legislation, and the critical date comes at five months, after which it is widely regarded as being almost impossible to dismiss an appointed employee on grounds of professional or administrative incompetence (as distinct from misconduct). Accordingly records are read at five months, discussions held with the officer's SPO and with the officer her/himself; if necessary, guidance is given about ways of improving performance, and occasionally warnings may be issued about the need for significant improvement. At eleven months, the final inspection is normally carried out and, if all is well, the officer is confirmed in post.

What happened to these officers during their first year? 65 per cent of our total sample said that they had received good supervision from their senior probation officer; 35 per cent had not. A slightly higher 75 per cent said that their SPO had given them good support during the year, and 86 per cent had had good support from their colleagues in the office. This would seem to suggest that a majority of newly qualified officers were a part of a pleasant working environment with good social relationships, but that almost one third did not receive what they considered to be satisfactory supervision from their line manager.

The probation service has always prided itself on being in the forefront of postqualifying training provisions in social work, and 69 per cent of the officers were entirely satisfied with the training and discussion facilities available to them during their first year. Some had been on staff induction courses; some had participated in first-year officer groups; and others had simply had access to the programme of courses on practice topics available to all officers in their area.

We know how the process of entry to the probation service involves many people in a very long period of personal commitment. (It can sometimes require not just two years of training but also a period of employment in the service, maybe taking a first degree as a mature student, and, even before that, sitting A-levels at night school.) How then did these entrants feel when they had reached their goal? Satisfied or disillusioned?

We asked our respondents whether they had become so disillusioned as 'seriously to consider leaving the service during their first year in practice'. As many as 25 per cent said 'Yes'. A key factor in their feelings was found to be whether or not the senior probation officer had given them support during the period; neither SPO supervision nor colleague support were influential, but the presence of support by the SPO significantly reduced the sense of disillusionment in the new officer, or at least helped her/him to overcome it. For example, in those instances where colleagues were supportive, and whether or not the officer received supervision, the presence of SPO support meant that only 15 per cent had considered leaving, whereas its absence produced a proportion of would-be leavers three times as high. Where the new officer received neither colleague-support nor SPO-supervision, the presence or absence of SPO-support was even more crucial: where the SPO was supportive, the would-be leavers group was only 21 per cent; where s/he was not supportive, an astonishing 72 per cent said that they had seriously thought of leaving the service in their first year (Chi-square = 63.675, df = 7, p<.001).

In a series of follow-up interviews with some of the would-be leavers, it was found that the circumstances of each officer's moment of crisis was always unique but that there were some common dimensions and that in every case it had been a very painful episode. Some said that training had ill-prepared them for the pressures and the stresses of the job; some found themselves in an uncomfortable or hostile office environment; some felt specially exposed by the combination of the confirmation process and the heavy workload; all of them expressed concern that there had seemed to be nobody to turn to in their time of need. (A note of the follow-up interviews can be found in Appendix 1(II).)

Given the heavy investment in the training of probation officers, the present study would seem to point to the need for a review of first-year arrangements if the preparation of recruits to the service is to be rounded off in an appropriate and efficient manner; the role and responsibilities of the local senior probation officer need particular attention. The apparent importance of a supportive style (with or without a supervisory agenda) has important implications for the hierarchical structure within which the probation officer operates. It may well be, of course, that a supervisory approach is necessary for the maintenance of high quality performance in the office; but so far as the morale of staff is concerned, it looks very much as though the provision of informal support with the SPO operating as 'first among equals' is more effective. If, on the other hand, it is thought important to distinguish between the supervisory hierarchy and the provision of emotional support, then the probation service may need to consider the model established by the Metropolitan Police in which an independent internal counselling service is available to any officer in serious need of help. Such a facility would of course be available, not just during an officer's first year, but throughout her/his career.

XIII   Conclusion

The experiences and opinions reported in this survey throw a unique light on the reality of probation training and staff development in the late 1980s, and the findings have implications for the Home Office as sponsors, for course managers and teachers, for probation service chiefs and their supervisory staff and, not least, for present and future recruits to the service. These findings are further illuminated when read alongside the results of our intensive interviews with a sub-sample of recently-qualified officers presented in Chapter 2 together with the conclusions drawn in the studies of long-serving officers described in Chapters 3 and 4.

Appendix 1

I Methodology

We set out to sample all those who had completed their training in 1985 and 1986 and who were still employed as probation officers. After considering a number of options (including an approach through the Home Office to all those who had received sponsorship), we concluded that the simplest way of proceeding would be to seek the cooperation of chief probation officers, and to ask them to supply us with lists of those officers in their employment whom they knew to have finished training in 1985 and 1986. We received a high level of cooperation from CPOs and the lists they provided gave us a sampling frame appropriate to our needs.

We received lists from all but three probation areas, and a total mailing of survey forms reached 538. We had responses from 457 probation officers, a response-rate of 85 per cent. The results are therefore based on information provided by a very high proportion of the total population of those officers in the service who completed their training in 1985 and 1986.

We had a higher response-rate from the more recent output of students: 43 per cent of our sample had finished in 1985; 57 per cent in 1986. This may have been due to a greater willingness to respond among those for whom training was a more recent memory; but one large probation area did not provide us with its 1985 entrants and that omission accounts for a significant part of the difference. We did a check on any variations in responses from the two years: there were no significant ones, and this means that the arithmetic gap is of no great consequence for our findings.

The questionnaire was extensively explored and piloted, and the design worked well. Analysis was done by means of an IBM compatible micro, using Dbase, Wordstar and Microstat software, and included data transfer to the University of East Anglia mainframe in order to utilise SPSSx.

Copies of the research schedule employed in the study are available from the authors on request. It must not, however, be used or adapted for use without their express permission.

II Some notes on conversations with probation officers who considered leaving the service during their first year

Telephone interviews were conducted with a 16 per cent subsample of the 112 officers who had told us they seriously considered leaving the service during their first year in post. All our interviewees confirmed that it had been a critical time for them, and some were still intending to move to another job when the opportunity arose - usually to one in an associated social work sphere.

Each individual's experience had been unique, but the common elements were to do with a feeling that training had inadequately prepared them for the realities of the job, that work allocation was either inequitable or inappropriately heavy for new officers, that they did not receive sufficient supervision from the senior probation officer, or that the process of confirmation had been unjust.

Training

The main problem was that training had simply not prepared the officer either for the weight of the workload or for the nature of the probation task. One officer said that his placements had been in a social services office and a probation student unit; neither gave him any idea of what he had to expect in a frontline probation office. Another officer was fine until a problem arose over a type of case which prompted feelings of panic in her: "No-one had taught me that it's OK not feel at ease, OK to ask for help". More than one officer said that their training had simply not prepared them either for the authority aspects of the job or for the confrontational nature of some of the work; it was as though an ideological conflict existed between the perspectives taught by the course and the reality of penal system social work in the statutory sector. The routine pressures of the office - working with colleagues, making good use of clerical staff, handling a heavy caseload, coping with large numbers of court report demands - were all jobs which students felt inadequately prepared for in training.

Work allocation

Some officers felt that the allocation of work was unfair to first year officers. Obviously this varied from area to area, and the problem was exacerbated in offices characterised by staff shortages and/or high turnover. We know from other interviews (see Survey 2) that some officers thrive in such a challenging situation, but it is clear that others are panicked by it and feel that they have

31

been ill-treated by their employer. One officer said that, in his area, inequitable work distribution had seemed unfair because it created different circumstances applying to different officers each faced with the same confirmation process.

Support/supervision

We have shown at the end of Chapter 1 how critical the SPO's support is, and this is confirmed in our interviews. Many of the officers who went through a first-year-crisis said that they lacked access to a sympathetic senior at the crucial time. Some felt the SPO was either too distant or simply viewed their problems in a coolly hierarchical manner. One senior was said to have viewed the confirmation process as a charade and had refused to write reports at the appropriate time.

Confirmation

Whatever the substance of the confirmation process, many officers are made nervous by it, and they resent any signs that it is unfairly handled, unprofessionally conducted or unjust in its outcome. Inevitably, some of the officers to whom we spoke (though not the majority) had been criticised in the confirmation process, and felt demeaned and damaged as a result. Clearly, given the symbolic importance of the process, it is important that it should be carried out in a way that commands general respect. One or two officers complained that their area had not organised an effective induction process for new officers.

Personal dimensions

Of course, some problems in the officers' first year were purely personal - to do with moving home, being away from family, buying and selling houses, illness, bereavement, and so on. In such cases, strong feelings against the service or its management may be viewed as psychological displacement, but they also reinforce the idea that, in some instances, it must be good employment policy to arrange matters so as to accommodate pressures and enable the newly-appointed member of staff to overcome initial difficulties and become a fully-functioning member of the practice team.

Conclusion

It would be wrong to conclude that any of these problems are unique to probation or that all are to be viewed as institutionally soluble; some may indeed stem from weaknesses inherent in the employee, with consequential implications for recruitment. But two conclusions do seem to be appropriate: that training for probation must aim to prepare students for the *realities* of practice; and that, with one in four officers likely to experience a crisis in their first year in the service, senior probation officers must be alert to the possible need for intensive counselling at the appropriate time.

32

2 Becoming a probation officer: through training and into practice

I Introduction

This chapter focuses on a series of in-depth interviews with a sample of newly qualified probation officers. It is intended to be complementary to the previous chapter, 'Probation training: a consumer perspective', and further explores, in Sections II – IV, the experiences of training, learning on placement, and the college and placement assessment procedures. Sections V – VII consider the first year in practice, induction programmes and training, supervision provided by the senior probation officer and, finally, confirmation which is an important element of the first year.

The sample consisted of 46 probation officers all of whom qualified during 1986. They were employed in five probation areas in England selected to reflect an urban/rural and regional mix. Each area had already supplied a list of officers in connection with the earlier mail survey and permission to approach the relevant officers with a view to interviewing them was sought from chief officers in the selected areas. Each officer was given an absolute right to decline to participate and all were given assurances of confidentiality and anonymity. In four areas all officers within our sampling frame were approached and only one declined to be interviewed. The fifth area did not supply a complete list of officers qualifying in the relevant year. However all those named were approached and only one was unavailable. Nevertheless the size of the sample proved appropriate for our purpose and provided a suitable mix of male/female and graduate/non-graduate officers. Appendix 2 provides the focused interview schedule utilised with this sample.

II   The officer's view of training

There was widespread criticism of CQSW courses for their lack of practicality in preparing students to become probation officers. That was a clear conclusion to be drawn from these interviews with officers who had attended a range of courses in a number of locations. The college syllabus was subject to particular criticism concerning its relevance to social work and probation practice, especially in the social science component. Generally college teaching was seen to focus on issues rather than skills and techniques for working with the clients of social work services. By contrast to the overall view of the college course the practice placements received a strong vote of confidence for preparing students for practice. Linked to this, pre-training probation experience was seen by some as a pre-requisite to adequate preparation for practice and by others as an important complement to the course as a whole.

1   The college syllabus

At best the college component of the CQSW courses was intellectually stimulating; capable of challenging ideas and beliefs; and able to increase the students' awareness and knowledge in ways which stimulated a thoughtful approach to practice. Courses were not often of the highest quality, however, and were commonly criticised for lack of relevance to social work and probation practice.

Whilst most aspects of the syllabus were subject to critical comment, the core social science subjects – sociology, psychology and social policy – were particularly vulnerable:

> The college course was inadequate – poor teaching. There was no attempt to put social work into a multi-racial context ... The core subjects [i.e., psychology, sociology and social policy] were a waste of time ... they weren't related to either social work or probation.

A number of other comments were made which echo this theme:

> Some parts of the course were a waste of space – for example welfare rights every week for a year; psychology could have been more geared to social work.

and,

> In college sociology and psychology were not particularly related to social work and sessions on various need groups – the young and the elderly – were not particularly relevant to probation.

A focus on issues   An important distinction which our respondents made in discussing the college syllabus was the tendency of courses to focus on issues concerning the background and context of social work rather than the teaching of skills and techniques for working with clients. This also applied to the probation and practice courses which will be discussed later. The emphasis on issues extended on one course to a radical critique of social work which occurred during the first term of a two year programme. One officer, who had found this course 'stimulating, interesting and challenging', discussed the timing and effect of this critical analysis:

> It should have come later – after the students have been out on placement and can handle the issues in the context of their experience of practice. The effect of a Marxist analysis ... was variable: on those students who were sympathetic to it, they tended to throw the baby out with the bath water; those who were unsympathetic simply got confused.

Another officer, who attended the same course, said she was furnished with a political background and a focus on issues rather than skills. By the time she went out on her first placement she felt she had been stripped of any skills she possessed and contrasted her position unfavourably with another course where the students were given 'a big bag of tricks' to try out during their first placement. Similar comments were made by others; for example one gained 'interesting academic insights' and was made aware of issues in criminology but,

> It was just assumed that you had skills; the question of what skills you need was never addressed. 'You get by by being a nice person,' seemed to be the message.

Although one thrust of the respondents' comments is the focus on issues rather than skills , the principal criticism of the college syllabus centres on the lack of applicability to probation work of much of the teaching. Thus in the context of being well prepared through training for eventual professional practice, serious criticisms emerge. So, whilst there was an appreciation of a wide ranging education, the plea for greater relevance in the college syllabus dominates:

> I enjoyed [the course] and got a lot out of it, but it wasn't related to what I do as a probation officer. I expected more on criminology and on the nuts and bolts of how to do the job. The time wasn't used effectively.

Another officer experienced the course as,

> Social work training which didn't sufficiently address probation issues. The academic input didn't get to grips with specific problems or issues. It was too broad and not of immediate practical application.

One officer, who did not think that the college teaching contributed greatly to her preparation for practice, commented on the balance and range of part of the syllabus:

> There was too much on child care and on welfare rights – because it changes so rapidly. Psychology was Freudian based and not objective –

35

having not studied psychology before, I was expecting a range of ideas and theories. I felt it was out of date.

Theory and practice   If the recipients of qualifying training are to develop into competent, thoughtful practitioners, then the college syllabus must be expected to contribute to the students' theoretical understanding of social work and their place in it. At a personal level, the individual's values, beliefs and ideas about the world are an important element in their practice. As we have already seen some found their courses provided a challenge to their assumptions but for others this process was lacking and they were critical of this omission. They did not argue that a single ideology should be imposed but rather that their personal value systems and beliefs should be tested out.

Some respondents were critical of the college syllabus because 'it was all theory and didn't deal with practical issues' and wondered whether the theory really applied in practice. One suggested,

A lot of it seems to have gone – maybe it's implicit in what I do.

Another officer alluded to the value of theory emerging over a period of time. Through sociology and criminology he was introduced to theories and ideas which made him question previously held assumptions. He commented:

The theoretical base seems at the time to have little or no relevance but it does stay with you. It seems to underpin what you do.

One officer said that because of pressure of work he found it difficult to apply the theory he learnt on the course because he 'just had to respond to circumstances as they happen.' Whilst this comment probably misrepresents the role of theory, it does reflect some officers' uncertainty about its role and value in practice. Again this must be another dimension to the respondents' perceptions of a lack of relevance in the college syllabus and a failure (at the level of the college, student or agency) to integrate theory and practice in a comprehensible way.

The teachers – lecturers and practitioners   What did our respondents think of the people who provided the input to their courses? A clear distinction was drawn between those who were 'in touch' and those 'out of touch' with actual practice – the former clearly being preferred. Some admired good 'professional' lecturers (not all of whom were CQSW holders) but thought that some social work tutors who had left practice and 'gone into teaching late' were inept by comparison. Others inclined to the view that some former practitioners had become too removed from practice and developed an 'ivory tower' mentality. By contrast practitioners coming into the college to teach did not generate 'the same feeling of detachment from practice.' But as one officer who appreciated the use of practitioners on her course commented, 'not all social workers are good lecturers'. The particular value of practitioners is in providing input and in engaging in discussion and debate drawing on their own practice experience.

This approach to teaching was welcomed for bridging the gap between college and practice.

In spite of the criticisms of the social sciences, these subjects had a place in qualifying training, according to our respondents, provided they were made more relevant to the needs of social workers and probation officers. Course input on issues about actual practice was particularly valued, especially where practitioners were brought in to the college. So the plea being made by the vast majority of these officers was for a more tangible link between the college syllabus and the 'real world' of social work practice. It is not therefore surprising that their comments about the practice placements highlighted the overwhelming value and necessity of this element of the course in preparing them for practice.

2 The placement is everything

> It was the placements that taught me all I know. In the first placement, I was learning ten times more each week than I had been in the college course. The course staff were living in a rarefied atmosphere. I hated going back there after placements. I just wanted to be prepared for a career that I knew was going to be stressful.

This statement reflects most starkly the views held by many officers in the sample that the placement is indeed everything in terms of preparation for practice. Others were perhaps not so negative about the college component but most comments give pride of place to the practice placements. They were 'invaluable', 'taught me how to work with clients', 'were very good and equipped me well.' By some they were seen as a complement to the college teaching: 'the course did a good generic training job. The placements prepared me well for practice.' Another officer spoke of being prepared 'reasonably well' by a combination of the college course and the placements. For others though the placements were compensatory; for example, 'the placements made up for deficiencies in the college course' and 'probation was neglected on the course although I got a lot out of the placement which compensated to some extent'. Placements also gave a sense of the day to day work of the service and for one officer 'made the course. That's when I learned about probation.'

Practice teachers   The practice teachers are obviously crucial to a successful placement and many positive and complimentary comments were made about them. For example, they helped students raise their standards, helped in 'building confidence', provided 'good role models', gave 'help and encouragement' and were 'challenging and stretching'. Not all our respondents had a positive experience of each placement. One had a clash of values with her practice teacher which detracted significantly from the placement. Another was placed with a civil work specialist unwilling to supervise the students' criminal work. Difficulties of this type, experienced by a small number of our sample, may be overcome by better selection and matching of practice teacher to student. However problems with the supply of placements and the time available for arranging placements may make it difficult to eradicate entirely such negative experiences.

Student units   Without exception, those respondents placed in a student unit spoke highly of the experience. One officer, when asked what elements had helped to make him the sort of probation officer he is said it wasn't the training course, but the student unit which was fundamental and had 'made him' professionally. Despite the positive comments some limitations were highlighted. For one officer the unit had the advantage of enabling her to get a breadth of experience of the types of work undertaken by the service but the limitation of not seeing a probation team at work. In another case the college course was seen as enjoyable but unrelated to the work of a probation officer, so the student opted for a student unit placement because 'they are geared to preparing students for practice'. Other comments were also made about the units making up for deficiencies in the course teaching. The unit supervisors were highly regarded and were particularly appreciated because they 'provided a lot of teaching' at a level not usually experienced in office based placements.

Pressure and protection   One problem which does emerge with both student units and office based placements is the lack of preparation for coping with greater volumes of work and the pressures encountered as a qualified probation officer. One officer, interviewed after the completion of his confirmation year, still felt he was struggling with this aspect of the job. It is a matter for some debate how far placements and colleges can prepare students for this, or the extent to which probation services should protect first year officers to ensure a smooth transition. But that there is a difference between working as a student and as a qualified officer which requires adjustment is made clear in the following comments :

> There was a big leap from being a student to being a probation officer. As a student everything was closely supervised and you could learn a lot from other probation students – all had pre-course experience. But in the job it is lonely and isolated. Everyone else seems so busy and harassed I couldn't turn to them for advice.

> They tended to teach you to be an ideal social worker or probation officer; in practice you have to face the reality that you can't do wonderful casework with all your clients

This raises a dilemma concerning the degree of protection students need from the pressures of practice in order for the placement to be a suitable learning experience, whilst also ensuring a sufficiently realistic view of probation work to enable them to function in their first post as qualified officers. Clearly an important element will be the nature of the work environment they enter after training, including the protection, supervision and in-service training they receive – about which more will be said later.

Block and concurrent placements   A number of comments were made about concurrent placements where students spend part of the week in college and the rest in an agency. All of the officers who mentioned these placements identified limitations compared to the block placement model. One officer said:

> Concurrent placements were worse than useless – it's disruptive trying to come to terms with working with clients and in the next breath saying you won't be available on Thursdays or Fridays.

Another officer, whose final placement was concurrent, commented,

> I missed out on some court work and couldn't go to court with clients if I wanted to. You don't really get an impression of what it's like to work in an office full time.

The practice of courses requiring the submission of essays during concurrent placements was also criticised. One officer felt the pressure detracted from the main purpose of the placement.

Amongst this sample of officers, the placements appear to be the most popular component of the qualifying training particularly when they are well organized and a constructive relationship develops between student and practice teacher. Student Units were valued for the teaching they provided and experience they gave, although this was limited in not giving the student the opportunity to experience working in a team of probation officers. Attachments to an office based team can overcome this although a concurrent placement is likely to impose limitations on the experience. The ideal for students intending to enter the probation service may be to undertake a student unit placement and a team based block placement.

3   Prior experience: a distinct advantage

A number of respondents had pre-training experience as probation assistants, community service officers, hostel assistant wardens and volunteers. All felt this was valuable but for some it proved to be essential in enabling them to function in their first post after qualifying. One officer, who considered that his course was primarily concerned with education and not training, alluded to its weaknesses as a preparation for practice:

> I appreciate the value of education. I've got the rest of my life to put it into practice and learn to be a probation officer ...[He'd been a community service officer prior to training and therefore 'knew a lot about probation work'] ... I'm glad the course didn't seek to turn me into a probation

officer but if I'd had no previous experience, practice would have been difficult.

Another officer commenting on her first post said,

If I had not had previous work experience in probation and had had poor placements I would have been in a real mess.

Thus she identifies a crucial link between relevant pre-training experience and the placements. If the latter are poor, the former is essential if the student is to be capable of functioning adequately on qualifying. As it was, this officer needed that earlier experience to 'fill the gap' between the social work perspective she acquired and the probation perspective she sought from her training.

The value of relevant pre-training experience was highlighted in another account:

The course worked well for some people: it was best when it built on what you brought with you. I don't think it could teach basic social work successfully to anyone without prior experience in a relevant field.

One officer, on a one year course, felt those students with prior experience were at a distinct advantage, whereas on another course whose 'relevance to probation was poor ... students without pre-course probation experience were floundering.' For another respondent prior experience might have enabled her to select 'more useful things' from the course – 'CQSW is so general and probation was just tagged on at the end'.

The criticisms of courses implicit in many comments about prior experience do not extend to criticism of generic training per se. Our respondents clearly recognize common elements in the training needs of students destined for a variety of settings. However in terms of preparation for probation practice, prior experience in the service is seen as valuable in itself, but it also makes up for course deficiencies (and so would be less important if courses were better)

4 The lack of practicality

The course didn't appear to understand the requirements of being a probation officer: it certainly didn't work to match those requirements.

The time wasn't used effectively. It was all geared towards social services although there were thirteen probation students.

These comments about two courses reflect the feelings of the vast majority of our respondents that as probation students they were marginal to the course. This sense of marginality was not only perceived by the probation elective group. One officer recalled the students being asked to comment on their course, 'Even some of the social work students thought that probation had been pushed out.' Another commented that nearly one half of the student group followed the probation option but they 'certainly didn't get proportionately that much teaching.'

When considering how well their courses had prepared them for practice our respondents suggested that the marginality of probation meant that they acquired a general social work orientation rather than an adequate preparation for probation practice. One officer said that at the end of his course he 'was a social worker not a probation officer.' In practice this meant that he did not 'assume the role, status and functions of a probation officer in the first few months.' In particular he found courtwork difficult, especially relationships with solicitors and court clerks. He didn't understand their respective functions or how the probation officer fitted in. Another respondent from a one year course commented that the role of the probation officer was lacking in his training, which 'does not prepare you to be a probation officer from day one: there's still another phase to go through of adapting to the setting.'

So, what did the colleges provide by way of a probation component? A clear distinction emerged on the two year courses, attended by the vast majority of our respondents, between the first and second years. Over one half of the officers mentioned such a distinction and of these two thirds indicated that the major probation input occurred during the second year. Only one officer, whose course only had a second year probation element, said that the provision was sufficient. For others, the probation component might have been 'very good' but insufficient time was devoted to it. One officer said,

> There wasn't enough. It was very much down to squeezing the last drop you could out of it. There wasn't enough on probation law, on structures, administration, aims, criminology or criminal justice.

The element of the probation component most commonly referred to was some form of seminar or workshop on 'probation practice' or 'social work with offenders'. Usually this comprised an exploration of and discussion about the range of tasks the service is engaged in, for example, hostels, community supervision and civil work. Sometimes courses required students to present topics for discussion or practitioners from the local service were brought in. In some cases a probation tutor provided a significant proportion of the input or was present to co-ordinate the sessions and provide continuity. The focus was more likely to be on 'issues' than on 'how to work with clients' and some officers were critical of this. However, this form of probation input was generally welcomed and considered to be appropriate.

Other subjects which might be considered relevant to a probation option, such as criminology, penal studies and juvenile justice, were mentioned less frequently. On a couple of courses criminology did not merit a separate course but was included in psychology or sociology. The law course sometimes had a discrete element for probation students; but probation law was often included in the 'practice' course (when a distinct probation element was provided).

Comments on specific deficiencies in the courses focused particularly upon the inadequate preparation for pre-sentence report and court work and the lack of sufficiently relevant law teaching. One officer referred to a college course on court reports being 'geared to the needs of local authority social workers.' Another remarked,

> There was very little about courtwork or the court culture. You could almost forget that probation officers had any role in court ... The role and function of others in court did not come up; it wasn't really addressed on placement either!

Concerning the law sequence one officer said,

> Teaching on the law was all child care – very little about courts at all.

Another commented similarly,

> A lot of the law teaching related to child care but I don't recall anything on probation law, for example, disposals, orders, the tariff – which would help to give you more confidence.

The principal criticism of law teaching concerns an over-emphasis on child care at the expense of court procedures, sentencing and the legal framework for probation officers' duties. Whilst this balance might be appropriate for some social work students, our respondents found that it failed to meet their needs as intending probation officers. At least one officer made the point that probation officers do overlap with professionals in the social services and mental health fields, so knowledge of these aspects of the law is necessary. That is unlikely to be contentious for those critical of law teaching because the thrust of their comments is that a more appropriate balance needs to be achieved between the needs of social work and probation students.

Conclusion: 'It's different being a probation student.' This clear unequivocal statement not only reflects the felt marginality of probation students, but also strikes at the heart of the concept of generic training. However, not one of the respondents argued against genericism and a number expressed positive support for it. The chief criticisms were based on the inappropriate balance between the component parts of the training and the relevance of course teaching to 'specialist' interests like probation.

So, while many officers were enthusiastic about their course, the majority were critical of it for its failure to prepare them adequately for practice. Although some did not think this mattered, most would have preferred more relevant theory and academic teaching, geared to achieving a better integration with practice learning and experience, and a more direct focus on probation work.

III Learning on placement

The practice placements were a significant part of the training courses for many respondents as was shown earlier. We therefore sought to discover what they actually learnt on placement. Their responses will be examined under five headings: pre-sentence report work; interviewing and counselling skills; the agency and office setting; self-development; and finally, methods of learning on placement.

1 Pre-sentence report work

For most officers this was a significant area of learning on placement and the source of some satisfaction because it involves a finite piece of work with an end product. By contrast, due to the comparative shortness of placements, developing skills and techniques for working with clients over much longer periods is simply not feasible.

Assessment skills are clearly fundamental to pre-sentence report work although they were by no means always learnt in probation placements. One officer discussed what he meant by assessment skills:

> The ability in a relatively short time to try and analyse what problems there are and their nature and to start to try and find ways out of the problem. You do it through interview and using knowledge that you've acquired.

He said that at first his knowledge of psychology and sociology led him to a 'social history' approach to report writing. However, on placement he realised that there was a need to look more at the 'here and now'. He continued,

> The knowledge comes from life experience, an understanding of people's needs (through developmental psychology) and an ability to interpret that in relation to the client's current position – that is the court, the offence and the tariff.

Another officer said that developing assessment skills,

> is partly about awareness of what is available in the community and knowledge of what the court can do. It is also about looking beyond the purely social work element to the offence and what that is all about.

Clearly, possessing certain knowledge is an essential element of acquiring and developing assessment skills, but that is only one element. The following accounts give some sense of the range of abilities involved in pre-sentence report work.

> I learnt about interviews and writing reports. Setting up a structured interview; gaining information; being concise; blending in knowledge

about previous convictions, the current offence and the tariff; writing a report that has a theme and leads logically to its conclusion.

Report preparation work involves interview skills – I had these to some extent already but was able to practice them on placement. It involves pulling together relevant information: for example, details of previous convictions, the offence, a sense of the tariff. I followed other officers' models by talking to officers and reading their reports. I was given a list of things to ask by my practice teacher and was told to leave the way open for a second interview. Pulling the report together was difficult – particularly trying to make it concise. I'd improved by the end of the placement. It helped to have someone go through the information with me and help me sort it out and make sense of it.

The relevance of knowledge about sentencing and the tariff features in both accounts. Some officers made reference to the need to avoid 'second guessing' what the Court is likely to do and recommending a disposal accordingly. Given the development of community-based sentences and the concern to avoid imprisonment wherever possible, the rationale for making particular recommendations is obviously important. The respondents seem to be describing a process of assessing the individual, determining what needs may exist and whether intervention may be appropriate, and examining the offence, its seriousness and the likely range of sentences which might be imposed. On the basis of all this information a conclusion is reached. It is manifestly not just a question of determining whether a 'need' exists and, if it does, and the client is willing, recommending social work intervention.

One officer gave an example of the way experience on placement altered her practice behaviour. Prior to training she had been a trainee probation officer and in that capacity had prepared pre-sentence reports. During her probation placement she said she learnt about issues relating to the tariff and sentencing, which no-one had explained to her before. As a result of this she began to focus more strongly on the offence and less on family background.

In the process of learning about report writing some officers said they developed a format for interviews and for writing reports which they internalised. In essence this seemed to provide them with a sense of direction and structure but sufficient flexibility to enable its application in a variety of situations and types of case. Of course, however much is learnt and experienced on placement, qualified probation officers may well encounter situations of which they have little or no previous experience. The internalised format for preparing reports is still of value, but the knowledge the officer processes may be deficient. For example, one respondent described how after qualifying he was requested for the first time to prepare a report on a serious sex offender. He felt quite unsure of how to proceed and uncertain about the basis for making an assessment. Whilst there are a number of areas in which students will be expected to gain knowledge and experience during training – some respondents mentioned child abuse and working with homelessness as examples

– no training course will be able to prepare every student for every conceivable eventuality.

The task of preparing a pre-sentence report does not begin and end with assessment. Several respondents referred to writing skills as being essential and some had clearly experienced difficulties in this area. References were made to the need to be able to translate ideas onto paper; some said they were given help with grammar and others with developing a concise style and structure to their writing. One officer became conscious of the need to be careful in the use of language and to avoid words having emotive and moralistic connotations. There was some sense of the respondents developing writing skills to enable them to communicate appropriately with a given audience, for example, magistrates and judges.

The court is an important arena for the probation service and as was shown earlier, some respondents were critical of their preparation for work in this area. However, a number mentioned courtwork as a setting in which they gained experience and competence during placements. Spending time in court led one officer to comment upon what she saw as the clear distinction between the participants – their dress, demeanour and location in the courtroom. It taught her 'how clients might feel in court' and she also gained some insights into the situation sentencers are in. As a result she could see the probation officer's role more clearly as being to represent 'the client to the court in terms of presenting information and an understanding of his social situation without acting as his advocate.'

Another officer who spoke mainly about courtwork in relation to learning on placement said,

> Your demeanour in court is important. You need a full knowledge of the law relating to probation; you need to be able to project confidence and competence; you need knowledge of how you come across to the bench.

At first he had to learn basics 'like where the PO sits in court; discovering who the various people in the court room are and what they do.' He commented that he learnt more about speaking in court on in-service training than during the CQSW.

The development of skills in courtwork, an element of which is a process of assimilation to the culture of the court, is of course important to fulfilling the role of court duty officer and being able to participate appropriately in proceedings. But the knowledge gained feeds into the development of report preparation skills particularly relating to the offence, the tariff and sentencing. Knowledge and understanding of the forum in which the report will be considered is certainly felt to be essential.

2   Interviewing and casework skills

As one officer said, 'interviewing skills are absolutely necessary to effective practice.' Many respondents discussed them in relation to pre-sentence report work but they also apply at other stages of intervention and form an important element of the communication skills which respondents said they developed during placement. Interviewing skills apply particularly to encounters where the officer is seeking information for a particular purpose, but communication skills are equally applicable where the officer is engaged in longer term casework involving task centred, problem solving, or counselling techniques. These in fact are all examples of approaches learnt during placements.

Conducting an interview is not a one sided affair, as one officer soon realised. The client has a part to play as well and some of what was learnt was directed towards maximising the participation of the client in an appropriate way. For example, developing awareness of and sensitivity to non-verbal cues; developing the ability to pursue important issues; being able to put the client at ease and learning how to ask difficult questions. Clarity of role and purpose and the ability to communicate this to the client was considered to be important.

Some respondents described learning useful skills in settings other than the probation service. For example, one described 'cold calling' on a placement with the education welfare service:

> I learnt how to win confidence and trust quickly. You knock on the door and you're just another authority figure: six 'cold' calls a day. When I began I'd spend two hours on a visit; the others laughed about it, and one said, 'If it can't be said in twenty minutes, it can't be said at all.' I got better and gained confidence. I exercised greater control over conversation – became more brutal. When I began, I'd let people go off at tangents, but I learnt how to focus the interview.

This ability to maintain focus is important to the probation officer in undertaking a variety of tasks. The focus may be on offence behaviour or particular problems or issues which the officer is trying to assist the client with, or in respect of which an assessment is being made. It will be noted in a later section how in the first few months, some newly qualified officers felt they had to try and meet all the demands of their clients and solve all their problems. However, some did confront this on placement and were able to put the issue in perspective. For one officer this came from a clearer idea of her role and what she should and shouldn't do as a probation officer. This, she said, 'is partly about giving clients responsibility and helping them to solve problems rather than doing it all for them – which is sometimes easier.'

Placements provided an introduction to groupwork for some and for others gave them the opportunity to develop existing skills. One officer, who had been disappointed with course teaching on groupwork during the first year was able to learn practical skills during his second year placement, for example, 'letting the members take charge; keeping it on the topic; assessing what group members got out of it.' Another respondent achieved a transformation from being a volunteer working in a group (reflecting his pre-training experience) to being a group leader. He commented that group work skills involve a combination of counselling, therapeutic and co-working abilities.

Groupwork was also mentioned in relation to community work skills. In this context skills of planning and starting groups, using statutory and voluntary agencies to meet needs and representing those agencies to individuals and vice versa were discussed.

Experience in a number of other areas was also gained from placement relating generally to interviewing and casework skills. For example, one officer developed skills in welfare rights work and budgeting. This was seen to involve a combination of interviewing and assessment skills; counselling; skills in advocacy; and knowledge about the benefits system. Developing ways of working with adolescents was a significant element of another officer's placement learning.

Whilst all the respondents had at least one probation placement it was by no means the only setting in which useful skills were developed. This suggests that much of what we were told about the skills learnt and developed on placement could apply to other fields of social work. However, the opportunity to develop these skills in a probation context is an important element in learning to be a probation officer.

3   The agency and office setting

The development of skills is an important aspect of placement experience, but the probation placement particularly is partly about adapting to the culture of 'an office' and 'the service'. The respondents described several elements to this process: learning to function within the probation service and adapting to its role and functions; learning about procedures and administrative responsibilities; and learning specific procedures, for example in the area of child abuse. At a local office level: getting to know the office routines and local procedures; getting to know colleagues; learning to work with them; and accepting responsibilities to each other.

The probation officer's time is a key resource so managing this time efficiently (skills in workload management) was seen as important. However, the development of skills in this area was limited as will be seen in a later section. Clearly not all students face a level of pressure which will test their abilities at workload management to any significant degree. Indeed it may be argued that too much pressure early on will be to the detriment of learning 'the basics' of probation practice.

Some found that the office culture had a strong bearing on the way certain tasks were performed. For example, one respondent said that because of the routines in offices she had worked in (as a student and officer) she had never used or been encouraged to use a dictating machine to assist in keeping records or writing reports. Whilst this may seem rather mundane compared to other areas of skill development, learning about office practice and establishing working relationships with clerical staff are obviously important aspects of doing the job. Without good organisational abilities it might be concluded that, whatever the other social work skills possessed by the student, it will not be possible to do the work of a probation officer well.

4 Self-development

In the course of discussing their placements several respondents commented on their personal development and its bearing on their capability as probation officers. There is clearly a link here with the other skills already described, particularly so far as they concern interaction with others. An increase in self-awareness leading to an improved use of self was noted by some. This involved, for example, becoming more conscious of the impact they had on others (part of which was being made aware of one's mannerisms), learning how to handle silences or how to be more or less assertive and controlling in interviews. Through placement practice some respondents felt more in control of the way they used their own personalities than they had done previously.

Another important element was the development of self confidence. One officer had felt her confidence decline whilst in college but experienced the reverse on placement. Another said he got the confidence to do the job from the placement whereas he felt the college course had been disabling.

For some the placement saw the beginnings of the development of a professional identity encompassing a sense of realism, honesty, persistence and clarity about the role of the probation officer. Some found this particularly helpful in dealing with difficult interviews. For one officer this sense of professional identity meant making himself available to clients and not avoiding them as he felt some colleagues did occasionally. Another officer also mentioned learning how not to be 'conned'. It seems a rather enigmatic quality but 'is partly a matter of experience and confidence. The way you relate to people has a bearing on it – maintaining authority whilst allowing them to be truthful and showing you're not a fool.'

5 Methods of learning on placement

Several references were made to the ways in which skills were learnt and developed during placements. Many spoke of 'learning by doing' and 'practice' is obviously the essence of training placements, although by itself is not enough. For some learning what to do and how to do it came partly from observation and role modelling. Discussion and analysis of work in open team meetings, other groups or with the practice teacher was another important element. Some drew on particular techniques involving the use of audio and video tapes and role play. Supervision should run through the placement and provides another context in which learning takes place. Some respondents were particularly appreciative of constructive criticism and being challenged, although not all experienced this. Finally, simply being in the probation office and mixing and working with other officers was valued as a setting in which to learn and develop skills and absorb the culture of the service. This reinforces the comments made earlier about the value of a block placement in a probation office.

IV Assessment

We explored with the respondents the assessment processes they had undergone during training, looking at assessment both in college and on placement, and their opinions about these processes.

1 Assessment in college

Our sample of 46 officers had attended CQSW courses in 19 colleges (universities, polytechnics, colleges of higher education) and it was notable that there was no common pattern in the assessment package. At one extreme were those institutions which placed a heavy reliance upon examinations as the primary means of assessment supplemented by coursework assessment, whereas others subjected their students to no examinations preferring to assess solely on the basis of coursework.

Some colleges had high expectations of students producing lengthy written pieces including dissertations of up to 20,000 words. Indeed, one officer estimated that during his course, taking account of all assessed pieces of work, he had to write in excess of 50,000 words. There was no evidence from the officers that they were being taught to write succinctly or in ways which matched expectations of writing in practice. Many respondents were required to undertake case studies based upon work done on placement and whilst these came closest to practice based expectations of writing, even they were in a different form and much longer than many of the case records and reports which probation officers are required to prepare. So the written work requirements of the courses failed in any significant way to contribute to the development of writing skills appropriate for practice.

One subject which was most frequently mentioned as being assessed by examination was law. But again there was some variation in the format ranging from a traditional unseen paper to an 'open book' exam or even questions being supplied sometime in advance of the exam. Some officers, who mentioned that they did not have a law exam, were required to submit an essay on a legal topic but this certainly did not test knowledge or understanding across the range of legal topics of which probation officers may be expected to have some basic understanding.

Overall we gained the impression from these respondents that college based assessment was heavily academic and this applied indiscriminately across a range of institutions.

2 Placement assessment

When we turned to discussion of placement assessment we once again found considerable variation between courses. The range of methods employed for assessment purposes was much greater than in college where reliance upon the written word dominated.

Certainly the vast majority of officers made specific reference to their written work – case records, pre-sentence reports and in some cases process recording – as being a central and significant element of the assessment. However, mention was also made of other techniques such as the use of audio and video recordings of interviews, direct observation by the practice teacher and informal observation by the practice teacher or another officer through co-working or groupwork. Reference was made also to feedback being received about the student's performance from third parties such as workers in other agencies and, in one case the views of a client were sought by the practice teacher. The opinions of other team members were also taken into account in some cases, and this would seem to be particularly important in relation to the student's ability to form appropriate relationships with colleagues.

As has already been suggested there is some overlap between placement work and college based assessment through the medium of the case study. One interesting variation on this was given by an officer who said she was required whilst on placement to keep a diary of work done and her perception and feelings about the work. Back in college the students were given a list of skill areas and they had to extract relevant experiences from their placement diaries and write about them.

Some officers referred to course documents which spelt out clearly the basis on which the assessment was to be made and the areas in which some degree of competence had to be demonstrated by the student. This approach was generally well received especially where there was open discussion about what a particular placement could offer and the expectations of the parties involved. In some cases this preparatory work was formalised in a placement 'contract' between the student, practice teacher and college tutor.

An explicit and formalised approach to placement assessment was certainly appreciated by some officers and there are parallels here with the experience of supervision and confirmation during the first year in practice in those probation areas which have clear guidelines and expectations about officers' performance and the standards to be met. A further dimension to this is that some officers adopted the model used in supervising them as students in supervising their clients so the very nature of the assessment and supervision process during practice placements influenced subsequent practice.

3 The students' opinions

Perhaps inevitably opinions varied about the value and rigour of the assessment processes in determining competence to practice. The majority believed the process to be appropriately rigorous, although a small minority rather doubted the strictness of the assessment procedures. Some found the course as a whole and the assessment in particular to be quite stressful. In a few cases the form which assessment took on a particular course determined whether some aspiring probation officers applied for that course in the first place. This was particularly true in relation to exams which a few wanted to avoid at all costs. However, some found that continuous course assessment exerted pressure on them throughout the whole course rather than for a shorter concentrated periods which they would have expected with exam based assessment.

Of course the approach adopted in this study could not provide an accurate assessment of how efficiently the procedures described worked. However, after early exploratory work we did wonder whether it was possible to complete the course without the probation options being assessed. Generally this was not found to be so although in a few cases the level of work required to be submitted on a probation topic was minimal. As might be expected of people wishing to enter the probation service on completion of training their interest in the service led them to select options for assessed pieces of work which enabled them to develop their knowledge and understanding of probation practice.

Finally, returning to the notion of rigorousness of assessment, we asked the officers whether they could 'think of any probation student on your course who you think should have been failed but wasn't'. Out of the 19 CQSW courses represented by our sample, respondents from 10 of those courses answered yes, they could think of someone who had passed and entered the service in whom they would have little confidence as a practitioner. In nearly all cases the criticisms were based on the personality and values of the individual, for example, arrogance, unwillingness to examine weaknesses in self, being overtly racist, and possessing values conflicting with social work.

Of course, these are personal judgements by individual practitioners about people they trained with. But what is especially interesting about their responses is the dominance of personality as the factor on which they base their judgement. This would seem to be an area in which qualifying courses are less able (or willing) to identify weaknesses and if necessary assess as unsuitable for practice. One officer said to us of her course, 'They try desperately hard not to fail people. They should be trying harder to stop incompetent people getting in.' So if courses are not being rigorous in their assessment of potential practitioners, by giving the benefit of the doubt to the student they are compromising the right of the client to be served by a competent social worker or probation officer. By doing the former they are necessarily failing to protect the client.

V   The first year in the probation service

1   Introduction

Each newly-qualified officer comes into a unique situation and brings with her/him a unique set of experiences, but our interviews nevertheless reveal some common patterns in officers' experiences. For some location is particularly important: one expressed excitement and pride at being in the heart of the inner city; another was conscious of being in an unfashionable office thought of as a backwater where 'you don't do real probation work' and this had an unsettling effect on him. One officer, already with two job offers to his name, was pleased to have been able to secure the post he wanted in a city team. By contrast another officer ended up in a small suburban office and resented it. For some the location was completely new, literally only arriving in the town the day before taking up post. One officer who wanted to live by the sea for a change wondered whether he was opting out by not going to an inner city. After a year in post he's sure he isn't. For others the area was well known to them either as their home town or place of previous employment. For a few starting work as a probation officer involved not just a new job but the first permanent job they had ever had and they recognised that this presented additional problems in settling down.

Some, though appointed to a particular probation area, were not immediately allocated to a permanent post. Whilst waiting for such a vacancy to occur they undertook a variety of work. One spent ten weeks doing predominantly pre-sentence reports which was 'a nice self-contained piece of work.' This was the most usual type of work undertaken during temporary placements but one officer spent four months as deputy warden in a probation hostel and another was located in a prison probation team for three months. These experiences were not always positive ones: one officer felt 'on the edge of the team' and another simply found it 'daunting'. Having been unable to secure employment in the probation service local to her course, one officer spent three months working in a social services department after qualifying before finding a post in an adjacent probation area.

Some probation officers remember the welcome and introduction they received to their new offices. At best this involved being given information about the area and its resources and having time to find their way around the patch. Not all were so fortunate and some went into offices disrupted by staff changes and experiencing particularly high workloads.

2   Protected caseloads

A number of probation areas have developed policies designed to 'protect' the newly qualified probation officer in terms of workload. This is sometimes linked to attempts to spell out in detail the range of work that officers should undertake and become competent at doing during the first year. As such it is linked to the process of confirmation. In describing their experiences of the first year a number of officers mentioned the protection policy operating in their area and the effect it had on them.

Several officers referred to having protected caseloads whereby they could commence work with a relatively low number of cases – for some no more than 15 – which would gradually increase during the first year, by the end of which it should be comparable to that of other officers in the team. Some also mentioned protection in relation to pre-sentence reports but guidelines in this area appear more likely to yield when demand for reports is high.

The pre-existing situation in the office to which the newly qualified officers were attached clearly shaped their experience. Some were able to build up a new caseload whilst others took over from a departing officer and to a greater or lesser degree started with that caseload. Sheer volume of work in a particular team area, whether through staff shortages or an overall increase in work, inevitably had an effect and there is undoubtedly some pressure on newly qualified officers to take on work over and above agreed or suggested limits for the first year. This is not always seen as a problem by the officer concerned but that begs the question of the desirability of this situation.

Some officers were especially conscious of a team dimension to issues relating to first year protection. For example, one officer, who described his office as 'understaffed and overworked' said that he could have used the protection policy to control his caseload. However, he chose not to do so because, regarding himself to be a team member, he felt some responsibility to 'take the strain of the office workload.' Another officer was very conscious that caseloads were 'a big issue in the office' and because she had a protected caseload, others were carrying more cases.

A clear contrast was noted between training and practice by one officer who commented:

> Nothing on the course can help you achieve an accurate perception of what the first year is like – the big difference is the protection you get as a student ... A protected caseload cannot be a reality here ... you want to be a part of the team so you offer to help out.

Some officers were not aware of a protection policy operating in their area and whilst not all were concerned about this, others found the job stressful because of the lack of protection.

Policies governing the first year experience seek to protect officers from high caseloads and more complex types of work and to some degree protect clients from inexperience. An inevitable consequence of this seems to be that some first year officers find the effects of the policy restrictive. For example, one officer who had undertaken Crown Court duty during training was not permitted to undertake this during her first year, nor was she allowed to do civil work (which, incidentally, her course had not prepared her for). By contrast another officer in the same area was introduced to civil work at nine months and took on a parolee during her first year (again, normally restricted).

This occurred because a current client was released on parole and it was not considered appropriate to transfer the case to a more experienced officer.

This discussion of protected caseloads does raise a number of points. Clearly difficulties can arise in teams suffering for one reason or another from high caseloads and the first year officer can be vulnerable to pressure to accept a workload in excess of the guidelines. This very practical problem has implications for the number of first year officers that can be absorbed into one team and the degree to which protection can be a reality.

3 From training to practice

For some entry into the service was the culmination of a long held ambition and for one officer it was the beginning of a new career in a new country. Arrival in the service was not always a positive experience. One officer, whose initial appointment was temporary, was struck by the thought that she was 'going to be doing 'this' for the next thirty years.' She missed the course and college life, whereas for a colleague in a different office, 'leaving college was like a breath of fresh air'. He had not been keen on academic life because 'it's too artificial' and so 'enjoyed getting down to the job.'

The speed with which the officers adapted to their new settings varied. Some started out full of confidence but most edged into it and took time to learn the routines. It was not uncommon during the first few months for officers to feel that they had to respond to every demand made upon them whether appropriate or not. For one officer a number of factors combined to make the first five months 'really bad'. She said supervision from her senior probation officer was 'awful' and she did not grow or develop at all during that time. It was only through having had previous experience in the service and a good probation placement whilst training that she felt able to cope. Whilst 'at first I felt I had to respond to everything, which put me under a lot of stress', she no longer does this and now feels more confident in her practice. Another officer made a similar point, saying that at first she wanted to be all things to all people. This continued for several months, but now she says she's settled into a routine and is more settled in what she tries to do.

During their first year a few suffered a crisis of some sort. One officer completed her course knowing she couldn't change the world but nevertheless had high expectations of herself. Because of this she suffered a crisis of confidence during which time she found it increasingly difficult to commit her assessments to paper or to write pre-sentence reports. Her senior probation officer was very supportive and helped her through this period. Another officer had a similar difficulty after about six months in post when she developed a 'block' in report writing which she too needed help in overcoming.

These experiences of crisis were the exception rather than the rule and, although none of the officers put it this way, there was a clear sense of responsible newcomers realising that they had a major task of becoming absorbed into a new and complex cultural setting. Most knew they still had a lot to learn and were only too keen to have experienced officers help them.

A particular problem facing some officers during their first year involved workload and time management – a set of skills which many felt their courses had failed to help them develop. Even their placements, otherwise highly regarded, had given them an artificial workload and so left some of them floundering during the first few months, especially if the exigencies of the local situation demanded that they cope with a relatively high caseload. For example, of two officers placed in the same office one described how after four months in the post he had 'everything' thrown at him; he could no longer do long term planning with clients, and had to operate on a day to day basis. There was a complete changeover of staff during his first twelve months and a period of staff shortages. His colleague first year officer also described the year as being 'a very difficult time – not enjoyable. Lots of evening work.' She was grateful for her experience as a trainee probation officer in another county prior to training in helping her through this period.

Elsewhere an officer for whom the job was her first experience of paid employment suggested that she had to consciously manage her workload in order to cope with it. She implied that without active management she would lose control of the job. Indeed this is precisely what happened to the officer described earlier undergoing a crisis over writing assessments. She felt 'helpless and hopeless' and suffered a high level of anxiety. Through her senior probation officer helping her with the organisation and management of her work she 'began to feel more in control.'

One officer, who completed his training without a clear idea of the role and function of the probation officer, said of his first year:

> It's been stressful because there's been no protection. The difference between training and the job is the pressure – court reports become shorter, more to the point, more punchy. Organising my time was difficult; there was so much more to do.

At the time of interview he still found this last aspect of the job difficult but felt he was coping better than hitherto

Several comments were made about the contrast between the nature of practice during training and the realities of a probation officer's work.

> Clients are the ones who get squeezed out when the pressure is on

commented one officer, who also expressed a sense of frustration at having learnt 'good methods and high standards from the student unit' but was unable to apply them consistently because of the pressure of work. He reported taking over thirty cases at the start of the year which 'was a struggle'. Another officer said,

> Things which I thought would be important are not, for example, administration and record keeping tend to dominate to the detriment of helping people which requires planning and time with the clients.

For her the main contrast with training was that,

> Client need does not come first. The need for the service to look good in
> public predominates – for example court reports being prepared on time,
> records being up to date ... what you actually do with clients need never
> be seen or assessed.

In another account it was said that,

> The main difference between the course and the job is time – there's so
> much less of it to do actual work with clients particularly because of all
> the meetings you have to go to.

This officer regretted the lack of time for working with some clients with
whom she felt she should be doing more.

The elements of 'time', 'protection' and 'pressure' emerge as key areas in
which newly qualified officers will need to adapt to the realities of practice:
dealing with more clients whilst experiencing less protection and support and
having less thinking and working time per client or task than on placement. As
one officer put it completing training and starting work 'was like passing your
driving test and going out on your own for the first time'.

4   Learning the routines

Although all the probation officers interviewed had undertaken at least one
probation placement, they still had to start from a relatively low point in
learning the routines of the job. Two areas of work – pre-sentence reports and
record keeping – featured strongly in their accounts of the first year in
practice. For a number, especially those initially given temporary appointments
pre-sentence report work made up a significant proportion of their work. For
example, one officer reported writing 17 reports in one month and another 25
reports in six weeks. Record keeping also features as a significant element of
the officers' workload. In one case, because of a personal issue which dominated
the first year, the officer concerned felt that she had to keep her records
'scrupulously up to date so management wouldn't have an excuse to dismiss'
her. Others found that the paperwork involved with record keeping and
administration detracted from time which could otherwise have been spent
working with clients and, as one officer put it, 'records are the bane of my
life'. Of course records are one aspect of public accountability and are one of
the tangible manifestations of the officers' work which managers can assess.

Several officers also referred to the style of management in their areas
particularly as it related to the degree of autonomy they experienced. Some
entered the service believing probation officers had a great deal of autonomy.
One officer, who had spent three years working in a hostel prior to training,
came to this conclusion and was envious of their status. However, in practice
she did not feel there was much autonomy but thought that was a good thing.
Another officer said of her area,

> It's patriarchal and caring towards its officers. Unlike other areas you can do your own thing; you don't have to follow strict guidelines – for example not preparing a pre-sentence report if the client misses two appointments ...

This she had experienced on placement and she clearly preferred being able to take a more flexible approach. Elsewhere another officer described his first year as 'excellent'. He had good support from his senior probation officer and colleagues and liked having the freedom to develop his own ideas in the job. By contrast an officer in a different area found the role of the senior crucial in determining his level of autonomy. His first SPO who was due to leave a few months after he arrived, allowed him 'space to develop' and to 'get on with the job'. The new senior however was 'anxious about her reputation at HQ' and as a result he experienced an erosion of autonomy which he regretted.

Linked to the issue of management style and autonomy was the question of the extent to which the individual officers' values were compatible with the ideology of the probation service as perceived by those officers. A small minority of officers commented on this. One, who clearly liked the autonomy of the job was still wondering after a year in practice whether she agreed 'with trying to get people to conform'. She said she was doubtful about what they were supposed to conform to, 'particularly if you try to take on board all society's norms'. Another officer said she had,

> qualms about some things – pushing people into conformity and encouraging the unemployed into job schemes. It's OK for the individual, but it's difficult politically when you take a broader view of what it is actually doing.

She clearly recognised that there could come a point at which she would not feel able to remain in the service because of a conflict between her own beliefs and the functions of the service.

Two other officers reflected upon slightly different problems. One found difficulty in keeping in touch with clients in a run down inner city area and questioned whether she needed a CQSW 'just to send people threatening letters.' This really reflects a sense of impotence after professional training but another officer found it difficult to reconcile her desire to help people with the non-interventionist strategies she encountered particularly in the juvenile field.

The vast majority of officers interviewed expressed no such problems over ideology and values when talking about their experience of the first year in practice.

The extent to which a number of these officers had been drawn into specialist functions during their first year was quite surprising. Reference has already been made to pre-sentence report work being undertaken in temporary posts and several officers referred to specialising in work with juveniles. This was not always undertaken with enthusiasm however. For example, one officer felt she had been 'dumped' and another said she had been pushed into this area of work: 'I had no choice about it.' It was an unpopular specialism in the office and she felt powerless and bitter about her situation but said there was not much she could do about it. Worse still, her qualifying course had not taught her about work with juveniles and so she had to rely on knowledge she had from pre-training experience.

Another officer said her first shock on taking up post was working with juveniles: she did not feel she knew enough for example about cautioning and inter-agency working. She lacked awareness of the structure and procedures of other agencies and it took her time to adjust. This theme of lack of preparation for the task is echoed in the account of an officer in another area who found himself in a specialist juvenile post. He said he was not well prepared for this initially; he did not do any juvenile work on his placements and his legal knowledge was inadequate. Furthermore, he insisted on having work other than juveniles as well during his first year in order to get a reasonably broad experience. However, he described his first year as being 'excellent' and clearly the difficulties he experienced with juveniles did not militate against this positive experience to any significant degree.

There was some concern about moving into specialist teams, or specialist posts, because of a feeling that the first year experience would be too narrow as a result. One officer, in a team supervising only clients over 21 years old, was particularly worried about this but was told by her Chief Probation Officer that if she moved into another field she would be given induction training. She was not altogether convinced that this would happen or that the training would be adequate.

Of course, where there is a conscientiously applied 'protection policy' in tandem with guidelines concerning the range of work the first year officer should experience, such problems might be minimised. But as was shown earlier some officers felt such policies to be too restrictive and the situation which the officer enters in a particular office may demand that certain tasks are performed by the new officer. Indeed, some offices were going through an upheaval when the new officers arrived and a surprising number experienced a high turnover of staff during the year. For example, one office received an influx of six newly qualified officers within a few months – virtually one half of the complement of maingrade officers.

Some officers went into what can best be described as an 'historically difficult' situation: a number of offices were referred to as 'problem offices' and were characterised by high staff turnover and a high concentration of newly qualified officers partly because, it was alleged, experienced officers refused to work in them and those officers placed there left as soon as the opportunity arose.

Whilst some found this type of experience unsettling and detrimental to their first year, for others the changes provided opportunities and challenges which were stimulating and on which they seemed to thrive. Such disturbances, whether viewed positively or negatively, certainly were capable of disrupting an organised introduction to the service. However, given sufficient self-confidence and ability, the autonomy of each officer's work situation allowed the vast majority to survive unscathed.

There were clear examples of offices changing for the better during our respondent's first year and successfully living down the reputations they once had. Indeed, a supportive environment characterised many of the offices visited during this survey. One officer who was able to 'bargain' his way into a city team said the office had previously had a 'bad reputation' but all that had changed. The team had a new young senior probation officer who worked closely with the team in making team aims and objectives. As a result they all had a clear idea of where they were going and what they were doing. Another officer placed in a small team where 'everybody has to know a bit about what everybody else is doing' commented favourably on the way team members met together informally at lunchtime, shared professional information and discussed difficult cases. Others also referred to the value of a staff meeting room in facilitating informal discussions between colleagues although this was far from being a reality for all officers:

> I didn't expect to feel so isolated ... pressure of work, lack of clarity and cohesion in the area and lack of support are factors ... some people want to work behind closed doors all the time.

Another officer commented,

> The hardest thing is working in a room on your own – you miss out on learning from others – especially after the student unit.

Again she didn't expect to feel so isolated in the job. But by contrast one officer initially wanted his own office but found himself sharing during the first year. It was 'wonderful' as he always had someone to turn to and he also commented favourably on the staff room being well used. It was a place where colleagues could discuss their work informally. One officer also mentioned a formalised 'pairing' arrangement between officers in the team as being useful because she was able to learn a lot from her more experienced 'pair'.

Of course a number of our respondents had previous experience of working in the probation service. The extent to which this helped them during the first year varied and for some it was not as significant as expected. One was surprised how little he knew about probation from having worked in a bail hostel for two years. 'It's a very different job.' Another with three years hostel experience was surprised to find the probation officer has less autonomy than she expected. For one respondent the contrast was in terms of the level of responsibility borne by probation officers compared to probation assistants. In the context of discussing the experience of the first year in practice only one officer referred to her previous probation experience as a community service officer as essential to survival in the job. However, most felt their earlier experiences had been of benefit and they would have been worse off without them.

VI Induction training and supervision in the first year

1 Induction training

We found wide variation in the nature and style of induction training in the five areas visited. In part this reflects the size and geographical layout of each area, and the number of first year entrants in each service. Comments made by the officers about their training during the first year will be examined by looking at each area in turn.

Large metropolitan area This service comprised a large urban/inner city area and surrounding towns and had the highest intake of first year officers in our sample. A two part induction programme was provided. The first part of three days duration provided an introduction to the area; looked at the organisation of the service; the responsibilities of management and probation officers; conditions of service and the consultation process. This was followed up some two months later by a further two day course which focused more on practice issues such as pre-sentence reports, court work, management of cases and child abuse. Most officers also mentioned that they were required to attend courses on race awareness and health and safety.

Some criticisms were made over the timing of the induction programme in that it came too late after starting work for some officers. But one felt it was good to have some time away from the office after six months in post. Comparisons were made with their professional training and for one officer the 'most striking thing about in-service training' was that it made her realise how good her CQSW course had been. Another commented:

> The management perception of the CQSW was very limited. It felt as though no research had been done into the needs of first year officers. The whole thing is overladen with a feeling of being monitored.

A third officer said that it failed to take account of previous work experience. Other reactions to the course content ranged from the positive and appreciative, through those who thought it superficial, to the cynical, 'Management came to do their bit and went away feeling better for it.' Undoubtedly the parts which were best received were those with input on probation practice especially when they made up for weaknesses in qualifying training. Overall most officers welcomed the opportunity the course gave to make social and professional contacts with their peer group.

The criticism that induction training fails to take account of what has been taught in qualifying training appeared to have some validity. However, the sheer variety of CQSW experience and the minimal probation input on some courses clearly made induction training problematic in terms of satisfying all participants. The problem was further aggravated because some officers, who were given a good introduction to their local office and rated their Senior Probation Officers' skills highly especially with regard to supervision, felt

60

little need of further support at area level. Those who lacked these advantages, however, looked to the induction programme to compensate for their experiences, possibly to an unrealistic degree.

Shire county service   An organised induction programme ran in this area comprising a one day introduction to the area and a three day course which looked at different aspects of the work of the service and included input from staff working in day centres, community service and hostels. Some officers referred to attempts to run a first year officers group and most would have welcomed a successful outcome. However, the group was abandoned, one officer suggesting this was due to budget constraints and another that other matters had a higher priority. Mention was also made of locally arranged induction programmes, geared to the needs of officers in a particular location. A couple of officers also mentioned going on other courses – for example, a breach proceedings workshop and one called 'Alcohol and Women.'

Attitudes to the training varied. Some were quite enthusiastic:

> It told us where resources were and talked about types of practice used in the county. It was a good link between training and work.

and one made a general comment upon the value of in-service training:

> Courses are important not just for the knowledge you gain but in putting time aside to discuss and think about issues.

However, the induction course didn't have a great impact on this officer although she appreciated the importance of the formal input.

Again a popular by-product of formal courses was the opportunity they provide for informal contact between officers which in this county was also reflected in the interest in developing a first year officers group. Another dimension to this interest may be that those who experienced poor supervision and support in their offices hoped that such a group would compensate for these local deficiencies in their experience.

Rural shire county   This service covered a large and predominantly rural area but had too few new officers to warrant a formal induction programme. The two officers interviewed both said they were able to avail themselves of training opportunities offered to all staff and neither commented adversely on the lack of a formalised countywide training programme for first year officers.

Small shire county   A compact area, including a sizeable county town, from which we received the most positive feedback about induction training. The pattern here was of a single induction day for all grades of new staff; a first year officers group; and a range of courses which were not exclusively for the first year entrants to the service.

The range of courses available to these officers received very favourable comment as did the first year group, although one officer felt it ran too long.

Again the informal social element of the group was appreciated. One comment reflected quite well the feeling of these officers:

> Contact with other first year officers was good. It has been a very unfettered experience of training. You could do whatever you felt helped.

Indeed one officer said she attended a course on working with sex offenders as a result of which she jointly set up and ran a group with a colleague.

Metropolitan county area   All the officers in this area who were interviewed believed an induction course was planned, or took place, but for some reason said they were not invited. It transpires that because of the absence through sickness of the manager responsible for the course, it did not take place. Some officers attended an induction type course after they had completed 12 months service and others mentioned that they would be attending a post confirmation course.

Both officers who mentioned attending the late induction course said it was good but should have happened sooner. One listed the topics covered: the transition of student to probation officer; court work; parole and life licence supervision; magistrates and crown courts; the probation order; breach proceedings; 'managing the task'; caseload control and supervision and support. Certainly a comprehensive programme.

Did those who missed out on any induction training or post-confirmation training feel that they had suffered as a result? One officer commented that because of the good supervision she had received and the supportive colleagues in her office she didn't feel she had missed out. This again suggested that the better the local supervision, induction and support the less would be the felt need for sophisticated induction and training programmes countywide. Certainly the level of morale amongst officers appeared to be more affected by the climate of individual offices than by the strength or weaknesses of an areas' training programmes. However it is difficult to judge precisely what effect the lack of induction training had on these officers.

Conclusion   The descriptions of induction programmes in the five areas visited show a wide variety of approach. The task of course organisers is not made any easier by the fact that newly appointed probation officers come prepared in varying degrees for probation practice. They also start work at different times of the year although the majority presumably start in the autumn. It is also apparent that the happier the officers are in their work setting – in terms of supervision, support and local induction – the less inclined they are to give high priority to area induction programmes. Maybe if qualifying training syllabuses improved practice relevant content, the induction course organisers could merely concentrate on providing an introduction to the employing service and making adequate provision for a support group in the first year. This could, amongst other things, focus on various aspects of the probation officer's duties. With regard to other training opportunities, the officers interviewed were overwhelmingly appreciative of the opportunities for access to post qualifying training which the probation service offered.

2   Supervision

Our respondents were asked about their first year experience of supervision and their comments reveal a wide range of styles in operation. A major contrast is the extent to which supervision is seen as being structured or unstructured and linked to this, to some degree, is the frequency with which supervision sessions occur. In fact all those who described supervision which was structured said sessions occurred 'regularly' or at least fortnightly. However, frequency alone does not seem to determine the degree of structure for there were those who had frequent but unstructured sessions. Generally those who had frequent and relatively structured supervision tended to be more positive about their experience.

A good example of a structured approach to supervision is given in the following description:

> The senior probation officer was very good in supervision. We had weekly sessions at first; fortnightly later on. We started by looking at pre-sentence reports and record-keeping and once those areas of work were satisfactory we looked more closely at work with clients and the way I was working. We had a 'contract' for supervision so sessions were well planned. That model helped me in supervising my clients.

Another officer described how his SPO had coached him on 'where to put my effort in'. For the first five months he was taught aspects of practice and was given case supervision thereafter. These sessions occurred weekly for the first eleven months.

Both of these officers give positive accounts of regular structured supervision, but not all officers shared this experience. One who had fortnightly sessions said of them,

> The senior would come in; we'd have a cup of tea, we'd go off at a tangent; there was no agenda; the 'phone kept ringing and he wouldn't get them to stop it.

In this case there is little sense of direction or purpose and others also commented upon the absence of an agreed agenda; on sessions lacking direction; and, for a small minority, sessions being frequently interrupted. Generally this style of supervision was felt to be unsatisfactory but the majority who were receiving regular supervision thought it better than no supervision at all.

A majority of officers lacked regular supervision, some experiencing gaps of weeks or even months between formal sessions. However, this was not always a matter for critical comment as the following example shows:

There is no formal supervision in this team, but the SPO is nearly always available.

They did not have 'a team way of working' but there was a lot of informal discussion about the work each team member was doing. The SPO had worked in the area for a long time and knew many of the clients and their families well.

The style of the office allows you to get on with the job but the freedom may not always lead you to the most effective way of working.

Clearly a number of respondents appreciated their SPO being accessible on an informal basis between formal supervision sessions. But there was some dissatisfaction where the first year officer was expected to take the initiative in seeking help with problems. One officer commented that the lack of oversight would enable him to get into 'a bad mode of practice' without being challenged. Not all officers felt able to seek advice from their senior officer outside supervision and some – a small minority – were distinctly wary of the process in any case. These officers were notably reluctant to reveal any weaknesses or negative feelings in supervision for fear that such disclosure might be used adversely during their confirmation assessments.

During their first year a number of officers experienced a change of SPO. This arose for a variety of reasons such as retirement, maternity leave, sickness, or moving to a new post. Also most officers who were initially given temporary appointments changed SPO when taking up a permanent post. The effect such changes had on supervision varied. Some were critical of the inadequacy of interim arrangements for supervision although this was not always found to be a problem. However, the change could come at a critical point for the officer. For example, one officer whose SPO left after 10 months felt he needed supervision most at that time because his caseload was rising rapidly. Another problem that arose was a senior taking over responsibility for officers located at a separate office several miles away which created difficulties in making arrangements for supervision. The problems were exacerbated for one officer because the senior had little knowledge of his specialist area of work.

The contrast between SPOs is highlighted by the accounts of two officers who experienced a change during the first year. One described her first SPO as 'very good, thorough, careful and exacting.' However her second SPO did not find time for formal supervision because he was helping the team out with the work, it being under considerable pressure. He made himself available informally if officers needed to consult him but she feels that her 'development has suffered because of a lack of supervision and the clients have missed out as a result.'

Another officer described how her first SPO had sold her to the team 'as a wonder woman' before her arrival. She was treated as if she could handle any situations and cases and early on she was without formal supervision for about two and a half months. After a change of SPO, however, she found she was getting supervision which examined her work critically – something she appreciated – and she had confidence in the SPO which she considered important.

Changes in SPO can clearly lead to very different forms of supervision and the absence of supervision can leave a newly qualified officer feeling vulnerable to changes in the office. To some degree the officers' expectations of supervision were conditioned by their experiences of the process during training placements and some specifically contrasted the two situations. One officer who said supervision from his SPO was 'poor' commented:

> On placement, supervision had been about how I was performing and the methods I was using; here it's about philosophy, policy, the organisation – very little about practice issues.

Another, who although she liked her SPO, said,

> His supervision wasn't wonderful – not a patch on that I'd had from the student unit supervisor.

The purpose of supervision was not always clear and one officer felt that overall her SPO 'was not challenging enough, particularly compared to supervision in the student unit.' Whilst some did find similarities in the quality of supervision between the two settings, a number of unfavourable comments were made particularly relating to the lack of 'in depth' and 'challenging' supervision they received as qualified officers.

Supervision, according to our respondents, varied widely in style, structure and content: it was sometimes concerned with case supervision; with policy and organisational matters; with administration and record keeping; and with general 'chat' of an office based nature. The comments contrasting it with the experience of supervision during training reflected in part the transition from student to officer status – the differing style and intensity of supervision was one element of a job which encompasses a different set of pressures, responsibilities and expectations from those the newly qualified officers have previously experienced or have been led to expect.

Overall there was a general feeling (with some notable exceptions) that senior probation officers did not adopt a rigorously organised approach to supervision. Most seemed to be feeding into the idea of probation officers being autonomous professional creatures from an early stage of their career. Indeed the probation service may see this as an appropriate way of weaning its newly qualified officers from the relative dependence upon practice teachers during training.

VII Confirmation – process and event

The first year in the probation service is a confirmation year during which time the newly qualified officer is formally evaluated. Usually this occurs twice: between 4 and 6 months and again before 12 months service have been completed. The basis for confirmation used to be laid down in the Probation Rules, but the 1984 rules make no reference to it although there is now a requirement that new officers should posses a professional social work qualification approved by CCETSW. The foundation for the process would now seem to be the employment legislation, particularly relating to unfair dismissal, and it also ties in with the ongoing process of evaluation and assessment of all officers beyond the first year in practice.

Our respondents were asked to talk about their experience of the confirmation year as a whole and specifically about the formal assessment interviews, usually with an ACPO but in one area with the CPO. The pattern was similar in the five areas represented although some relied explicitly on written guidelines or a form of development checklist to assist in the evaluation process. These were also used to ensure that an appropriate range of work was undertaken during the first year. Linked to this is the protected caseload which was discussed in an earlier section and which some officers referred to in connection with confirmation.

1 The process

The confirmation year then is a formalised and central part of the newly qualified officers' experience. All go through the process although not all are aware of the nature and purpose of it from the outset. Some officers were conscious that if they did not reach an appropriate standard of practice 'they can sack you' but very few made such an explicit comment.

As an experience several found the confirmation process and the formal evaluations 'stressful', 'threatening' or even 'traumatic'. However the following comment is more reflective of the majority opinion:

> It's a slightly worrying process, like waiting for exam results. A mystique builds up about confirmation and I thought it would be more difficult than it was.

After the first year in practice however, many wondered why they had been so apprehensive and there was a clear sense of the anticipation being more worrying than the reality of confirmation. Some officers were not apparently given a clear idea of the purpose and nature of the process by their line managers or through induction training. They found out about it from colleagues or talking to friends also in the service. One officer thought that 'college should have given us some idea about the process.'

Where written guidelines existed for the first year, their very existence was a source of anxiety for some. One officer wondered, 'What if I don't cover everything on it?' Others were less concerned about this but apprehension about the confirmation process could promote a tendency to 'over-record because you're anxious not to leave anything out.'

For some there was a sense of disappointment and frustration that after two years of training they were still not secure in the job for a further twelve months.

The awareness of being judged and assessed also had an inhibiting effect on the openness with which some officers felt they could communicate with their SPO. One commented that she couldn't complain to her SPO about having too many PSRs to do as it would be interpreted as meaning she could not cope with pressure. Some also felt that to reveal weakness in supervision might lead to adverse consequences for the confirmation assessment. Thus the supervision process is seen to be linked to confirmation. Some officers took confirmation in their stride, describing it as a positive experience as in the following example,

> I did not find confirmation stressful nor did I feel constrained by it. I'd had regular and good supervision and felt confident of being confirmed. I thought the process was fair and the questions to be tackled were spelt out clearly in the area's guidelines.

Another officer said,

> It pinpointed my weaknesses. It's not nice to go through; uncomfortable; but standards have to be set. No-one likes it but probation is the type of job where you have to stand back and see where you're going.

This really reflects the experience of those who, while recognising the appropriateness of the confirmation process nonetheless felt it was a difficult experience to go through. Others suggested they were relatively untouched by it; they were not especially anxious or threatened by it and sometimes, by comparing themselves to other officers, they became convinced that they would have little difficulty in making the grade.

In discussing their experience of the confirmation process none of the officers argued against it as a system. Some were more ambivalent than others but no-one was hostile to it. One officer questioned whether confirmation is in practice 'a weeding out or developmental process'. He argued that it should be concerned with the development of professional ability but was doubtful that this was always the case. Others agreed that it should be a developmental process and some saw a link with their training. For one it was the 'final hoop to jump through' in becoming a probation officer whilst another said that the first year can be used to,

> finish off the education process started on the CQSW. Confirmation provides an anchor and positive strokes as well as pointers for progress.

Two officers related the need for confirmation to their feelings about the lack of rigour in CQSW assessment:

> It's important because the placements aren't a good enough test of your probation competence.

and

> It's easy to get through the CQSW and the service should have a responsibility to see how probation officers are coping and to help them develop.

The assertion of agency responsibility for the individual in these examples was given less prominence in another account:

> The idea of confirmation is good for both the agency and the individual. It helped me to see that I was competent and allowed the agency to check me out.

Although this comment recognises the value of confirmation for the agency, only one officer played down the primacy of the individual to a greater extent when he said,

> The process is necessary because probation officers have to be capable of working on their own, especially in [rural areas]. If there are problems it reflects on the credibility of the service as a whole.

Some officers clearly had a sense of pride in passing their confirmation year and becoming a part of the service. It was a boost to their confidence which enabled them to relax and undertake their practice with a greater degree of competence. By contrast others were left with a sense of disappointment because confirmation was experienced as a rather routine process which was not challenging. Their disappointment reflected a feeling that it had not been taken seriously by their managers.

It emerges from these reactions to the process that confirmation is one of the mechanisms by which officers are assimilated into the culture of the service. Another dimension to confirmation in this respect is the way it is used in some cases to identify aspects of the officer's practice which do not fit into the local service's expectations, and to seek to modify those practices. For example one officer was told to reduce the number of home visits he was making because of other pressures on his time. This was a compromise he did not like making because the basis for his practice was the high standards he felt he had been set during his training. However, because of the exigencies of the local situation he was under pressure from his line managers to modify this aspect of his work. In two other cases officers were criticised in respect of pre-sentence reports – one for making recommendations which were considered to be unrealistic and the other for failing to deal sufficiently with offending behaviour.

The confirmation year really consists of supervision by the SPO; the absorption of the officer into the culture of the service; and the formal confirmation assessments carried out before the completion of 6 months and 12 months in post. Several officers considered that the confirmation process was intrinsically interwoven with supervision. This became more apparent when they talked about the formal evaluation by the ACPO or CPO which was preceded by the preparation of a report by the SPO. Some referred to the SPO preparing them well for confirmation through the process of supervision. In such cases a typical comment was,

> I didn't experience any shocks – any difficulties would have come out in supervision first.

But as was shown in an earlier section not all officers felt they received good supervision and in these cases apprehension about the ACPO interview and evaluation 'wasn't helped by the difficulties with supervision.' For some, though, there was compensation in the ACPO assessment in that it provided 'constructive comments' and gave the officer a sense of confidence after having 'little feedback' from the SPO about performance and progress. This point, and the contrast between SPO styles, was highlighted by one officer who experienced a change of SPO during her confirmation year:

> The first SPO's report was late; it was shallow and meant nothing. There were no criticisms in it so it couldn't help her development. The ACPO was the first person to look at her work critically. The final SPO report, by her new senior, was very good – 'a lot of meat in it' – and provided a constructively critical analysis of her work.

A further dimension to the ACPO evaluation was highlighted in another account,

> The ACPO assessment was two months late, and was confrontational on both sides. It concentrated on *me* rather than my work. The ACPO's report contained a double message – one for me, and one for the SPO: that he should concentrate more on what I actually do.

Although this officer did not describe a positive experience of the confirmation year she made the point, which others support, that one element of the ACPO evaluation seems to be directed at the senior probation officer's performance. Another officer commented,

> I hate to think what level of supervision I'd have had if there had been no confirmation process. The ACPO was checking up on the SPO as much as me.

There is a clear feeling that the existence of confirmation raises expectations about receiving supervision and to some degree protects newly qualified officers from infrequent and inadequate supervision.

2   The event

The confirmation 'event' involves formal written evaluations by the SPO and ACPO. By comparison with assessment methods used on some CQSW courses, no one mentioned the use of audio or video taped work in evaluations. The confirmation assessment is dominated according to our respondents, by a reliance upon case records and reports – in other words, the written manifestation of the officer's work. Some officers were conscious of the limited perspective this gave to their work, as the following examples show:

> Confirmation was essentially two sessions of a prolonged and detailed files inspection. The first evaluation at five months was superficial – they looked for the fact of entries in records, not at the content

At 6 months the ACPO came. She said she had no major concerns. What were the minor concerns then? The ACPO couldn't quite put her finger on it. Eventually she said I'd not filled in my front sheet properly. Well, I could see that. I was upset, angry, felt let down.

If there were genuine shortcomings in this officer's performance, what is notable in her description is the lack of any real specificity in the criticisms made of her by the ACPO. Such tangibility as does exist in these officers' accounts is related mainly to records and report writing. One officer said that he had to go through his files with the ACPO and SPO using a checklist 'looking out for, for example, whether the file was up to date, type of case, number of home visits made.' This type of procedure certainly reinforces the feeling that the thrust of evaluation is about the written manifestation of the officer's work and apparently less concerned with the content. Another officer said his 'success rate' in having pre-sentence report recommendations accepted was measured. After some criticisms early on, he said 'By the end of the first year my success rate ... was virtually 100%' Of course it would be possible to achieve this by 'second guessing' what the court was most likely to do. Whilst this is not necessarily the case here, the officer was certainly moved to modify his practice behaviour to conform with certain expectations.

Some officers were clearly disappointed that certain aspects of their work did not appear to be considered. One said no-one looked at her work with juveniles and another made a similar comment in relation to her correspondence with prisoners.

Notwithstanding these comments about confirmation some officers had positive experiences and were given what they felt to be helpful advice on ways of improving their work. One had pointed out to him by the ACPO that he was failing to work with the families of youth custody inmates. The officer was able to remedy the omission and commented, 'That kind of targeting of areas to improve is useful'.

3 Confirmation as quality control

The final confirmation assessment before the first year's end is the culmination of what is in essence a probationary year. Viewed as a form of quality control is the confirmation process effective? According to our respondents there is some doubt about this. Some were sceptical of what the process could do and how it could handle 'marginal' cases. Comments were also made to the effect that it should be more rigorous.

Confirmation is important, but I worry that the service is too eager to confirm. I see nothing wrong in confirmation being put back if there is a reason ... perhaps it should be a bit more painful.

Another officer said, 'It's quite easy to cover up bad practice', alluding to the basis on which evaluations are undertaken and the relatively private nature of probation practice.

The confirmation process has been seen to be more effective in terms of identifying and seeking to modify and improve certain identified aspects of practice and in assisting the process of socialisation into the service. But our respondents are less certain about its ability to deal with any officers who do not achieve appropriate standards of practice. It could be argued, as by one officer, that 'the CQSW should give you the basics before you start in the job.' On the assumption that it does he argued that 'if supervision is operated properly you shouldn't need the confirmation process'. In any event his experience was that a two year CQSW and the confirmation year 'seemed like a three year course'. Similar comparisons were made by others and if officers do have to go through 'a further stage of learning' and development post-qualification does this need to be recognised explicitly perhaps in the form of a third employment based year of the CQSW? Alternatively, if the confirmation process is found to have serious weaknesses cannot the existing system be improved to ensure probation officers achieve satisfactory standards of competence and performance?

VIII Summary and conclusions

Although the concept of generic social work training is not criticized by the respondents there is dissatisfaction with courses for their lack of practicality in preparing probation students for practice. The principal plea is for a more direct focus on probation work involving more relevant theory and academic teaching geared towards a better integration with practice placement learning and experience. Given the value of relevant pre-training work experience there is an arguable case for making such experience mandatory for probation students.

Student training units are particularly valued for the level of teaching they provide in a practice setting. Probation office based block placements are far more satisfactory than concurrent placements and aid the assimilation of the student into the culture of the probation service. Therefore the ideal may be for probation students to undertake a student unit placement and a block probation office placement.

The majority see the assessment process as suitably rigorous although a minority doubted the strictness of the procedure. The principal weakness identified was the perceived inability (or unwillingness) of courses to assess students as unsuitable for practice on the grounds of personality, values and attitudes. These are important elements in making a good probation officer according to the respondents.

During the first year in practice induction training was generally well received. It appears less important to those who are provided with a good

71

office induction and have supportive colleagues and good supervision. However a first year officers' support group as a forum for discussion and sharing experiences is valued by the majority.

The quality of supervision provided by the senior probation officer varied and caused some respondents concern. Frequent and structured formal sessions together with opportunities for informal contact are appreciated but there is a general feeling that SPOs do not adopt a rigorously organised approach to supervision.

The extent to which caseloads and workloads are protected is an issue of particular importance to the first year officer. Is protection necessary and if so to what extent can it be a reality? If a protection policy exists should it be more than a statement of 'good intentions' which can be overridden at any time? If new officers are to be protected there may well be implications for the number of such officers who can be absorbed into one office.

Some officers are unsure about the nature and purpose of confirmation and others feel their managers do not treat it with the seriousness it deserves. If it is to be an important element of the first year this cannot be an acceptable situation. Indeed, supervision, caseload protection and confirmation are important and linked elements of the first year experience and appear to require some further thought and clarification. Significantly, there were no arguments against confirmation although a few thought it superfluous given the existence of professional training.

Professional social work training in the way it has been described by our respondents is not primarily skills based although the development of skills of assessment, intervention, communication and organisation are essential for probation practice. These skills are not unique to probation work, however, and do not distinguish it from other social work occupations. Clearly training must, in part, be concerned with the development of skills but should also facilitate the acquisition of relevant knowledge.

Our respondents came from a variety of backgrounds and brought with them to training and the probation service a wide variety of life experiences. Together with their personal qualities, these experiences were important in determining the kind of officers they became. Some considered them to be as influential, if not more so than the training itself. So given this variety of backgrounds and qualities what drew the respondents together corporately as probation officers? Arguably there are three elements: the unique role and function of the officer is one; the professional identity with social work which many (though not all) see as crucial is another; and the penal system within which they work is the third. Within this framework the kind of probation officer any woman or man will be depends in large measure on personality. Cultural absorption into this framework of role and function, professional identity and agency context should be helped rather than hindered by the training process.

Appendix 2:
Focused interview schedule

Outline of topics

1 Basic data: name, age, course, dates, place of work.
   [These should be available on the written questionnaire; if so, move to question 2]

2 Tell me about your experience of practice so far.
   (Minimum prompts)

3 What kind of supervision and training have you had since finishing your course?

4 What about the confirmation – process and event?

5 Looking back on it now, how well do you think the course as a whole prepared you for practice?

6 Tell me about the probation component. What was it like? (Clarify details of syllabus, etc.)

7 Now I'd like to talk about the assessment process. Could you briefly describe the system(s) of assessment – both in the college and the placement? *[Prompt: How rigorous do you think it was?]*

   Would it have been possible for you to have done the course without being assessed for any topic directly related to probation practice?

   Can you think of any probation student on your course who you think should have been failed but wasn't? *[Approach warily!]*

8   I'd like to talk with you about the kind of things you learnt on the placements: skills, knowledge, tricks of the trade ... In what way did your practice behaviour change as a result of your placements? *[Basic information should be in the questionnaire.]*

9   What sort of skills or other qualities do you think are needed in a good probation officer?

10   What elements have made you the kind of PO you are (e.g. life experience, training, etc.)?
     [Prompt: From training, where did the main influence/impact come – course teaching, placements, role absorption, etc? How would you be different as a PO if you had *not* been 'trained'?]

Thank you very much for your help.

3 The changing face of probation

I The changing shape of the probation service

Astonishingly, there has been no general review of probation practice since 1962, when the Morison Committee's Report started from the assertion that 'the supervision of probationers was the purpose for which the probation service developed; that this supervision constitutes the great bulk of its work; and that the men and women who seek to enter it do so primarily, and perhaps wholly, with probation in mind' (Report of the Departmental Committee on the Probation Service, 1962).

However the report also acknowledged that probation officers had 'acquired a variety of other functions', some recognised by statute, some not, and many of long standing; they anticipated that 'the demands on the service must increase'.

The Morison Committee's review of the evidence led them to the belief that, for all practical purposes, officers gathered a general caseload based on territorial boundaries. Somewhat tentatively, their report endorsed the practice, 'which we understand to be growing, of taking account of officers' special aptitudes, interests and experience in allocating work to members of a group' (para 215, page 83), but they had no hesitation in concluding that 'the scope for specialisation in the probation service is severely limited', and they ruled out 'any general movement towards specialisation in particular types of work, such as after-care or matrimonial conciliation' (Conclusion 73, page 155).

Times have changed. The single most important finding from the survey of probation practice which forms the foundation of this chapter is that almost a half of all probation officers are employed in specialist duties; only 52 per cent describe themselves as field team POs working with a mixed caseload. (Table 3.1)

Table 3.1
Principal functions of serving probation officers

Field team PO	52%
Civil work PO	9%
Prison-based PO	8%
Court-based PO	8%
Probation centre PO	5%
Throughcare specialist	3%
Community service PO	3%
Hostel-based PO	2%
Other specialisms	10%

N = 785

[The 'other specialisms' group includes 42 officers who have a wide-ranging variety of full-time functions (juvenile work, drug/alcohol/substance abuse, homeless offenders, sports officer, staff development and training, etc) and 34 who combine work as field-team officers with one or other of the mainstream specialisms (for example, six officers share field-team duties with responsibility for community service). For research purposes, the category is very heterogeneous and an unsatisfactory one for detailed study; although the numbers are included in 'full-sample' analyses throughout the chapter, the 'other specialisms' category will not be further explored in its own right; a majority of those included within it seem to share the characteristics of field-team POs rather than those of other specialists.]

As well as asking about the officer's principal function, we asked whether they also have specialist knowledge or expertise which either leads to them being allocated special cases or being used in a consultative capacity by other officers. We found that 57 per cent of all officers said 'yes' to this question, listing an astonishing range of particular fields of interest and expertise. The following represents only a brief selection of those topics mentioned:

groupwork	women offenders
probation rules	knowledge of drugs
welfare rights	sexual offending
psychodynamic casework	the care of the forensic
adult literacy	psychiatric offender
alcohol abuse	foreign languages
working with	prison procedures
black offenders	debt counselling
Christian counselling	Guardian ad litem work
shoplifters	outdoor pursuits
victim support	AIDS/HIV

The most common specialist skills available are in alcohol and drug abuse. In this and in other respects, it is clear that the probation service contains within its ranks a large reservoir of expertise that possibly may not everywhere be being fully utilised by the penal system.

II The front-line fieldworker

All probation officers are likely to be field-team workers at some stage in their career; most will take a field-team post on completion of training, but very few remain there throughout their time in the service.

The pattern is seen clearly in table 3.2: 83 per cent of those in their first two years in post are in field-team jobs, but the proportion falls rapidly until after five years it is less than 50 per cent.

Table 3.2
Proportion of officers in field-team posts at different stages of their career

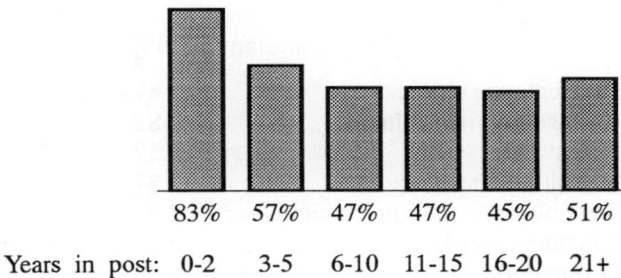

	83%	57%	47%	47%	45%	51%
Years in post:	0-2	3-5	6-10	11-15	16-20	21+

The continued use of field-team officers in large numbers varies greatly from one area to another, and is clearly not determined solely by the size of an area (though the number of penal establishments in an area will certainly determine the number of prison-based officers employed there). Taking six areas to exemplify the situation, our respondents fell into field-team categories in the following very different proportions:

West Midlands	24%
Devon	32%
South Yorkshire	35%
West Yorkshire	63%
Hertfordshire	71%
Middlesex	78%

No comment can be made on whether there are efficiency implications in having a greater or lesser concentration of specialists among maingrade staff. The figures simply show that areas have responded to changing organisational demands in different ways.

Tasks and methods

Probation officers in fieldwork posts carry mixed caseloads, prepare pre-sentence reports, do courtwork and undertake office duty. We wanted to get an idea of the way that field-team officers set about their work and the respective priorities they see operating in the course of their daily duties; we offered them a list of nine tasks and methods that are known to be relevant to probation practice, and we asked them to indicate their relative importance on a scale from 0–3.

Table 3.3 shows the results, averaged out for all field-team officers, in rank order.

Table 3.3
Tasks and methods in field team practice[1]

[Very important = 3.00]

Pre-sentence reports	2.87
Counselling individuals	2.82
Courtwork	2.37
Workload management	2.37
Dealing with other professionals	2.24
Keeping records	2.17
Groupwork	1.67
Co-working	1.53
- -	
Family therapy	1.36

[Not at all important = 0.00]

N = 411

As the topics offered were all tasks and methods that had emerged, in the course of an exploratory study, as being in some way central to probation practice, it is not really surprising that they were all described by some officers as being very important. Indeed, only family therapy fell – marginally – below the mid-point average level of 1.50, and as a result becomes labelled as marginally unimportant overall.

The interest in the list derives from relative emphases. At the top, court report preparation and counselling are crucial aspects of work for all field probation officers. The dominance of pre-sentence report work is especially striking, and illustrates the primacy of the officer's role in the sentencing process and the high degree of seriousness with which s/he approaches it. 88 per cent of field officers gave it the highest rating. This fact is reinforced by the high position of courtwork in the list.

Workload management is ranked third-equal, a reflection of the fact that POs see the need to organise their working lives in such a way as to enable them to cope with the multifarious demands that are made upon them; it is also a reflection of the high degree of autonomy which they enjoy – a privilege that brings with it parallel responsibilities of self-direction.

Surprisingly high, perhaps, comes an emphasis on the importance of dealing with other professionals – a recognition that the probation officer's work can only be done within the context of complex social settings, and that they have to be accomplished in their working relationships with colleagues outside the probation service – in the criminal justice and penal systems, of course, but also within the social welfare network and the private and voluntary sectors.

Keeping records is seen not just as a bureaucratic chore imposed on the officer from above, but as an important task in its own right – linked, presumably, with workload organisation, but also intended to maximise efficiency in work with clients and in dealings with colleagues both inside and outside the probation service.

It is striking that, of the social work methods listed, counselling one-to-one still reigns supreme. Groupwork has its enthusiasts and is rated very important by 24 per cent of the sample, but 42 per cent thought it unimportant. Co-working (that is to say, undertaking casework in partnership with a colleague – sometimes working side-by-side, sometimes apart) has a significant number of supporters: 15 per cent rate it very important, 37 per cent fairly important. Family therapy was said to be important by 41 per cent of the fieldwork sample, but the majority rated it unimportant, and this takes it below the mid-point overall. Each of the three 'lesser' methods have their advocates but all the officers remain heavily dependent on counselling as the primary practice mode.

We invited officers to 'write in' any tasks and methods that they thought were important in field-based practice that had not been included in our list. Although a large number of highly specific, individual items were mentioned, only three seemed to expand on the range to a significant extent:
1   Liaison with the local community and its agencies – for example, the social services department, the income maintenance system, hostels and landladies, hospitals, law centres.
2   Office duty
3   Understanding and dealing with management

Areas of knowledge

What do probation officers need to know in order to do their job properly? Following an exploratory study, we drew up a list of eight probable areas of knowledge. Table 3.4 shows the results when we asked our field team respondents to indicate, on a scale from 0–3, how important to their work was each topic. (A score of 3.00 would indicate maximum importance; a score of zero no importance at all.)

Table 3.4
Areas of knowledge required for field team practice

[Very important = 3.00]

Sentencing principles/tariff	2.68
Local resources	2.67
Court procedure	2.63
Welfare rights	2.21
Appropriate law	2.18
Social work methods	2.14
Psychology	1.95
Sociology	1.66

- -

[Not at all important = 0.00]

N = 411

Once more, the primacy of the court setting in the probation officer's work is immediately apparent: we are told that knowledge of the principles of sentencing and of court procedure is virtually indispensable in the job; a little less crucial, but still important, comes appropriate legal knowledge. In all of this, one senses the emphasis of serving probation officers on having colleagues who can be relied upon in a public setting to uphold the standards of the service in a way that will enhance its professional reputation.

The two areas of knowledge which split the court-based topics and which share with them the top of the table are both pragmatic, atheoretical and heavily tied up with the primacy of experience. Knowledge about local resources – where to get help from, whose support to enlist, where the job opportunities are, which landlady will take which types of client, and a multitude of similar questions – is something which can very easily get taken for granted; and yet, here we have probation officers explicitly recognising its critical role in their work. Similarly, knowledge of welfare rights – knowing as they do that many probation clients will be unemployed, in receipt of benefits and in need of frequent material support – is rated a high priority by our respondents.

Only then, when the pressures of a competent court performance and a down-to-earth approach to client need have been established, do the officers recognise the importance of background knowledge – in social work methods, psychology and sociology. None of the subjects are said to be *un*important by the sample as a whole (that is to say, they all score above the mid-point on the scale), but their relative position is a salutary reminder of the dangers of over-academicising social work training programmes. The research method we used allowed our respondents to rate all the areas of knowledge equally highly; they did not *have* to mark down the more theoretical topics. And, yet, they did so. Sociology, in particular, was cast somewhat adrift, though its value in terms of background knowledge for practice is supported by the figures: 12 per cent rated it very important, and 48 per cent fairly important. But in comparison with the rest of the list, it emerges rather weakly.

When we invited the field-based officers to add to our list of knowledge that was useful in practice, two areas stood out in particular: knowledge about alcohol, drug or substance abuse, and knowledge about the whole field of psychiatry and mental health. Two other, more pragmatic areas were mentioned: knowledge about the hierarchies and decision-making structures in other agencies, and knowledge about the availability of national resources (hostel places, therapeutic regimes, and so on).

Skills and qualities

Finally we offered our field-team respondents a list of eleven skills and qualities that had been reported to us in the exploratory study as being relevant to good probation practice. Officers were asked to rate them on a scale 0–3 indicating how important each one was in their present job. Table 3.5 provides a succinct summary of how probation officers judge the relative importance of different qualities and skills necessary for good fieldwork practice. The top five certainly, and probably the sixth, can be regarded as prerequisites for professional competence, seen through the eyes of those in the front-line.

Extrapolating from the six top items listed, it can be concluded that anyone appointed as a probation officer should, as a minimum requirement, have good interpersonal skills, a high standard of literacy, personality traits which incorporate resilience and the power of persuasion, and a combination of learning and life experience which have produced a high degree of sensitivity to human behaviour and its social context.

Table 3.5
Skills and qualities used in field team practice

[Very important = 3.00]

Writing reports	2.88
Counselling 1-to-1	2.77
Influencing court decisions	2.75
Making assessments	2.74
Coping with client emotion	2.72
Getting on with colleagues	2.39
Writing records	2.14
Groupwork	1.69
- -	
Organising meetings	1.24
Public speaking	1.19
Practising family therapy	1.17

[Not at all important = 0.00]

N = 411

These five elements can be described in a little more detail.

1 Interpersonal skills The officer has to be able to relate (talking, listening, sharing, giving, receiving, tolerating, understanding, empathising, inspiring trust), not just to clients and their networks, but to all those with whom s/he has dealings, especially, it would seem, to close colleagues: probation practice requires cooperation and collaboration, and the officer must be capable of such a working style. Whereas interpersonal skills may be said to be advantageous in many occupations, probation officers seem to be saying that their job is utterly dependent upon them – that, quite literally, you cannot *be* a probation officer unless you can relate to other people in an effective and purposeful manner.

2 Writing skills Given the primacy of pre-sentence report work and the crucial nature of the relationship between probation officers and decision-makers (mainly in the courts, but also in the Parole Board and in the wider sphere of social welfare), it ought not to surprise us that probation officers put the art of writing reports at the very top of their list of desirable skills. Included in this must be the whole business of gathering relevant information, keeping it in note form, turning it into a convincing and professionally impressive document and incorporating in it an appropriately arrived-at recommendation. Such work demands literacy skills of a high order.

3 Persuasiveness If 'influencing court decisions' is seen as having a high priority, then the art of persuasiveness becomes an important quality in its own right, both through the written and the spoken word: knowing when to use it and when not to use it, how to prepare the ground properly and how to follow it up afterwards.

4 Resilience Coping with client emotion is a task not unique in probation or social work; police, doctors and nurses all need resilience in the same way – perhaps to an even greater extent. But our respondents are clear that the nature of *their* job is such that an unduly thin skin would make someone unsuitable for a career in the probation service.

5 Sensitivity to human behaviour and its social context If the officer is to make appropriate assessments quickly and accurately and if s/he is to achieve professional competence as a counsellor, then the probation officer needs an amalgam of experience, personality and accumulated knowledge, including some coverage of relevant aspects of psychology and sociology. The high-level skills required, however, are almost certainly more likely to be a product of supervised practice than of critical or detached book-learning.

Groupwork has both its advocates and its detractors (25 per cent of the field work sample see it as a very important skill; 51 per cent say it is unimportant); it requires quite different skills from those used by counsellors.

Right at the bottom of the list, family therapy has nine per cent who see it as very important and 24 per cent who say it is fairly important; it has a literature, a tradition and, increasingly, a reliance on technical expertise that make it almost unique in community-based social work; but it has not yet become a dominant force in probation practice and cannot be described as an essential skill for all or most officers.

Finally, probation officers are not, it seems, normally required to do much in the way of public speaking or organising meetings. There are, of course, exceptions to this, and some may choose to develop both skills in the context of their own workload. But neither is seen as a prerequisite for good practice – though each may, of course, be regarded as important in the context of longer-term career aspirations.

III The emergent specialisms

We have identified seven areas of specialist activity, each of them accounting for between two per cent and nine per cent of our sample (see Table 3.1). Some of the specialisms have evolved out of long-standing probation traditions – court-based work, throughcare and civil work; others are a product of changing practices and penal innovations – probation centre work and community service; the rest – prison-based work and hostel-based work – originated as a result of government policies which gave to the probation service responsibilities which had previously been borne by other organisations.

It is not the case that specialist functions are themselves particularly new. What is different is that they now exist in such proportions that they can no longer be regarded as marginal to the organisation of the service, nor as irrelevant for the purposes of probation training – though whether the implications are for basic training or for post-qualifying courses (or for both) is a matter for discussion.

In this section, we shall briefly review each of the specialisms in turn, noting in particular the extent to which they differ from mainstream fieldwork in respect of identified tasks and methods, knowledge, or skills and qualities said to be important in their execution, and drawing on the further information volunteered by our respondents when asked to describe their work in more detail.

1   Civil work

Probation officers allocated to civil work (now known as Family Court Welfare) duties move out of the criminal justice and penal systems altogether and take on the mantle of welfare officers in the civil courts together with associated conciliation and reporting duties. Their work is largely concerned with marriages in the process of breaking up and with the consequences of divorce and separation for the welfare of any children; questions of custody and access loom large.

Civil work is not something to which new officers are allocated:

Number of years service	Proportion of POs doing civil work
0 – 2	none
3 – 5	4%
6 – 10	10%
11 – 15	13%
16 – plus	11%

The main distinguishing characteristics in civil work are to be found firstly in the way in which family therapy is rated highly as a method relevant to probation practice, and secondly in the high priority given to co-working (even higher than counselling one-to-one which gets a lower rating from civil workers than from all other specialisms except community service officers). (Table 3.6) Both of these emphases reflect the complex psycho-social interactions operating within marriage and family life which civil workers have to handle, and the fact that they have discovered the advantages of a more systems-based approach to exploration, assessment and – possibly – therapeutic intervention.

Civil workers do not use group work, and they tend to place less emphasis on record-keeping than is generally so elsewhere in the service. Courtwork is seen as the top priority, and relations with other professionals are also of great importance.

In addition to the tasks and methods listed, civil workers identified conciliation and mediation as being significant in their work; and the writing of reports for the civil courts is crucial.

Table 3.6
Tasks and methods in civil work practice

[Very important = 3.00]

Courtwork	2.53
Dealing with other professionals	2.50
Workload management	2.35
Co-working	2.35
Family therapy	2.24
Counselling individuals	2.10
Keeping records	1.69
- -	
Pre-sentence reports	1.44
Groupwork	1.08

[Not at all important = 0.00]

N = 70

The knowledge that civil workers say they use (table 3.7) is governed by two elements in their work: on the one hand, the court setting requires detailed knowledge of law and court procedures; and on the other, the complexity of family dynamics and a focus on the interests of the child lead to an unusually high emphasis on both psychology and social work methods, while even sociology, which comes low in most probation officers' priorities, is seen as bringing a relatively important added dimension to civil work practice.

The civil worker does not need to have any knowledge of sentencing patterns, and practical knowledge about welfare rights or local resources is said to be largely irrelevant.

In addition to the items listed, civil workers said that a knowledge of child development (and of child psychology generally) is essential in their work. They need an understanding of the theory and practice of family work in its various forms, and especially an awareness of the effects of separation on the different parties involved. They need to know about the law and practice of marriage and divorce.

Table 3.7
Areas of knowledge required for civil work practice

[Very important = 3.00]

Court procedure	2.67
Appropriate law	2.59
Social work methods	2.24
Psychology	2.21
Sociology	1.79
- -	
Local resources	1.49
Welfare rights	1.16
Sentencing principles/tariff	0.42

[Not at all important = 0.00]

N = 70

How does the civil work specialist rate the skills and qualities that we identified in our study? (Table 3.8) S/he needs, above all, to be able to handle client emotion – anger, anguish, pain, distress, and the consequences of loss. Family therapy skills are rated highly by 71 per cent of civil workers.

Table 3.8
Skills and qualities used in civil work practice

[Very important = 3.00]

Coping with client emotion	2.90
Writing reports	2.84
Making assessments	2.80
Getting on with colleagues	2.54
Influencing court decisions	2.49
Practising family therapy	2.07
Counselling 1-to-1	1.82
Organising meetings	1.77
Writing records	1.55
- -	
Public speaking	1.26
Groupwork	0.99

[Not at all important = 0.00]

N = 70

Skills of assessment, of report-writing and of being able successfully to influence court decisions are essential for probation officers specialising in civil work. An ability to organise meetings is also said to be important in the job, but public speaking, record-writing and groupwork are not.

Perhaps surprisingly, counselling skills, though required, do not occupy as central a position as they do in most other areas of probation practice.

The main skill that civil workers mentioned specially (in addition to those listed in table 3.8) was the ability to communicate with children.

The distinguishing characteristics of civil work   As a way of further exploring the nature of probation practice specialisms, we asked officers to tell us how their job differed from work that they had undertaken in other parts of the probation service. The answers give us a profile of the distinguishing characteristics of each specialist field.

When asked to identify the characteristics of civil work which most clearly differentiate it from other probation functions, our respondents mentioned, in order of priority:

1 They work mainly with families and children. While the children are not often parties to the court proceedings, they are frequently seen as the focus of the officer's work. The principle of the welfare of the child being paramount is strongly defended.

2 They work in different courts and tackle different issues. The duties of working in a different court setting – magistrates domestic courts, county divorce courts and the High Court – require a different style of practice. And the range of issues dealt with – custody, access, wardship, guardianship – require different knowledge and different skills.

3 The use of conciliation, mediation and family therapy are all practice methods which are strongly identified with the civil work specialist's duties. Some see their role as being to achieve 'family conflict resolution'.

4 A number of lesser factors were also identified as being 'different': the fact that clients come from a wider social spectrum than in criminal work, that the tasks are almost always more clearly defined, and that the service provided tends to be county-wide rather than patch-based.

2   Prison-based practice

Probation officers have worked in prisons since 1966, initially called welfare officers, but later reverting to their normal occupational designation of probation officers. They are now located in all penal establishments, undertaking liaison work with field-based colleagues and theoretically available to all prisoners at any time of day. Their work is particularly concerned with the need for prisoners to maintain links with the outside world and to prepare themselves for release, either on parole or otherwise.

There is a marked association between age and the chances of a probation officer being located in a prison: 3 per cent of officers in their twenties are located in prison, compared with 6 per cent of officers in their thirties, 9 per cent of those in their forties and 12 per cent of those aged 50 or older. This distribution only partly reflects length of time in service, and there appears to be a tendency for younger officers to be protected from work in the prison setting for as long as possible.

The tasks and methods identified by prison-based officers differ in only one significant respect from those identified by officers in the field: courtwork and court report preparation cease to hold centre-stage; indeed they almost disappear altogether. The importance of dealing with other professionals is emphasised, but otherwise the nature of the tasks performed does not differ as much as might have been expected; only the work-setting is different. (Table 3.9)

Table 3.9
Tasks and methods in prison-based practice

[Very important = 3.00]

Counselling individuals	2.69
Dealing with other professionals	2.68
Workload management	2.23
Keeping records	2.02
Co-working	2.01
Groupwork	1.85
- -	
Family therapy	0.68
Pre-sentence reports	0.33
Courtwork	0.18

[Not at all important = 0.00]

N = 62

When asked whether there are other tasks and methods that characterise their job, prison-based officers drew attention to the paradox of two extremes: on the one hand, they have more time to engage in deep casework with serious offenders and to become involved in long-term groupwork – for example with sex offenders or with alcoholics or drug-abusers; on the other, a lot of their duties in reception interviews and in responding to welfare requests are seen as being superficial. Much of the work may involve domestic enquiries, but, even here, the probation officer often sees her/himself as doing no more than passing messages.

The reports that prison-based officers write are mainly concerned with home leave and parole applications.

What kinds of knowledge do prison-based officers say is important? Knowledge of court procedure is peripheral, although an understanding of sentencing principles remains relevant. Psychology is given greater emphasis; social work methods (at a fairly high level) and sociology (at a low level) are unchanged; knowledge of welfare rights, the law and local resources are seen as being significantly less important than is so in the field. (Table 3.10)

Table 3.10
Areas of knowledge required for prison-based practice

[Very important = 3.00]

Social work methods	2.21
Psychology	2.15
Welfare rights	1.90
Sentencing principles/tariff	1.79
Local resources	1.71
Appropriate law	1.70
Sociology	1.68
- -	
Court procedure	1.18

[Not at all important = 0.00]

N = 62

The main additional kind of knowledge required is said to be knowledge about the prison system – the regime, rules, regulations, current departmental policies, the parole process, lifers, pre-release procedures, and so on. A second specialist area mentioned is to do with the availability of national resources for discharged prisoners (like hostels and drug rehabilitation units). Knowledge of the internal workings of Home Office departments is also said to be useful ('Who to telephone with what query').

Thus the emphasis is almost wholly on matters of system and procedure. The prison-based officer needs to be able to find her/his way around if good quality practice is to ensue.

When we look at the skills and qualities used in prison-based work, (table 3.11) there are again fewer differences to be seen than might have been anticipated. Skills in coping with client emotion are pre-eminent (because probation officers are often involved both at the start and the end of a sentence and in the context of liaison with the outside world where, very often, the prisoner's family may be in difficulties or where a relationship may be ending); there is more use of groupwork, but all the normal skills – counselling, assessment, writing reports and records – remain much as they are in the field. Those skills which have low priority outside – organising meetings, family therapy and public speaking – are similarly rated inside. The art of influencing court decisions is something which the prison-based officer can largely forget about during her/his tour of duty.

Table 3.11
Skills and qualities used in prison-based practice

[Very important = 3.00]

Coping with client emotion	2.90
Counselling 1-to-1	2.79
Making assessments	2.76
Getting on with colleagues	2.60
Writing reports	2.56
Writing records	1.97
Groupwork	1.88
Organising meetings	0.98
Public speaking	0.85
Practising family therapy	0.52
Influencing court decisions	0.23

[Not at all important = 0.00]

N = 62

In addition to those listed, prison-based probation officers said that you have to have skills in assessing risk and in dealing with aggression (or 'challenging behaviour'); but, by far the most important skill is in the area of liaison and negotiation with other people – with discipline staff in the institution, with colleagues and other agencies outside the prison, with prisoners and between them and their families.

Lying behind the liaison and negotiation role is the objective of improving the regime for the benefit of prisoners, obtaining greater commitment from field-based POs and sustaining the private lives of prisoners while they are inside. The prison-based probation officer is, in every sense, a go-between – diplomat, enabler, facilitator. The qualities required may be those more often found in the realms of industrial arbitration.

The distinguishing characteristics of prison-based practice   Probation officers working in prison say that it is the location of their base that has the most powerful effect on what they do and how they work. The job of providing a social work service from within a penal institution is, they say, unique to them. Moreover, this is further affected by the variety of types of prison in which they might work or by the precise location within the institution of the probation office. Their approach to the job is, for example, influenced by whether they are in a remand prison, on a hospital wing, in a unit for 'vulnerable prisoners', a dispersal prison or an open prison: all have their own special characteristics, and all presumably require a period of adaptation for the newly-attached probation officer.

Another factor stems from the close – if sometimes ambivalent – relationship that probation officers have with the uniformed staff who dominate their working environment. The PO has to work under the direction of the prison governor and is often a part of the wing management team. Despite this, some officers still see the prison as a hostile, even an alien environment, and one in which they are most decidedly not in control. They have to work within rules and regimes that are determined by and imposed by the Prison Department of the Home Office. Several told us that they are in constant battle with the institution and that they do not find the work setting conducive to good probation practice: objectives are frequently determined by the needs of the institution rather than by those of the client-prisoner.

A third feature impinging on the work of the prison-based PO is, though not unique, certainly different in degree. The caseload is made up wholly of prisoners and their families. It includes a high proportion of hardened offenders and high-risk clients – lifers, serious sex offenders, professional criminals, prisoners with severe psychiatric problems and men and women convicted of serious crimes of violence. The prison-based officer's clients are seen as being more aggressive and more alienated than those of the field-based officer.

Fourthly, prison-based officers are constantly having to respond quickly to demands made upon them. They see themselves as frequently having to make a 'first-line response'. They are always available, and say that they see clients face-to-face much more intensively during the working day than is the case outside the prison walls. It is more like residential work than community social work. The job is 'demand-led' – they are faced with demands for attention, for counselling, and for the resolution of practical welfare problems. Because of this, probation officers in prisons do not, they say, take initiatives; they just respond.

Finally, however, some officers say that they are glad to be out of what they describe as the increasingly bureaucratic structure of the community-based probation service. They find, in prison, (perhaps ironically) fewer hierarchical pressures, and say that their work is less susceptible to Head Office interference.

Eight per cent of our respondents told us that they were specialist court-based officers – many of them located in Crown Courts.

Among officers who have served up to 15 years in the service, only about 6 per cent specialise in court-based practice; after that, though, the proportion rises to 13 per cent. The court-based specialism is a function particularly likely to be allocated to the long-serving officer.

It goes without saying (or rather it is tautologous to say it) that court work is the paramount task, with the writing of pre-sentence reports also dominant. The high priority given to dealing with other professionals reflects the liaison role of the court-based PO. Counselling, workload management, keeping records and co-working are slightly less important than they are in the field. Groupwork and family therapy are marginal. (Table 3.12)

Table 3.12
Tasks and methods in court-based practice

[Very important = 3.00]

Courtwork	2.98
Dealing with other professionals	2.80
Pre-sentence reports	2.66
Counselling individuals	2.21
Workload management	2.09
Keeping records	1.78
Co-working	1.50
Groupwork	0.65
Family therapy	0.58

[Not at all important = 0.00]

N = 60

In providing additional information, court-based officers confirmed the central place of liaison and public relations in their job; they are the medium through whom a great deal of information is communicated – involving court staff, magistrates, judges, lawyers, defendants, witnesses, field colleagues, workers in other agencies (like social services departments) and members of the public.

They have to support other officers' pre-sentence report recommendations in court and assist outside colleagues in respect of court-related matters. Their duties require them to spend a much higher proportion of their working life actually in court than would be the case with most probation officers.

Their contacts with clients are usually quite brief. They may well have no caseload of their own, and although they will sometimes do full pre-sentence reports, they may also be called on to do short-term assessment work in the body of the court and to report back after stand-down enquiries.

Knowledge of court procedure and the law is seen as absolutely essential for court-based officers, but the overall pattern of knowledge required is almost identical to that offered by field-based officers. (Table 3.13)

Table 3.13
Areas of knowledge required for court-based practice

[Very important = 3.00]

Court procedure	2.98
Sentencing principles/tariff	2.92
Appropriate law	2.68
Local resources	2.43
Welfare rights	1.86
Social work methods	1.69
Psychology	1.58
- -	
Sociology	1.28

[Not at all important = 0.00]

N = 60

Beyond this, court-based officers did not add greatly to our information about the knowledge required to do their job. Some said that you had to know about the attitudes of the judiciary or the magistracy towards different kinds of offences; and others implied that court-based officers were expected to be experts on the effects of addiction on offenders and even on psychiatric symptoms – this presumably so that they could advise the bench on whether to seek specialist advice before passing sentence.

When we look at skills and qualities, however, although there are many similarities in the order of priorities, there are significant differences in the weight given to some of them. (Table 3.14) In particular, the court officer is one of the functional categories for whom public speaking is considered important, whereas much less emphasis is placed on counselling than in fieldwork. The ability to influence court decisions (naturally) and the ability to get on with colleagues both emerge strongly as requirements of the job.

Groupwork, family therapy and even record writing are not rated overall as important.

Table 3.14
Skills and qualities used in court-based practice

[Very important = 3.00]

Influencing court decisions	2.93
Making assessments	2.72
Getting on with colleagues	2.68
Writing reports	2.58
Coping with client emotion	2.53
Public speaking	2.29
Counselling 1-to-1	1.78
Writing records	1.41
Organising meetings	0.90
Groupwork	0.62
Practising family therapy	0.48

[Not at all important = 0.00]

N = 60

The liaison role of the court-based officer requires inter-personal skills and, we were told, perhaps a higher level of integrity than in other parts of the service; these specialists are very conscious of their role in representing the interests of the probation service in a very public setting, and they would look for skills and qualities that could guarantee good-quality practice.

Court-based officers should be able to undertake short-term work, to make rapid assessments and to respond with quickly-produced but carefully thought-out recommendations; some see this as a form of crisis intervention; others said that it was largely a matter of identifying realistic recommendations bearing in mind the climate of the court.

The distinguishing characteristics of court-based practice The main distinguishing characteristics of court-based practice are those already outlined above: the primacy of the court setting, and the fact that the officer spends much of her/his time there; the role of liaison and communication and the responsibility of maintaining the reputation of the probation service in the criminal justice system; the absence of a full caseload and the focus on short-term work, with a particular need to make competent assessments and to produce rapid recommendations under pressure.

4   Probation centre practice

Probation centre work had its statutory origins in the Criminal Justice Act 1972 (though there had been some tentative ventures before then); then, under the CJ Act 1982, Schedule 11 provisions (amended by the CJ Act 1991) built it into the routine fabric of the probation service. All areas were given access to capital funds, and this enabled probation service managers to create a wide range of day centre facilities designed to put offenders into community-based regimes of varying degrees of correctional intensity.

Probation centre work is one of the few specialisms which is more likely to be done by younger officers – especially by those in their 30s and 40s; it is almost entirely monopolised by probation officers with between three and fifteen years service behind them; it is more likely to be done by men than women, and by graduates than by non-graduates. In this sense, it is a specialism with a PO-profile that distinguishes it from most of the others.

This distinctiveness is reflected in the central place accorded to groupwork and co-working as tasks and methods in probation centre practice. The five per cent of probation officers based in these centres clearly have to adopt a quite different approach to their work when they arrive there from the field. Counselling remains important, but the preparation of pre-sentence reports and courtwork have a lower priority. Family therapy is marginal. (Table 3.15)

Table 3.15
Tasks and methods in probation centre practice

[Very important = 3.00]

Co-working	2.78
Groupwork	2.73
Dealing with other professionals	2.54
Workload management	2.28
Counselling individuals	2.20
Keeping records	1.63
- -	
Pre-sentence reports	1.33
Courtwork	1.27
Family therapy	0.59

[Not at all important = 0.00]

N = 41

In their open-ended answers to our questions, probation centre staff confirmed the importance of groupwork as a method – either working with formal and

95

structured groups or with unstructured groups depending partly on the types of offender and partly on programme aims.

Probation centre workers find themselves faced with the task of supervising staff (including non-professional employees) and with a public relations and liaison role – seen as important both during the development of the centre and once it is in full operation.

Table 3.16 appears to suggest that the knowledge base of probation centre practice is not appreciably different from that used by field-based staff. However, when we draw on the additional material supplied by our specialist respondents, we learn of a number of variations. The use of quasi-educational methods in probation centres means that the officers have to use non-social-work perspectives in many of their plans. Probation centre officers also said that knowledge about alcohol and drugs, knowledge of the principles and methods of groupwork, and – in particular – knowledge about management are all important.

Table 3.16
Areas of knowledge required for probation centre practice

[Very important = 3.00]

Local resources	2.61
Sentencing principles/tariff	2.56
Social work methods	2.39
Welfare rights	2.32
Court procedure	2.05
Appropriate law	2.03
Psychology	2.00
Sociology	1.71

- -

[Not at all important = 0.00]

N = 41

The skills and qualities outlined in table 3.17 reflect the differences in probation centre methods: the staff need to be more skilled in groupwork, better able to organise meetings and competent as public speakers; getting on with colleagues is a pre-requisite of effectiveness. Writing reports is not something that probation centre workers do as much of as they do when based in the field office.

Management skills were especially emphasised by respondents in the additional information provided. They say that running a probation centre requires them to be skilled in programme planning, in recruiting and supervising staff, in centre administration and budgeting, in team leadership and in planning the future development of the centre. They also need to be able to handle publicity and relationships with the media.

Probation centre specialists say that they need skills in working with other agencies and organisations, a special awareness of the signs and symptoms of alcohol and drug addiction, and an ability to get involved in problems of accommodation.

A number of probation centres seem to have built in research and monitoring elements, and the officers felt that this added yet another dimension to the skills they were expected to have available.

Table 3.17
Skills and qualities used in probation centre practice

[Very important = 3.00]

Making assessments	2.85
Getting on with colleagues	2.78
Groupwork	2.76
Coping with client emotion	2.63
Influencing court decisions	2.49
Organising meetings	2.34
Public speaking	2.23
Writing reports	2.08
Counselling 1-to-1	2.03
Writing records	1.83
- -	
Practising family therapy	0.55

[Not at all important = 0.00]

N = 41

The distinguishing characteristics of probation centre practice   Probation centre workers see themselves as mini-managers and team leaders; they carry significant administrative responsibilities. Their professional work is very much groupwork-focused and there is a real educational dimension to it. The all-day, five-days-a-week approach means that they have a more intensive involvement with the clients – many of whom will be serious offenders.

5   Throughcare

Throughcare requires officers to specialise in work with prisoners both before their release and afterwards. They are based, not in the prison, but in an area probation office. In theory the focus begins at the time of sentence, but the concentration of activity tends to come later – especially when the question of release on parole is first scheduled. Some officers specialise in young offender cases; others are allocated specifically to work with homeless or rootless offenders. Throughcare officers tend to be aged over 40 and to have a minimum of six years service behind them.

Throughcare specialists are inclined to downgrade all the tasks and methods offered to them in our enquiry; only workload management is rated (marginally) higher than it is by field-based officers. The order of priority is broadly in line with fieldwork practice, except for pre-sentence report work and courtwork, of which throughcare officers do less. (Table 3.18)

Table 3.18
Tasks and methods in throughcare practice

[Very important = 3.00]

Counselling individuals	2.76
Workload management	2.52
Dealing with other professionals	2.20
Pre-sentence reports	2.20
Keeping records	2.08
- -	
Groupwork	1.33
Co-working	1.32
Courtwork	1.16
Family therapy	1.12

[Not at all important = 0.00]

N = 25

The principal task mentioned by officers in addition to the tasks offered to them by the questionnaire was concerned with resettlement and the provision of practical help. As well as writing pre-sentence reports, throughcare officers prepare home circumstances reports as a part of the parole review process; and a considerable amount of liaison with prisons is involved – usually with the probation officers based there.

As table 3.19 shows, throughcare specialists are enthusiasts for practical knowledge – about local resources and welfare rights, but all other fields of knowledge are seen to be of less importance than in the mainstream. They make less use of knowledge about the law, about sentencing principles or about court procedures, and they have less felt need for psychology, sociology or social work methods.

Table 3.19
Areas of knowledge required for throughcare practice

[Very important = 3.00]

Local resources	2.80
Welfare rights	2.52
Sentencing principles/tariff	2.40
Court procedure	1.92
Appropriate law	1.88
Psychology	1.60
Social work methods	1.52
- -	
Sociology	1.44

[Not at all important = 0.00]

N = 25

The knowledge that throughcare officers say that they need is mostly about systems and procedures: they have to know their way around the prison network, to know the regulations, the criteria for home leave, and the workings of the parole scheme. Some said that a knowledge of Home Office organization is invaluable – which person in which department to contact for which problem.

When working with prisoners and their families, knowledge about alcoholism, addiction and mental illness is considered useful, and some knowledge of ethnic issues and cultural perspectives is increasingly necessary.

So far as skills and qualities are concerned, throughcare specialists follow much the same pattern as applies in the field. They make extensive use of counselling skills and have to be able to absorb client emotion; they see the ability to do assessments and to write reports as key elements in their work. (Table 3.20)

Influencing court decisions, getting on with colleagues and writing records are all important, though slightly less so than are the qualities required in the course of client-contact work. Groupwork, organising meetings, doing family therapy and public speaking are not, for the most part, core skills required of the throughcare officer.

In addition to the qualities listed, throughcare officers say that they need to be good judges of character, to be able to assess client potential, and to be prepared to accept a less social-work-orientated role than is appropriate elsewhere in the probation service: their job is very heavily concerned with protecting the public, often from very serious offenders, and this is a duty that they take seriously.

Table 3.20
Skills and qualities used in throughcare practice

[Very important = 3.00]

Counselling 1-to-1	2.84
Writing reports	2.80
Making assessments	2.76
Coping with client emotion	2.72
Influencing court decisions	2.20
Getting on with colleagues	2.04
Writing records	2.04
- -	
Groupwork	1.20
Organising meetings	1.08
Practising family therapy	0.92
Public speaking	0.84

[Not at all important = 0.00]

N = 25

The distinguishing characteristics of throughcare The two main characteristics mentioned by our respondents concern:

1 The fact that their clients are almost all in custody or subject to licence. This means that the officers spend a lot of their time visiting prisons or otherwise liaising with institutions. They tend to see themselves as having more clearly defined tasks than have fieldwork officers, and much of the work has a very material focus.

2 They see their specialism as being very correctional and only marginally geared up to a social work perspective. The emphasis of their work is on protecting the public, especially when they are responsible for supervising serious, high risk or life sentence offenders. They are very conscious of the fact that they may be held accountable if something goes badly wrong.

6 Community service practice

The pattern of managing community service schemes has evolved to a point where some maingrade probation officers have been given delegated responsibility for local provisions. The POs are expected to run the scheme, to supervise non-professional and ancillary staff, to assess offenders referred for community service and to offer general oversight once an order is made. They carry some responsibility for liaison with the agencies offering work.

Table 3.21
Tasks and methods in community service practice

[Very important = 3.00]

Courtwork	2.83
Dealing with other professionals	2.79
Keeping records	2.74
Workload management	2.67
Co-working	1.59

- -

Groupwork	1.22
Pre-sentence reports	1.18
Counselling individuals	1.17
Family therapy	0.09

[Not at all important = 0.00]

N = 24

The officers are also expected to handle difficult client situations requiring professional expertise; these are especially likely to apply when breaches have to be dealt with and court appearances ensue.

Community service officers are among the most experienced of any specialist group; there are a disproportionate number of them aged 50 or older; and almost all of them have spent between six and twenty years in the service; it is not, in general, a job delegated to younger or recently qualified officers.

The focus of the work is reflected in the emphasis given by CS specialists to courtwork, dealing with other professionals and keeping records; they are engaged in procedural matters that do not require extensive use of counselling, nor much knowledge about social work methods or welfare rights. (Table 3.21)

The probation officers involved say that one of the tasks facing them is to maintain the cost-effectiveness of the scheme.

The most important knowledge required by community service specialists is to do with sentencing principles and the tariff, court procedures and the law. (Table 3.22) But they also say that a knowledge of local resources and of psychology are important: these, together, reflect the extent to which they have to achieve a good match between the potential performance of their clients and the need to preserve a steady flow of service opportunities in order to absorb them.

Community service officers say that they also require to be knowledgeable about trade unions and charitable trusts, whose cooperation and support are needed to ensure the smooth-running of the offenders' scheme.

Table 3.22
Areas of knowledge required for community service practice

[Very important = 3.00]

Court procedure	3.00
Appropriate law	3.00
Sentencing principles/tariff	2.96
Local resources	2.54
Psychology	1.63
- -	
Sociology	1.25
Welfare rights	1.13
Social work methods	1.13

[Not at all important = 0.00]

N = 24

The most important skills used by community service officers (so far as the proffered list is concerned) involve making assessments and influencing court decisions; they also do more in the way of organising meetings and public speaking than others do. (Table 3.23) Of low priority are family therapy, counselling and groupwork; and even the normally required skill in coping with client emotion is lower down in the list of priorities.

Table 3.23
Skills and qualities used in community service practice

[Very important = 3.00]

Influencing court decisions	2.83
Making assessments	2.83
Getting on with colleagues	2.83
Writing reports	2.50
Organising meetings	2.42
Writing records	2.38
Public speaking	2.17
Coping with client emotion	1.63
- -	
Groupwork	1.08
Counselling 1-to-1	1.00
Practising family therapy	0.08

[Not at all important = 0.00]

N = 24

In addition, the community service specialists emphasised in particular the management skills that they say they require: budgeting, staff supervision and training, and the evaluation and development of their programme. They need to be skilled at liaising with all manner of local groups, employment agencies, voluntary organisations and government departments. They need skills in public relations, and they must be qualified to assess risk in would-be clients. For the most part, skill in supervising clients is not said to be a prerequisite of the job.

The distinguishing characteristics of community service practice The importance of managerial duties and the primacy of the officer's role in court in respect of community service breaches are the two dominant elements that differentiate the job from that held by field-based officers. Community service officers carry a good deal of responsibility for running the scheme and for maintaining a good correctional model so far as its clients are concerned. They also feel that they have a higher public profile, because of the wide-ranging nature of their links with the community in setting up projects and carrying them through to a successful conclusion.

7   Hostel-based practice

Most probation officers based in probation hostels or bail hostels are likely to be employed as deputy wardens with an SPO-graded officer in the warden's post. Because of the shift system, they are often responsible for the day-to-day running of the hostel as a whole.

Table 3.24
Tasks and methods in hostel-based practice

[Very important = 3.00]

Counselling individuals	2.88
Dealing with other professionals	2.75
Co-working	2.63
Workload management	2.56
Keeping records	2.44
Groupwork	1.88
Courtwork	1.69
- -	
Pre-sentence reports	1.19
Family therapy	0.56

[Not at all important = 0.00]

N = 16

103

Hostel-based officers tend to be relatively recently qualified (44 per cent of them trained less than five years ago, compared with 28 per cent of the sample as a whole), though they are not particularly young.

Counselling and workload management are high priorities in hostels, as they are in the field; dealing with other professionals gets a higher rating, and co-working is very significantly more important as a method (though groupwork is not). Courtwork and the preparation of pre-sentence reports are not centrally relevant tasks, and family therapy comes at the bottom of the list. (Table 3.24)

In addition, officers told us that the need to hold a balance between care and control was one of the significant tasks that faced them in the job. Additionally they are involved with the full range of management functions (under the warden's direction), giving staff supervision and support, and providing staff training as required.

In general, hostel-based staff tend to rate all areas of knowledge more highly than do fieldworkers (table 3.25), but the rank order is broadly similar; the two main differences concern psychology and social work methods, both of which are more heavily emphasised (especially the former) as being areas of knowledge of direct relevance to the work that hostel staff are required to do.

Table 3.25
Areas of knowledge required for hostel-based practice

[Very important = 3.00]

Local resources	2.80
Sentencing principles/tariff	2.69
Psychology	2.63
Court procedure	2.63
Social work methods	2.56
Welfare rights	2.27
Appropriate law	2.19
Sociology	1.71

- -

[Not at all important = 0.00]

N = 16

In their open-ended answers, hostel-based staff said that practical knowledge (like how to change door locks) and managerial acumen (like ensuring the availability of sufficient laundry) out-weigh more theoretical fields of knowledge in importance. It is seen as an advantage if officers are knowledgeable about mental health legislation and practice, and information about the national network of hostels is also an asset.

104

Getting on with colleagues is an essential quality in the confined context of a residential setting, and the skills of assessment and coping with client emotion are also of increased importance. Writing reports is not something which hostel-based staff have to do a lot, and they do not need to influence court decisions very often; family therapy is hardly used at all. Organising meetings and public speaking, though not of major significance, are nevertheless called into use more often than in a field-based setting. (Table 3.26)

Table 3.26
Skills and qualities used in hostel-based practice

[Very important = 3.00]

Getting on with colleagues	3.00
Coping with client emotion	2.94
Making assessments	2.88
Counselling 1-to-1	2.81
Influencing court decisions	2.38
Writing records	2.31
Groupwork	1.88
Writing reports	1.81
Organising meetings	1.56
Public speaking	1.56
- -	
Practising family therapy	0.31

Not at all important = 0.00]

N = 16

The skills that staff mention when invited to add to the list include: stress management, the ability to defuse aggression, sensitivity to drug or alcohol abuse, and the art of residential work generally.

The distinguishing characteristics of hostel-based practice   The two primary distinguishing characteristics of hostel-based practice are:

1 The fact that the work takes place in a residential setting. The working hours are longer and often anti-social: they involve sleeping-in and weekend duty. Often the officer is the sole member of staff in the hostel and needs to be prepared to cope with whatever emergency arises. Even if not on duty in the hostel, the warden and deputy warden have to be available 'on call'. Residential work means 'living with the clients', participating in domestic tasks, and tends to require the officer to

concentrate on short-term crisis work, especially where the residents are on pre-sentence remand.

2 The fact that the role of the officer is very heavily management-orientated. The deputy seems to be given specific functions in many hostels – especially the supervision and training of staff and the maintenance of the accounts.

It can be seen that, although the focus of work is still on offender-clients, the nature of the job is quite different from that which characterises most probation posts.

IV   Tasks and methods, knowledge, skills and qualities: an overview

We found very little sign that officers' age, gender, length of service or graduate background were associated with their perceptions of what was involved in doing the probation job. There is a remarkably consistent pattern to what all officers say about the tasks they perform, the methods they use, the knowledge they draw on, and the skills and qualities that they consider necessary if the work is to be well done. Of course, individual officers vary in their attitudes and views, but these variations are to be found equally among men as among women, among graduates as among non-graduates, among the young as among the old, and among the recently-appointed as among long-serving officers.

As we have seen, the different specialisms that are now an integral part of the probation service create quite different working environments for officers and often require changes of focus, expertise and purpose to an extent hitherto not publicly appreciated. Even so, some elements remain common.

Tasks and methods

Two tasks are of paramount importance to all probation officers: the need to deal with other professionals, and the management of one's workload. All functional groups agree that they could not do their job properly without an appreciation of these two essential tasks.

Dealing with other professionals requires skills in interpersonal relations, a style and manner that is acceptable in the cultural setting in which the officer operates. Workload management requires an organised approach to one's duties. In effect, our respondents are saying that you cannot be an acceptable probation officer if you are a social isolate or a trouble-maker, or if you have a chaotic approach to your working life. The primacy of these two elements is particularly apparent in the light of the emphasis on managerial duties that has emerged in respect of hostel-based staff, in probation centres and in community service settings, and in the light of the emphasis on public relations that court officers and others make.

One other task – record-keeping – is seen as being almost always essential in the job. Courtwork is more variable: for most officers it is central to their daily duties, for some it is marginal.

So far as working with clients is concerned, counselling still predominates. With the exception of community service officers (who see it as having little relevance to their work), all probation officers use counselling as their main working tool with clients. Co-working and groupwork are drawn on by officers in one or two specialist areas – co-working, for example, by those in civil work, and groupwork by probation centre staff.

Family therapy is generally very little used outside of civil work settings where the focus is on marriage, the family, relationship breakdown and conciliation.

Knowledge

Some areas of knowledge recur again and again in our analysis. Those which, in the light of our respondents' answers, can be said to be essential for almost all probation officers include knowledge of the law, of court procedure, of local resources and of the principles of sentencing. Only officers based in prison would dissent to a significant extent; their felt need to be au fait with institutional life and culture means that their interest in the outside world of the courts and the local community is relatively slight. Civil work specialists say that, for them, a knowledge of the principles of sentencing is irrelevant – though they regard knowledge of civil court decision-making procedures as important.

These four 'essential' areas of knowledge are remarkably atheoretical. Only after them, do probation officers mention psychology and social work methods as subjects which any good practitioner must have studied. Their mention prompts the thought that we know remarkably little about *what kind* of psychology and *what aspects* of social work methods are most useful in probation practice.

At the bottom of the list of knowledge needed come welfare rights and sociology – though neither of them are dismissed by a majority of our respondents as being irrelevant.

Skills and qualities

Two skills are said to be of supreme importance by probation officers in all fields of practice: first, the ability to make assessments; and second, the ability to get on with colleagues.

Assessment requires perceptiveness of personality and behaviour, judgment and skills in decision-making. The ability to get on with colleagues requires a balanced approach to personal relationships and acceptable patterns of office behaviour.

Other qualities that are rated highly include skills in report-writing (requiring high standards of literacy), the ability to influence court decisions (demanding personal credibility and a facility to write or speak persuasively on the basis of a well-presented assessment), and a capacity to cope with client emotions.

Counselling skills are rated highly by four functional groups, though there are also four for whom they are not so important; writing records is regarded as a middling sort of skill. Public speaking, organising meetings and groupwork are required skills in one or two areas of practice, but less so in most. And family therapy is rated low by the majority of all our respondents.

Adding to our list, we were told that management skills, an interest in public relations and the ability to liaise and negotiate with individuals and organisations are significantly important in some settings.

V   Levels of work satisfaction in probation practice

We have seen how the shape of the probation service has changed over the past 30 years, and, in particular, how all officers with five years service behind them now have a fifty-fifty chance at any one time of being employed in a specialist capacity.

But how much do probation officers like the job that they do? What is their level of work satisfaction? We employed a specially designed questionnaire to explore these questions. The schedule consisted of 18 questions, broken down into six categories, so that we could distinguish between levels of satisfaction in respect of different aspects of work and working relationships.

The results are given in table 3.27.

We will consider, in turn, the six categories of questions that each officer answered.

1   *The work that POs do*

Probation officers score very highly on most of our work satisfaction indices, but the highest ratings of all come in response to questions about the work that they do with their clients.

85 per cent of them say that they like the sort of work that they do with their clients, and 87 per cent say that they enjoy working with the particular client group that they have 'now'.

These are impressively high proportions, and are not the less impressive because only 52 per cent express themselves satisfied with the results that they get in their work.

There are statistically significant differences in levels of work satisfaction between the settings in which probation officers work, though even those which come relatively low in the list still show an impressively positive statistic:

Table 3.27
Measures of work satisfaction

	Strongly agree	Agree	Undecided	Disagree	Strongly disagree
1 The work that POs do	%	%	%	%	%
I enjoy working with the client groups that I have now	29	58	9	3	0
I enjoy the sort of work that I do with my clients	24	61	10	3	0
I am satisfied with the results that I get in my work	5	47	34	14	1
2 Working colleagues					
I enjoy working with my immediate colleagues	26	59	11	3	1
I am satisfied with the supervision that I get from my SPO	14	39	15	22	10
I see a lot of my colleagues out of working hours	1	9	7	50	32
3 Relations with management					
I get the feeling that higher management have no idea what it's like to do my job	20	32	22	24	1
I am proud of being an employee in this Probation Area	9	42	33	13	2
Managers give me ample opportunity to use my own initiative at work	19	57	14	9	1
4 Pay and status					
Compared with other jobs, I think I'm quite well paid	2	29	17	38	13
Mine is a job which ordinary people think highly of	3	29	36	29	2
I expect to get promotion in the next couple of years	1	9	23	34	32
5 Professional pride					
I think that my colleagues at work do a good job	14	61	19	5	1
When I'm at work, I have a sense of pride in my profession	13	55	22	9	1
If anyone asks me what I do for a living, I sometimes conceal my occupation	2	20	4	40	35
6 A sense of alienation					
I am happier in my work than most other people I know	8	39	34	18	1
Most days I have to force myself to go to work	1	5	5	49	40
I really wish I was doing a quite different job	3	8	17	39	33

© Martin Davies 1988

When asked whether they enjoy the sort of work that they do with their clients, those in different functional groups answered 'yes' in the following proportions:

97% of civil work specialists
94% of hostel-based POs
93% of probation centre POs
87% of mainstream field team POs
79% of prison-based POs
78% of court-based POs
76% of throughcare specialists
71% of community service POs

Expressions of satisfaction with the type of client group produced a similar pattern, but a different shape emerged when we looked at who said they are satisfied with the results that they get in their work:

73% of civil work specialists
66% of court-based POs
63% of community service POs
59% of probation centre POs
50% of hostel-based POs
47% of mainstream field team POs
44% of prison-based POs
40% of throughcare specialists

From these three questions, it is clear that civil work specialists have the highest levels of satisfaction, throughcare specialists the lowest.

2   Working colleagues

Probation officers are fortunate in most of their working relationships: 85 per cent of them enjoy working with their immediate colleagues. But the relationships do not generally extend beyond working hours: only ten per cent claim to see much of each other outside the work setting, and many vehemently derided any such idea.

Just over half the sample say that they are satisfied with the supervision that they get from their senior officer.

3   Relations with management

Previous research has shown that job autonomy is one of the most highly regarded features of probation work, and we found that this is still largely available in most posts. Over three-quarters of all officers said that managers give them ample opportunity to use their initiative at work.

Most specialist functions seemed to carry a higher level of job autonomy: those working in hostels (100%) and probation centres (98%), in community service and in civil work (both 83%) were all more likely to say that they are given the opportunity to use their initiative. The only settings in which the proportion fell significantly below the average were in prison (66%) and in throughcare (68%). The extent to which officers feel autonomous is not related either to the officer's age or to the length of service.

A slight majority in the sample (52%) said that they thought management had little idea of what it is like to do their job.

51 per cent claimed that they are proud of being an employee in their local Area; 33 per cent were either undecided or neutral and only 15 per cent seemed willing to express positive dislike of their employing authority. In the specialisms, it was the probation officers located in the hostels (69%) and the courts (60%) who feel the greatest pride in their employer, and those in throughcare (44%) who feel the least.

4   Pay and status

A bare majority of our respondents felt they are not well-paid – just 51 per cent – but there was a strong relationship between these opinions and the length of time that officers have been in the service. Dissatisfaction with pay-levels is highest in the early years of service and falls over time:

65% of POs in their first five years are unhappy with pay;
53% of POs between 5 and 10 years are unhappy with pay;
51% of POs between 10 and 15 years are unhappy with pay;
32% of POs after 15 years are unhappy with pay.

There was a straight split in the response to a statement about how the probation officer's job is perceived by members of the public, with over one-third refusing to proffer an opinion. Again there is a relationship with age and experience: the longer an officer has been in the service and the older s/he is, the more they think they are well viewed by members of the public. In the functional groups, the greatest sense of occupational status is expressed by those working in prisons, 52 per cent of whom agreed with the statement that 'ordinary people think highly of my job'. Hostel staff, community service workers and civil work POs also feel that they are held in relatively high regard by members of the public; but the rest tend to think that their occupational status is not good.

Very few of our respondents were confident of getting promotion 'in the next couple of years': 10 per cent could be said to be optimistic in some degree, though only a tenth of these were strongly so. A large majority of the sample – 72 per cent – hold out no hope at all.

111

5   Professional pride

When they are at work, does the idea of 'being a probation officer' feel like something to be proud of? Our respondents, in general, think that it does. 68 per cent feel a sense of pride in their profession, and seventy five per cent think that their colleagues do a good job; only 22 per cent said that, if anyone asks them what they do for a living, they sometimes conceal their occupation.

6   A sense of alienation?

The work satisfaction index contains within it a batch of three questions which are intended to identify employees who appear utterly depressed by their work setting. Fortunately for the probation service, they prompt a response from only a small minority of officers: 6 per cent admit that on 'most days, I have to force myself to go to work'; eleven per cent really wish that they were doing a quite different job; and nineteen per cent positively deny that they are happier in their work than 'most other people they know'.

A significant 38 per cent of those in community service work say that they are less happy in their work than other people they know. The lowest expression of discontent – 5% – comes from probation centre officers.

VI   Summary

This study has shown that almost a half of all probation officers are now employed in specialist functions. The proportion is higher in some probation areas than others, and is greatest among officers who have been in the service for more than five years. Some thought ought to be given to the implications of this both for basic training syllabuses and for in-service, post-qualifying programmes. In any case, it seems likely that the emergence of specialisation has had and will continue to have a major impact on the probation officer's view of her/his role in society; at the very least, it challenges the hitherto homogeneous perception of probation officers as 'social workers of the courts', and, more radically, it may in the future be seen to have been instrumental in bringing about the total separation of probation from its social work roots. For the present, however, the majority of serving officers continue to describe their work in ways that would have been familiar to their predecessors

In mainstream fieldwork, the primacy of the court setting is a dominant feature, and determines many of the skills, qualities and areas of knowledge that officers say are important.

Pragmatic knowledge about court procedures, sentencing and the law, together with an awareness of local resources outweighs more theoretical fields of learning, though social work methods, psychology and, to a lesser extent, sociology are acknowledged as being important in their own right.

112

Five core skills and qualities are identified: interpersonal skills (for work both with clients and with professional colleagues), literacy, persuasiveness, resilience, and a sensitivity to human behaviour and its social context.

Specialist officers often have to adapt these same core skills to very different settings; in addition, some specialisms require skills in management and team leadership.

Counselling one-to-one remains the dominant method of working with clients, though some of the specialisms call for skills in groupwork, family therapy and co-working.

Probation officers enjoy generally high levels of work satisfaction, especially with respect to their contact with clients.

Note

1   In Tables 3.3 – 3.26, the broken line marks the mid-point on the rating-scale: categories above 1.50 are said, on balance, to be important overall; those below it are judged by the majority to be unimportant.

Appendix 3: Methodology

A questionnaire was mailed to 1200 probation officers selected randomly (using a random numbers table) from the current Directory. 38 questionnaires were returned because the officers had retired, died, were absent on long-term sickness or had been promoted out of the maingrade. The effective sample, therefore, was 1172, and the return of 785 completed questionnaires gave us a response-rate of 67 per cent – perfectly satisfactory for an investigation of this kind.

The questionnaire was designed following extensive exploratory and pilot studies which involved a large number of interviews with experienced officers and senior managers in different parts of the country.

60 per cent of our respondents were men; 40 per cent were women. 48 per cent of the sample were graduates; 52 per cent were not.

The age spread was as follows:

	%
20–24	1
25–29	7
30–34	15
35–39	21
40–44	20
45–49	12
50–54	12
55–59	8
60–plus	4

Length of service was equally widespread:

Years	%
Up to 2	10
3–5	18
6–10	27
11–15	25
16–20	14
21–25	4
26–30	2
31–plus	1

Data analysis was undertaken on an IBM compatible micro, using Wordstar, Dbase and Microstat software. Data transfer to the UEA mainframe allowed the major analysis to be done using SPSSx. Grateful acknowledgement is made to Steve Mosley, computing adviser in the School of Economic and Social Studies at UEA, whose skill and patience were indispensable to the successful completion of this study.

4 Holding the balance between court and client: the unique role of the probation officer

I The survey and the sample

The combinations of skills, knowledge, and qualities which experienced probation officers employ in their day-to-day practice are directed, in the main, towards a central mediating skill – that of holding the balance, in a variety of settings, between the court and the client. This is the nerve centre of the probation service upon which the core skills of communication, assessment, intervention, and agency professionalism converge. It is the consolidating skill which probation officers find the hardest to acquire, and with which many consider their qualifying training, on the whole, failed to equip them. This is the major conclusion of this in-depth qualitative survey of 62 experienced probation officers.

This fourth chapter centres around the views of a sample of experienced probation officers with a minimum of five years' service, in relation to the skills, knowledge and qualities they needed and utilised in their practice. Qualitative research methods were used. Whilst it should be read as a discrete piece of work, there is an extent to which it supplements and fleshes out the parallel statistical information in Chapter 3. Its primary value however lies in the extraction of detailed, individual and collective views from a varied group of well-versed probation practitioners about the factors which constitute the crux of their trade, and offer insight into the social reality of their practice as probation officers.

The sample of 62 probation officers was drawn from geographical areas which, it is suggested, were sufficiently balanced in character to be seen as presenting a reasonable cross-section of the population. These areas were Merseyside, Essex, Hereford and Worcester, and North Wales, from whom 26, 14, 12, and 10 main grade probation officers were respectively and proportionately drawn, via a random sample selection process. 32 officers were female, and 30 male. 25 officers worked with generic caseloads in mainstream district offices, and 37 were in full-time specialisms which covered throughcare, probation centres/packages, prisons, civil work, court work, community service, drugs, and hostel work. With five exceptions, all officers in the sample had been in a specialism at some point in their careers, which varied in length from 5½ to 24 years.

The questions in the interview schedule (see Appendix 4.2) evolved from a piloting process with 15 officers in the Merseyside, Lancashire, and Norfolk Probation Services, and two group 'brainstorming' exercises in the Merseyside area. One of the methods tested and modified for use in the 'Communication' section of the schedule was critical incident analysis which revolved around a detailed description of an officer's work with a particular case. For reasons of manageability it was decided not to adopt this method in its entirety, but some of the wealth of case material produced in the exercise has been used in illustration of some of the points made by the main study. Further to this, it was decided to follow up officers' views by observing the skills, knowledge and qualities actually employed in practice during the course of a working day, and two officers from West Yorkshire took part in this section of the research. Data from all the officers interviewed was collected via the written notes of the researcher. All participants were assured of confidentiality and the anonymity of themselves and the clients they talked about, and their contributions have been very much appreciated by the authors.

II   Communication with clients

1   Making human contact

Almost without exception, when recalling how they had established human contact with particular clients, the officers spoke of the importance of putting them at their ease, in order to create an atmosphere of trust and confidentiality in which the purpose of the PO/client contact could then be explored. Some officers felt it necessary to be 'up front' by stating their purpose immediately but most preferred to approach it more gradually, making formal introductions brief and trying to relax clients first, offering them coffee and informal conversation, establishing common human links, rather than store up problems of alienation by emphasising role differences early in the relationship.

As was the case throughout the interview schedule, some officers found difficulty in analysing processes which they regarded as skills, but felt they performed, for the most part, instinctively, sometimes automatically. Several officers, indeed, admitted that on an 'off' day, because of their long experience in the job, they could switch onto 'automatic pilot' in their communication with clients, though none of them was particularly proud of this ability. However, when pressed about the ways in which they put people at their ease, it became clear that many officers put considerable thought into this endeavour by asking their clerical staff not to interrupt them on the telephone, arranging chairs in a fashion calculated to aid communication, and then greeting the clients by shaking hands and giving them their proper titles. This is the beginning of a process which affords people status and respect, one of the traditional social work values, which these probation officers clearly still regarded as paramount in their work. Several officers mentioned the importance of signifying that they themselves were relaxed, particularly by the use of their own body language, smiling, making direct but unthreatening eye contact, and speaking in warm, reassuring tones. One described this process in the context of her work with a young female heroin addict whose drug abuse was out of control and who was reluctant to engage in discussion about her lifestyle when they first met. 'I needed to enable her to know I'd be there however often she failed. I wanted to overcome the restrictions of my office and my role – I didn't want my role to be another pressure on her. I wanted her to see me as friendly and unshockable. I used my own personality and warmth to give her the message, "I've got time for you." '

Some officers who worked in probation centres or had other informal settings available to them, spoke of the usefulness of establishing common human contact by sharing an activity, such as a game of pool, in which conversation which one described as being of 'a non-directive, non-intrusive nature', took place, where again an atmosphere of relaxation, and space-giving (also regarded as important by a number of people) could be created. The need for such a climate in client/officer contact was probably best justified by a prison probation officer who said, 'In a formal setting, a client may give you information, such as the fact that he split up with his wife in 1972. What you have to do is to create a sufficiently relaxed atmosphere for him to tell you how he *felt* about that, and to become more transparent.' Given that nearly all the probation officers spoke at some point in their interviews of engaging with clients' feelings, in order to help bring about real change in their lives, it becomes clear that the ability to relax people sufficiently to own their feelings is the first, and perhaps most crucial skill, upon which all subsequent probation skills hinge.

That this process has to take place in the context of a clear sense of purpose, seemed to be agreed by most respondents in the survey. They were aware that whilst they might be giving the appearance of engaging in aimless social chit-chat, they were in fact laying the foundations for the work which they hoped to be able to do with their clients. They were also employing what one civil work specialist called, 'a series of awarenesses – holding onto purpose, observing the effect you're having on a person, identifying the effect they're having on you – in fact using your learned skill of continuous social assessment. You assess all the time their statements, their actions, their living conditions if it's a home visit.' The more specific nature of this sense of purpose is discussed later on in the interview schedule, but having identified its importance, the skill of timing was one which seemed next to be brought into play. Officers spoke of the need for adaptability and flexibility in their approach, and whilst most had, over the years, developed a personal model for communicating with clients, it was one which allowed for the unpredictability of what might be presented to them. 'Starting where the client is at' was a phrase used frequently, so that if a client presented her/himself in a businesslike fashion, and was clearly more at ease with formality, and immediate discussion about purpose, role and function, then that would come first on the agenda. If, on the other hand, a client was visibly distressed, then both formal and informal discussion would be put in abeyance, whilst the emotion of the situation was directly addressed. In other words, the officers were concerned to keep down barriers and blocks to communication, so that they could begin to work effectively with their clients.

'Learning to listen, *really* listen' was how several officers emphasised another important communication skill. This referred to the uniqueness of the individual, and the danger of slotting them into pigeon holes without really taking in the meaning for them of what they are saying. Observing their facial expressions, body language, their silences, and interactions with other family members, was also an intrinsic part of *really* listening. One officer suggested,

> If you *really* listen, you provide yourself with the necessary clues about when to ask questions too, and when to gently prompt. You need to gain a lot of information about the client to be able to work usefully with them – it's like slowly painting a portrait and getting the shadings and angles right. You don't get a picture of quality by clumsily stabbing at it with a brush – you paint a bit here and a bit there when it feels right. It's the same with finding out about a client – if you overwhelm them with questions and talk, you might get some information, but it won't tell you much about colours or feelings.

The need to show genuine interest in clients was stressed by many officers, and the process of listening was again very important here. 'Honesty' and 'genuineness' were word used over and over again in the context of relationships with clients. It was clear that officers felt they must be accredited as human beings before they would be accepted and responded to as probation officers. This also involved appropriate self-disclosure, humour, sometimes anger, sometimes body-contact, issues which will be referred to in the next two sections. A minority but not insignificant skill mentioned was being able to communicate with deaf clients, and to speak clients' native languages, a situation that arose particularly with the North Wales officers. One of them, herself Welsh, pointed out that she is conscious of being better able to express her own thoughts and feelings in Welsh than in English, and that this must apply in much greater measure to those clients who speak mainly Welsh, and very little English. Some of the English officers had taken the trouble to learn some Welsh for this very reason – to aid relaxed communication. An issue which contains clear implications for work with any ethnic minority, this is another unexpected dimension to the diversity of responses which probation officers make to the establishing of human contact with their clients.

To help illustrate the practical applicability of some of these communication skills, here is the first section of a piece of work described by probation officer A, with his 32-year old client, Harry, on a 2-year probation order with a condition of attendance at a probation centre. His offences were assault, and threatening behaviour, arising out of a domestic dispute.

> My SPO did the court report, and recommended this sentence. There'd been a lot of publicity and newspaper coverage of the case. He'd been labelled 'the mad axe-man'. I felt real physical anxiety and worry before meeting him, so I got him to come to the office the first time. I dealt with the anxiety by putting what I knew of him out of my mind, and waiting to see how he responded to me. After about 20 minutes, I discovered he had a lot of insecurities, and was feeling threatened by my questioning, so I toned down the discussion, and we talked about more general things (like politics and the police) which relaxed the client. I did this to get him to communicate with me. At the end of the interview, my anxieties about his potential violence had ceased completely. I knew what I had to do with him was to be tactful, get him to relax, not threaten him, in order to get him to open up. Using these techniques actually put me in control of the relationship, so the way in which I communicated with him was of the essence.

2   Setting limits in the relationship

Officer B (specialising in homeless through-care cases):

> I set myself professional limits by not getting emotionally involved. It's the skill of appearing to be a friend but not actually being one – it's cheating! I would only breach someone, though, if they declared they were never going to turn up to see me. My authority lies in making someone accountable, via a softer approach, because we're also trying to help them. But there's a lot of lies in our whole approach to people, because we're trying to help, but if they don't accept help we'll be quite forceful in telling them they should have it. Converting something that's an obligation into something that's helpful – this is the essential skill of the job. Conversion! I couldn't have done it when I first came into the job without making a hash of it. Lay people couldn't do it without being very authoritarian. Only probation officers can do this – it's like no other job. You have to present the balance of personal and professional, and the personal has to come first. Their [clients'] happiness, fulfilment and self-realisation is your aim.

Officer C (working in a probation centre):

> I breach people a lot more here than I did in a district team, because you have to be absolutely consistent working with groups. There is a skill in

mixing the friendly approach and establishing limits within a rigid framework. You need to work through it, wrestle with it a bit, get it wrong a few times. Getting the balance right, becoming comfortable with it yourself – that takes time.

These two quotations highlight some of the common dilemmas probation officers have in keeping their communication with clients both human (personal) and businesslike (professional), and in attaining the right balance between the two. They also illustrate the differences which particular settings can make to effecting relationship boundaries. The ground rules of a probation centre are clearer because they are a restriction on liberty and they visibly apply to whole groups of clients. Similarly, most of the prison probation officers felt that the institution set its own firm boundaries for them, and the community service and civil work officers were, on the whole, of the opinion that the specialist nature of their tasks meant that focus and limits were much more sharply defined than in generic fieldwork. One fieldworker confirmed this view when he said, 'In the 22 years I have worked for it, the probation service has never sorted out when to breach people, though community service has. I do it more these days than I used to, but on two occasions the court didn't agree with me!'

Getting the balance right is a process, invariably seen as a skill, which these officers talked of constantly. In terms of limit-setting in communication/relationships, it is about offering the personal and the professional in the right proportion for each client, and adapting the proportions each time. Later on it is seen in operation between courts and clients, between clients and community. Quite importantly in its present context, it also points to the traditional care/control continuum which probation officers traverse with some uncertainty in their early years, but perhaps with more confidence as their experience increases. Only two of this group said they would never breach clients, others had established various thresholds of permissiveness with which they felt comfortable, and twelve (mainly specialists) were very firm about the need to breach when contracts of behaviour were broken. One probation centre worker established her limits via 'honesty about the nature and purpose of the relationship, the contract, and the authority invested in the probation officer. People breach themselves!' Several officers, however, expressed their frustrations with courts and the Home Office for not supporting their recommendations for breach action or for recall of prisoners on parole licence, and for the overall lack of teeth in young offender licences. It was difficult then, they felt, to go on demonstrating consistency in their relationships with their clients, or to receive credibility from them.

In their direct interaction with clients, a few of the officers saw themselves as mother or father figures, Dutch uncles, or the parish priest working the patch. One said, 'I come on like grandma. I convey that the iron hand is in the velvet glove.' Another (the only CS worker who saw her job as having a social work brief) spoke of mothering her clients. 'I tell them to come to me with any problems. That way we get unlikely people through their orders. I'm a soft touch, but they know I care.' A number of officers in their middle years felt that their age and colour of their hair conveyed its own limits! The officer who wanted to 'get back to being the patch parish priest' had been 'a very good salesman. I can charm people, sell ideas. I come to the point quickly.' In setting limits he suggested, 'You don't get down into the gutter with people. You maintain your own standards.' Indeed, a number of the officers talked of the need to be clear about their own values and standards, for self-awareness and self-knowledge in respect of who they were, what roles they played, and how they came across to others. This was a prerequisite of being able to set moral and behavioural limits for clients, or rather *with* them, as one person stressed was the ideal way to work.

Some more obvious ways of limit-setting included use of surnames, operating a firm appointments system, time limits on interviews and knowing how to draw them to a close. Learning to say 'no' or 'no more' and avoiding discussing your own private life were also mentioned, though more officers talked as suggested above, about knowing themselves and feeling sufficiently comfortable with that knowledge to reveal parts of themselves and their lives, which reminded the client that they were human too, but did not change the focus of work from the client to themselves. One civil work specialist said that he might for example tell clients that he too sometimes had rows with his wife or difficulties with his teenage daughter, but would never get into the intimate detail of any of this. 'You do it so that people know you're not an automaton with all the answers. But you have to know when it's helpful and when to stop.'

Because the probation officer's duty has traditionally been to 'advise, assist and befriend', they were asked how they thought clients understood their role. A prison probation officer said, 'I explain the notion of social distance – the difference between befriending and being a friend.' One female officer of 10 years' experience described a young male client, Paul, in a probation hostel who periodically sent her cards with hearts on.

> He said to me recently, 'You and my Mum are my only friends.' I had to say to him, 'Paul, I'm not your friend, I'm your probation officer.' I won't go for drinks with them. I won't let them control me because you have to respect yourself as well as them. Clients in this area control by not keeping appointments. I allow them some leeway for a few weeks, and then I have a showdown with them because they've contracted to come and see me. I increasingly believe that people have to take responsibility for themselves – a point I've reached both personally and through professional experience.

Another officer felt that people's practical problems, particularly those of women, had to be addressed step by step, before communication and explanation of limits could ensue. They needed to feel they could exercise control over their lives before they had something to offer to the relationship. Of limit-setting the officer said,

> It's quite difficult. I've developed it over 9½ years, almost defensively. At first I used to enter into more personal relationships, but I'm now more clear about the professional role and what I'm prepared and not prepared to do. I answer personal questions but only in a generalised fashion. I help them see I'm not just a friend who drops in for a cup of tea, that there is structure to it. You have to be able to bring things to an end.

The last two quotes, both from female officers, indicate that the limits they now set in relationships with clients have evolved over quite long periods of time, and they have both had to wrestle to some extent with role and balance in this area. A number of officers spoke of body contact with some clients, hugging them, or holding their hands if they were in distress – bereavement was a common factor in such situations. Others would use humour, and some display anger, as part of their humanity. One officer said, as an example, that in exasperation she would say to her client. 'Bloody hell, Pam, can't you see what will happen if you do that?' But she also felt aware of the need to be careful when she used herself in this way, because of the manipulativeness of some clients and the dangers of collusion with them. Knowing where to draw the line between the personal and professional and on the care/control continuum, seemed to be the main skills which these officers described in their answers.

In illustration of some of the issues in this section, let us return to the story of Mr A and Harry:

> Harry refused to do any cooking in the probation centre because he said it was woman's work. I knew him better by then so I tried to get a better understanding by asking trigger-questions. I explained the centre's requirements clearly, and that he was on a rota, so didn't have to cook every day, and it wasn't intended to humiliate him. I also clarified to him that it was a condition of the probation order. Clarity was very important with this client. But then he stormed out of the centre after a row with another offender, and wouldn't return. My SPO gave him a warning interview and he still didn't return. I had to continue working with the client, who was still coming to see me, and I had to breach him at the same time. I had to put this to him, with clarity and honesty, and he accepted it. I had to point out that he could get sent away, and yet at the same time he was going through a divorce and needed a lot of sympathy from me. I felt unhappy about his decision to be breached, rather than go back to the centre, but I came to a point where I had to accept Harry's own decision about his life.

3 Qualities needed for communication

Perhaps not surprisingly, discussion with the 62 probation officers on this subject produced an almost inexhaustible list of the qualities they felt were needed in order to be able to communicate with clients. The list is recorded at the end of this section. However, to give the qualities suggested some meaning in terms of probation officers' actual relationships with clients, the seventeen which were most frequently mentioned will be considered below. First, however, it is important to clarify that although the emphasis of the discussions was upon personal rather than professional qualities, it became evident that those interviewed thought that at least seven of the seventeen could be enhanced significantly by training and experience, given that the right unembellished elements were present to start with. This did not apply, however, to the two most popular qualities, honesty and warmth.

In the first section, both these qualities were briefly highlighted as constituent parts of the range of skills which probation officers use to communicate with clients. Because many of them feel that a sharing of humanity has to be established, before professional skills and knowledge can effectively be brought into play, they take the view that the raw material of the people they are is crucial in the overall dynamics of the relationship. As one officer put it. 'Honesty and warmth are qualities which cannot be learned. You are either honest and warm or you are not and the client will always sense it, and respond accordingly!' Another probation officer, who gave the same two responses to the question said, 'Warmth first. You have to be a people person and be genuine. Then honesty – feeling OK about making mistakes because you haven't always got the answers. Both these qualities help to cement relationships. I treat people in work the same as I do people in my private life though the boundaries are different.' Honesty, as another officer suggested, was also important in letting clients know what you can and can't do for them and clarifying mutual expectations. This was crucial, she thought, in 'generally finding the balance of the relationship with people', a wider skill which, as section 2 began to suggest seems to be at the heart of good probation work for these officers. Most of the qualities this officer mentioned, including warmth, respect for people, and sincerity, she was sure were 'sensed by people, and you need to have them inside you before you can learn any social work skills.'

In order of their popularity, the eight other qualities which the officers considered, on the whole, could not be learned if they were not already present in some measure were as follows: having a genuine interest in people; a sense of humour; an acceptance of people as they are; being genuinely caring and concerned for people; an ability to share one's own humanity; a diverse life experience; sympathy; realism.

Being genuinely interested meant to several, as one drugs specialist suggested, 'letting them know that you do want to talk and hear about *them*, not just what they are in relation to the probation order'. Again, it was felt that clients quickly distinguish between the bureaucrat who is just carrying out a set of organisational

124

requirements, and the person who cares over and above that, who the client is and what happens to her or him. In having a sense of humour, it seemed important to be able to laugh at yourself sometimes, and with the client, though never at her/ him. In accepting, the point was made by several officers that clients in addition to society being unable to accept them, frequently have difficulty in accepting themselves as people, and have low self-images. Probation officers, according to many of those interviewed, are often the only people who are able and willing to afford offenders acceptance and respect as human beings, and this quality as we shall see towards the end of this report, is one which appears to contribute a 'sine qua non' for the essential components of a probation officer. Most respondents who spoke of acceptance, however, emphasised that in accepting the client they did not condone the crime and that, indeed, the main purpose of their contact was to work with the client to ensure that criminal actions were not repeated.

Being genuinely caring and concerned was important to those who mentioned it because they felt it was sometimes possible to 'over-professionalise' these qualities in a caring agency, and again they were sure that clients do not respond to professional help when they sense that the concern being expressed is institutionalised rather than genuine. Sharing one's own humanity was described by one officer as 'being able to share some of your own experiences and emotions, which helps both probation officer and client break through the stereotypes. Most of the time we share more than we differ – for example loving our children – and this in turn conveys an acceptance of the client.' As suggested in an earlier section, most respondents felt that engaging in this process takes a maturity and confidence which ensure that the boundaries of shared humanity are appropriately drawn.

A diverse life experience was mentioned by several officers as being a prerequisite for 'understanding what it's like for people out there. It's not just about having to be a thief to understand why people steal. It's about seeing life in settings which aren't sheltered. You need to have made mistakes yourself and got through to the other side.' Sympathy was a quality put forward less often than that of empathy (a quality which most people consider can be learned), but nevertheless was seen again in the quite personal sense of genuinely sharing in someone else's trouble, rather than merely trying to put oneself in their shoes. Some officers thought you could both sympathise and empathise – sometimes the former followed on from the latter. One officer saw sympathy, empathy and realism as interlinked, 'because it's no good dishing out bucketsful of sympathy if it's misplaced.' Being realistic and knowing the limitations of oneself and the client was desirable in an occupation where quite a lot of idealism abounded, and again the issue of balance, in this case between the ideal and the attainable, was felt to be of importance.

The seven qualities which the officers, on the whole, considered could be learned if present in embryo were, in order of their popularity, as follows:

empathy; being a good listener; consistency; an understanding of people and their problems; (these last four followed honesty and warmth in terms of overall importance); self-awareness; confidence; and competence.

125

Empathy, as seen above, was about 'putting yourself in other people's shoes' or 'thinking yourself into someone else's situation instead of limiting your reaction to your own perception and experiences of the problem in hand.' This was very clearly viewed as a professional skill more objective than sympathy, and appeared to have been impressed upon people during training and their subsequent work experiences. Similarly, being a good listener was thought to be a quality which could be developed with time and training, and was an integral part of overall communication skills. The concept of *really* listening was referred to in this context in the first section, and 'being a good listener' is clearly the ideal partner for such a skill. One officer said, 'I'm a person who finds it all too easy to sit and chat to clients, but I know the value of listening, and I have disciplined myself to sit back and listen instead of carrying the interview. I'd say I'm a good listener now.' To her, this was not an instinctive quality, but one which she had developed through holding on to the purpose of her meetings with clients rather than coasting aimlessly through a series of friendly contacts.

Consistency, often linked with words such as reliability and trustworthiness, was viewed by many officers as being a quality which had to be continuously demonstrated to clients. Because clients themselves can be unreliable, unpunctual and often untrustworthy, at least in relation to their offending behaviour, these probation officers thought it vital to lead by example, and to make it clear to their clients that they could always be counted on to help when needed, and to stick to their part of any contract which had been negotiated between them. One CS specialist commented, 'I lead by example. They know that their timekeeping is important to me and I therefore make sure that mine is as good as I want from them. I'm honest and straight with them because that's what I expect from them. When I make promises I carry them out, and when I make threats I carry those out too.' Sometimes the officers had had to put a lot of effort into demonstrating consistent behaviour, especially if other clients were making simultaneous demands on their time, or if they themselves were not naturally punctual.

Having an understanding of people and their problems was a quality which contained obvious links with that of empathy, but also related to the life experiences of people in areas such as use of language and social values. It became a quality which some described as instinctive but which one could go on learning by continuous observation of human behaviour, and indeed by studying it during training. Self-awareness was a quality brought about by similar processes, but which involved often painful experiences of rigorous self-analysis and criticism. One probation officer thought it vital to know your own value system when you are implicitly working with the values of those who have offended against the norm. As a probation centre specialist, she had found herself working with one or two colleagues who, in her view, were not conscious that they operated delinquent value systems, seeking short-term answers to everything. Some attention to their own behaviour and thought

126

processes might then have the effect of an improvement in their levels of self-awareness.

Confidence and competence, two qualities which are often mentioned in tandem, are also seen very much as being attained through work experience, and the existence of one can frequently, though not always, imply the presence of the other. Competence was described by one officer as, 'Showing we can offer both understanding to clients and alternatives to imprisonment to courts.' At times, these can be two quite polarised requirements, needing again the skill of balance to hold the tension between the two. Confidence was 'showing you know your job, that you're well-informed, and that your judgement can be trusted.' Briefly continuing the story of Mr A and Harry, and remembering that Mr A has already described the need for qualities of honesty, sympathy, and acceptance in his work with Harry, he now goes on to tell us something about his use of competence and confidence in the court setting.

> Presenting the breach properly, and presenting myself confidently in court was very important, as was showing the care/control balance between doing the presentation and not making the client feel rejected by it all. I had to make the position of my probation centre colleagues clear, and I also had to compromise by suggesting community service as a non-custodial alternative, even though I didn't believe it was necessary. That was about being realistic. But because I think I'd both given the court what it needed to know, and presented Harry's situation as clearly as I could, they gave him a new probation order.

So here, Mr A is demonstrating his competence via his understanding of the client's plight, and his knowledge and realism in relation to alternatives to imprisonment. His confidence is shown in his court presentation, his ability to present information and use his knowledge and experience of the setting, and ultimately in the court's decision to trust his judgement. Like Mr A, however, most of these officers felt that a great deal of experience and knowledge were needed before they were able to feel confidence in their role. It is also the case that areas of competence required by probation officer can change, and confidence be eroded by events, so that they are both qualities which need to be continuously built upon and improved. The suggestion that confidence takes knowledge moves us towards the final section in the area of communication, which will follow the list of qualities put forward by the probation officers in this survey.

Qualities needed by a probation officer for communication

(Discussed above)

Honesty
Warmth
Empathy
Good listener
Consistent
Genuinely interested in people
Understanding of people/problems
Sense of humour
Acceptance
Self-awareness
Caring/concerned
Diverse life experience
Competence
Being human
Sympathy
Confidence
Realism

(Mentioned by small numbers only)

Integrity
Willingness to give time
Ability to use oneself
Firmness
Ability to interpret
Adaptability
Patience/sticking with people
Imagination
Sensitivity
Objectivity
Authority
Tolerance
Self-discipline
Ability to affirm/encourage
Willingness to challenge
Ability to be directive
Ability to balance care and control

4   The effectiveness of communication with clients

In this section, probation officers were effectively being asked what knowledge they possessed about the process of communication and its effect on their clients. Most frequently, this knowledge appeared to relate to interpreting the level of response from their client – whether their efforts at communicating messages or advice had borne fruit in terms of verbal reply or behavioural change. Three of them describe their views and experiences below:

Officer D

It's whether I'm heard; whether it's retained and seen as relevant. But it's not always what's said – it's the mood of the contact. For example, one client with great problems hid behind his hair and wouldn't look at me for weeks. Now he does look at me so I know I've had an effect. Another client went from not caring about himself to being quite positive, and is now saying he actually doesn't want to go to prison, he wants to be on probation. That is the result of years of probation officers sticking with that man.

Officer E

I have a probation client convicted of indecent assault on his teenage daughter and her friend. I know from his and his wife's response that they've followed my guidelines, taken advice. He was full of guilt and remorse, and I did a huge job of building his self-confidence and tried to get him back to work. He was very resistant but did go back. I push him, sustain him, support him all the time, and I and the social worker do joint interviews with him and his wife, to which they respond well. There's a lot of staying with people in this job.

Officer F

> The content, amount, and level of response tells you a lot. I have a schedule 1 offender with whom I've had to be very straight about child abuse procedures, almost at the expense of the relationship. But he will only come to probation when he needs help. He won't go to other agencies. He's recently begun to discuss his feelings – that's a big change in the level of communication!

These three probation officers and many others who gave examples of effective communication, have confidence that their interaction has produced change in their clients. Confidence, as we heard earlier, very often derives from knowledge, and whilst later sections of this report will tell us more about particular bodies of knowledge which probation officers need, these passages indicate the importance of a knowledge of human behaviour in communication. For example, demeanour, body language, and silence often say more than words themselves. Knowing that a missing ingredient such as self-confidence is crucial in helping someone to change; knowing that the quality of 'sticking with people' is often a prerequisite for gradual behaviour adjustment; knowing that an ability to discuss feelings indicates internal movement – these are ways in which experienced probation officers utilise the knowledge they have built up through training and experience. The third quote also provides an example of significant pieces of knowledge – the law in relation to Schedule 1 offenders, and agency guidelines on child abuse – which probation officer F needed to have at his fingertips in his day-to-day contact with that client and probably others too.

Many officers also considered that clients reacted to their efforts at communication by 'voting with their feet.' Most of them would give some leeway about attendance during probation orders, and therefore if attendance flagged, would look first at their own possible contribution to that state of affairs. Some made a point of asking for feedback at the end of each contact to see if they had understood and been understood. Others spoke of the helpfulness of unsolicited feedback from clients, who might write or visit them much later to thank them for their help, when often they had not been conscious of effecting much change. One officer spoke of a woman shop-lifter she'd worked with upon whom she had consistently impressed that Styal Prison was at hand if she did not change her ways. The woman later fed back to her that every time she went into a shop, she thought 'Janet!' (pseudonym for the PO), and it stopped her stealing. Also, one day when she found a purse, she

129

reported that her thought was 'Janet would want me to hand this in to the police station,' – and so she did. This was a clear reinforcement for Janet of the effectiveness of her communication with this client.

Other officers suggested that they would look for evidence of clients being able to trust them, perhaps by confiding very personal information, or bringing along their friends for advice. Some would look for the client being able to be honest with them. One officer pointed out, 'A lot of clients in this job have been in the system a long time, and can eat POs for breakfast. When you find them initiating communication, starting to think aloud with you, trusting you, even if they're saying they're still drinking or taking drugs, then you know you're getting through.' Several officers also cited the 'office grapevine' as being a way of hearing involuntarily how clients had perceived their contact with individuals, particularly where client groups or drop-in centres were attached to offices.

Most of the civil work officers saw the evidence of their own effectiveness at communication in the extent to which they were able to help separating couples reach agreement about the arrangements for their children. This is perhaps a more tangible form of measurement than exists in generic probation work, but as one civil worker said,

> If I'm getting lots of agreement, it's not just because I've got people who will agree, it's because I've got knowledge of how the system works, and skills in mediating, arbitrating, conciliating, negotiating, steering the middle course. But it's also that I show them empathy – getting across that I understand what they're going through – and consistency, because I do what I say I'm going to do. It also helps in this job to get on well with children through play, lego, drawing, cars, whatever props are around. It helps to be a bit of a kid yourself.

This quotation, perhaps, helps us to begin to see how probation officers in whatever setting, have to interlink their skills, knowledge, and qualities in order to produce a piece of work which begins with effective communication, and continues, as we shall see, into the areas of assessment and intervention.

In the final illustrative passage relating to communication between Mr A and Harry, we see how Mr A further develops his use of the same three factors and measures his own effectiveness as their post-court contact continues.

> After the new probation order was made, I was able to do some very good work with Harry. I got him doing woodwork in the probation centre. I helped him write letters applying for jobs. I got him working with old age pensioners on a voluntary scheme in the area and, of course, I had to liaise between Harry and the scheme about the nature of his offence. This was all to help him establish a structure and a routine whilst, as Harry put it, his life was 'falling apart'. In the meantime my face-to-face work with him was mainly therapeutic, letting him express his bottled-up feelings about the divorce he was going through, and his

mother's death from cancer. I had to build up his self-esteem through the voluntary work, and show him that I had some faith in him, by sticking my neck out for him in court, and generally giving him something to hold onto. The Order has ended now. Harry hasn't reoffended and I feel that the Order achieved its desired results.

The breakdown of Mr A's and Harry's story in terms of establishing human contact, setting limits in the relationship, the injection of personal qualities, and the effectiveness of the contact, has been an attempt to present a living example of some ways in which probation officers might utilise their network of skills, knowledge, and qualities in their day to day work with clients. The story is illustrative and pointed in its sequences, but it is not exceptional amongst the range of cases which probation officers in this study described. Their collective experiences and views have helped to build an initial picture of the essential components of a probation officer which, in terms of ability to communicate with clients, is someone with a sense of timing, and a series of awarenesses, who relaxes people whilst holding onto purpose, who really listens, tries to get balances between personal and professional, care and control right, who possesses qualities of honesty and warmth in particular, and has a good knowledge of human behaviour. The next section will show how, having established communication with the client, the probation officer adds to these primary components during the process of client assessment.

III Client assessment

1 The skills and knowledge for the task

The process of assessment, whether for report-writing or record-keeping purposes, constitutes one of the major tasks of the probation service. The majority of responses to the subject in this first section centred around interviewing and information-gathering skills, around practice wisdom and life experience, knowledge of psychology, sociology, criminology, knowledge of local resources, court procedure, sentencing and the tariff, offending behaviour, and relevant law. It was often emphasised that the communication skills described in the last section, having operated to relax the client, had to be continued and interwoven in the processes of assessment, so that the two sets of skills and knowledge were simultaneously at work.

The skill of interviewing itself appeared, in the main, to be a matter of structure – having a beginning, a middle, and an end, during which purpose was stated and hopefully fulfilled – in conjunction with an ability to ask the right question at the right time, to *really* listen to the answers (as with communication, but this time with correct assessment as a more specific end-product), and to gather, prioritise, analyse, and summarise information, ideally involving the client in the entire proceedings. One officer did speak of a particular formula which she always used in assessment, and which she described as 'Professor Rogers' 7-point plan' (though she was unable to provide the reference for this material). 'It is,' she clarified, 'a survey of a person's background, their family, family interaction, education and attitudes to it, innate abilities, religion and social morality. If there's a conveyance of feeling about something, you break off and discuss it. It's a diagnostic interview, and when it's done, you then put it against your knowledge of offending, sentencing etc. You often find it's normality rather than abnormality which causes people to offend.' Although other officers did not, in the main, work to definite formulae, many of them referred to the need to blend interviewing and diagnostic skills with particular bodies of knowledge, and to 'fit them all,' as one officer said, 'into the bag of tricks.'

A civil work specialist gave a useful account of such a process. 'Learning how to ask questions which don't pre-empt the answer. Getting the client to talk but not letting it turn into chat. Keeping the flow going by asking prompting questions in a way which doesn't seem controlling. Listening on two levels – first to the words that are fed back, and second to other indications like tone of voice, fastness or slowness of response, the ease or difficulty of it. Always weighing up if what the client tells you fits in with how you've perceived them. Applying a well-digested knowledge of human growth and development – not the kind you've just taken in and spat out again. For example, knowing that there are three levels (psychological, sociological and physical) of impact on a person of a condition like, say epilepsy – and that you have to respond to them. You may not always know what they are, but you know they exist and you know where you can go and look them up!' Another officer tried to clarify this linking of skills and knowledge by differentiating between how she would assess a client and how she would assess a friend:

> With a client, I establish that I'm in control. The process of assessment is continuous – one thing comes out of the thing before. It's picking up hints, body language, or why did that question make someone look uncomfortable? My job as a friend would be to get an idea of her problem, dry her tears and send her home in a good condition. But my job as a PO is more lateral, not always to be sympathetic, but to move things sideways, get them into another ball game, get clients to look at things differently with me.

Most people felt that the process of agenda-balancing, getting clients to state their own needs via asking, listening, then sharing, was very important. A through-care specialist described it as 'Asking and listening, *really* listening, and identifying people's own perceived needs. If they want a BMW I'll help them to identify acceptable ways of getting one. If they want to stop offending, I'll help them with that too. Often they ask for strawberry and get vanilla. Generally they're right about what they need, so I help them identify the possible steps to it, sometimes with diagrammatic explanations to simplify it for them.' Generally, it seemed to be the view that there was little sense to be made of the assessment process without placing genuine credence on the client's own perceptions of her/his needs and situations. This process is one which needs encouragement, however, as one officer pointed out. 'People may say something which you know needs drawing out, and we will say, "You seem to feel bad about that" or something similar. That is a skill which the person in the street doesn't have.' Or in another person's version, 'your listening is a *trained* listening – your ear gets trained by experience and you can follow patterns that repeat themselves. You put it to the client, "Do you think it could be this, or could be that?" – or "I actually think this may be a problem for you. What do *you* think?" You put all of this together with your own assessment, all the other things you know about them, and the offence, and you get the end product.'

Although there appears to be a skill in drawing out information, one officer nevertheless said she was 'constantly amazed at how much people will tell you about themselves' and whilst this is helpful in the case of many clients, it also calls for the skills of sifting and prioritising the information which is being given. On this subject another officer said,

> I need to be able to order the information a client gives into a sequential pattern, as soon as I can. This is often difficult, because people will present things in order of emotional importance. You have to give them time to say what they think is important, and in all of this you may find yourself using social work skills too – like being able to gauge when a person has given enough and to ask them to come back next time. If they are upset, you may have to deal with that before you get the information you need. You also need to sum up with them and for them at the end, explaining what will happen to the information they've given you, making sure they know the court system if you're doing a court report, discussing disposals and getting their reaction to them, being very clear what probation, for example, would mean for them. This takes a complex combination of skills and knowledge which are in parallel operation throughout.

Here there begins to emerge a process which is something more than an information-gathering exercise, and requires for its success not only the skills and knowledge of communication and assessment, but also those of social work intervention, which will be discussed in the next section. Here, it seems, is another balancing act for probation officers to perform.

Having gathered information from the client, from records, colleagues, other agencies, and made their own observations using what some officers referred to as 'the third ear,' and having sifted it according to their knowledge and experience of what is relevant, many officers spoke of the need to analyse, interpret, or 'break the codes' before finally summarising the information and saying what it meant. This was a skill, they felt, largely brought about by practice wisdom. For example, one officer said, 'I know if someone's being vague, saying they might be moving, or they might be getting a job in London, what they're really telling me is that they don't want to do the CS order I've suggested, so there's no point in my recommending it.' A civil work specialist talked of 'making assessments for the court in the context of a dispute that *apparently* is about arrangements for the children.' His life experience, and his 16 years of practice wisdom, he considered, were the factors which had taught him what was really going on in such situations, though 'bits of some training courses have given an insight. But a lot of getting to where I am in this job has been trial and error, seat of the pants stuff. You just take a deep breath and go. When you start to get things right, that gives you the confidence you need to develop.'

Judging attitudes, ability and motivation was an intrinsic part of the analytical process. One officer actually had a questionnaire which she used with some of her clients to assess this. Another officer said, 'These aren't just mental wanderings, and you're not just assessing personality. You're taking clients' views, needs and abilities, and assessing and balancing them.' Another, who had also spoken of the need to build up pictures of people's abilities and motivation commented, 'You couldn't do it on day one in the job. It takes experience, trial and error, of slotting ability and motivation into sentences and resources. People that we deal with often sell themselves short, and you need to be able to assess their potential. It's a long process of linking things up and developing with someone a blueprint for where you start.' It was also pointed out that one of the most frequent assessment tasks was that of compiling court reports and that, in the midst of information-gathering and analysis, there would equally be at work the probation officer in the role of 'intermediary', 'bridge', or 'honest broker', as variously described by three people. Holding onto this role amidst pressure from various sides was also, as we have begun to see elsewhere, a necessary professional attribute, which one officer described as being 'all the skills and knowledge of explaining the court and its procedures to the client – and vice versa, which is often much harder.'

The bodies of knowledge which these probation officers felt they needed in the assessment process have begun to be clarified above, and they will be more specifically outlined below with a few brief examples.

The necessity of knowing court procedures both for acting within them, and explaining them to the client, has been made apparent. For similar reasons prison and parole procedures need to be known and understood by those who work both within and without them. A wide knowledge of all sentencing disposals and the tariff system (even though unwritten) is considered vital for assessment purposes. So is a good awareness of relevant legislation – particularly that pertaining to court reports, probation and supervision orders, community service, life licences, hospital and guardianship orders, sentencing powers and the Rehabilitation of Offenders Act. Various Criminal Justice Acts, Theft Acts, and Children and Young Persons Acts were mentioned and, after many years experience, it was clear that a number of officers still felt under-equipped in these areas.

A comprehensive knowledge of one's local community and its resources was considered to be vital, and this often embraced a knowledge of welfare rights – social security, housing, etc. – in relation to local agencies and policies. Several field officers cited child abuse literature and guidelines as an increasing necessity, and a number of those interviewed, particularly people working in custodial settings, outlined the need for more knowledge of sex offenders and violent offenders with whom they had to work with increasing regularity. Outside of these areas, the three bodies of knowledge most frequently mentioned were those of psychology/human growth and behaviour, sociology, and criminology. In the field of psychology, areas particularly referred to were an understanding of people's defence mechanisms (an example was given of a client in custody for killing her baby, who was 'emotionally flattened and devoid of feeling'), life phases and changes, stress, crisis and transition points, and emotional effects of marriage and family breakdown and bereavement. A number of officers said they retained mental checklists of such issues which they checked off whilst assessing people.

In respect of criminology theories relating to peer group behaviour and subcultures were found the most helpful, and sociology helped people's understanding of environmental limitation. One officer said, 'Joe Bloggs in the street would assume that people have free choice. Our experience and our sociology training tells us that our clients' choices are limited. Typically, because of this, they have failed and have no experience of success. We need to understand why this is so that we can help them to broaden their choices and opportunities.'

The overall view, as suggested earlier by the officer who said that knowledge had to be well-digested, was that those three academic disciplines provided a necessary and helpful base, but were only one of many factors to be drawn upon as we have begun to see, and then on occasion, as one officer said 'rejecting them at first, but then maybe finding that they come back and make sense, and your experience helps you put them in context, which you couldn't before.' Another comment confirmed this. 'Your theoretical knowledge is bound up in a practice wisdom model rather than an "I've read a book" model, and you make heavy use of your experience of handling situations in the past.' All in all, therefore, this section highlights the importance of the blend of a large number of skills and knowledge for assessment which, ideally, are drawn upon in a balanced fashion to produce a well rounded portrait of the client in question. The following section will attempt to show what additional skills and knowledge probation officers use to ensure that their picture is an authentic one.

2 Making 'streetwise' assessments

It was clear from the bulk of answers given in this section that many respondents lived with some feelings of ambivalence on the subject of being 'conned', which ranged from accepting it as inevitable to nevertheless experiencing some hurt pride if it happened. Certainly, apart from one person who said he did not know any better now than twenty years ago whether he was being told the truth, and two officers who felt training had been the key factor, most officers agreed that their job experience had been the main factor in enabling them to discern authenticity when assessing people. Furthermore they considered it important to have this ability in situations where they had a duty to report honestly to the court. Here are four probation officers talking about the meaning of their experience and practice wisdom in acquiring the skill of being 'streetwise' with clients:

Officer G

My experience and knowledge of how people behave, over the last 18 years, told me that a family of a prisoner I was working with were 'conning' me, by telling me he would have a job to come out to if he were given parole. A letter came from someone, out of the blue, offering him this job, and somehow I smelt a rat. I rang the number on the letter, and spoke to the wife of the man who'd written it. She said her husband couldn't offer anyone a job, they were so hard-up themselves. My instinct had been right, and my experience also tells me that clients 'con' the most when they're trying to get parole.

Officer H (Homeless throughcare specialist) – on a similar subject.

Some clients play the probation/parole game, and you get to know this. *They* conduct the interviews and tell you what they think you want to hear. I had one who did that and I went back and looked through his files, wrote down all the differences in information, took it back to him, and asked him what *he* thought. It's important to confront them with what they're doing.

Officer I (Prison probation officer)

It's an inbuilt something that comes to the fore and you think, 'Ah!' You get this from experience, and your own awareness of how *you* try to 'con' people too! If I was locked up in one of these places, I'd be the biggest 'conner' out. If you don't ask you don't get.

Officer J

You don't always know, but I rely on intuition a lot, and I do know better now than I did eighteen years ago. I remember one guy who talked me into recommending a probation order for him, and after he got the order, he just never came to see me. But I'm at a stage now where I usually know when a client walks into the room if s/he's trying to hide something.

All these officers are effectively saying that a combination of their lengthy work experience and something amounting to intuition had given them enough knowledge of human behaviour to get a fairly good idea of whether or not their clients were telling the truth. Intuition is clearly a personal quality rather than a skill, and has always represented something of a mystique in the social work profession. Some officers who used the word were asked what it meant to them, and variously answered that it was the cumulative result of observing similar patterns of behaviour in people; or that it was knowing yourself sufficiently to understand why other human beings behave as they do (as Officer I acknowledged); or it was being sensitive and imaginative enough to perceive someone else's reality. Again, knowledge of self and of human behaviour, qualities of sensitivity and imagination, all referred to in the first section on communication, were seen as components of intuition. An officer of 24 years' experience described an intuitive moment made up of some of these elements, when a young man he was with was, 'telling me a pack of lies. I just looked at him. The lad broke down in tears. He said to me, "You knew I was telling lies, didn't you?"'

Nearly all the officers, however, spoke, in addition to the need for experience and intuition, of the importance of verifying information clients had given – with their families, other agencies, past records and the like – and of telling them (in some cases asking their permission) that these processes would take place. One officer saw this as a definite skill, which he described as 'detective work.' Another described an experience which had taught her to seek corroboration of her facts.

'I have learned now to double-check everything I can. Last year I did a court report and recommended probation with a condition of attendance at a probation centre on a lad who said his girlfriend was pregnant. He was rearrested soon after, and taken into custody. I went to see him and remarked that the baby must be due about now. He told me then that there never was a baby – he'd just spun me that line to help his case. I was furious!' Certainly it was a case of hurt pride for that officer! Another respondent outlined the situations in which he would be particularly careful.

'I am better at it now than I was at first. It's about being streetwise. If you get a lot of vagueness, you go over things with a fine-tooth comb. The same if their account is too neat or there are logical gaps with no explanation. Whether I feel pressurised – sold a line. You need to check even more with those people. The thing is they're often "conning" themselves too.'

Perhaps the police would have some skills to teach the probation service in its role of detective – though some probation officers would say, as did the last two respondents, that when clients are 'conning', they are usually 'conning' themselves, and that this is of far greater concern in the long run than the hurt pride of the probation officer. An officer working in a female prison starts most of her contacts with inmates by saying just this to them. 'I begin by saying it's pretty sad if they have to lie to me, but it's diabolical if they have to lie to themselves. Nine times out of ten they trip themselves up. Then I advise them to go away and come back with the right story. But you can't blame them for having a go – the parole process is horrendous.' (Note the similarity of view to that of prison probation officer I).

Because of their concern about clients 'conning' themselves, several probation officers felt it was important to begin by believing people until there was reason to alter their view. One civil work specialist said 'I work from the premise that people don't tell lies but that they say what they need to say to help make sense of their own worlds.'

A community service specialist (also an ex-magistrate) commented, 'You have to check facts and press people on information. But believing people is part of our job. I always approach a new relationship as if I'll be involved in the future so you need to build up trust. I'll often say, "It's important that you're honest" especially if I know they've lied in the past – because they're the ones that suffer from it ultimately.'

Another officer confirmed these two views. 'If you talk to people as they present you get to the real person later on. If they need to "con" there's a reason for that which you don't get by calling them a liar.'

Nevertheless, many officers do see it as important to confront those who are being less than truthful, and one officer saw this as 'the skill of challenging without demolishing – there's a fine line between the two.' It was also necessary to wait for the right time to challenge, as another officer pointed out, and went on, 'In the meantime you might play them along. We all manipulate, and they're in the business of surviving. It doesn't mean there's no basis for work. You still need to go into each relationship on a basis of trust – though you do learn to protect yourself over the years.' A further respondent confirmed and highlighted this view. 'The skill is starting where the client is, taking them at face value and how they need to present to you, dealing with that and working through it. It's about taking risks with people. I do tell people if I think they're being dishonest.'

One officer's experience of risk-taking had led him to a similar philosophy about what was presented to him. 'I've been "conned" by tearful middle-aged people and been too tough on the hard-faced cocky youngsters. Unless what people say to me doesn't match the way the world works (which I will confront), I tend to accept what they say.'

Another honest respondent admitted, 'I'm a terrible one for being "conned". After 22 years I seem to have an unreduced ability to give people the benefit of the doubt. But I'll always challenge people if I start to suspect it.'

Equally a civil work specialist of 16 years' experience said, 'I'm quite easily "conned" – because the alternative is to be cynical. It doesn't worry me. I'll say to people, "You can pull the wool over my eyes if you want, but I'll catch up with you eventually". But I'd qualify that by saying I avoid looking silly whenever possible. This means I'm gullible – so I have to be very thorough in my investigations.'

Many of the answers given above constituted qualified reactions to the question of how they knew they weren't being 'conned' following a quite frequent response of, 'I don't really know, but ...'. This suggested that knowing whether or not someone was telling the truth is a difficult and grey area, in which probation officers are never wholly confident, but develop strategies for working with. A lot of experience, intuition and knowledge of self and human behaviour seem to be required, as does the discipline of verification and the knowledge of where such information is to be found. Qualities of honesty and risk-taking are needed, too, for challenging and making and receiving opening statements of intent – 'a sparring movement' as a prison probation officer described it, 'during which a lot of "conning" goes on by both sides until each knows what the pay-off is.' Timing and balancing are again skills of some importance and the quality of acceptance, starting where the client is and working through the 'conning' process, is also once more to the fore. The last word on the skill of discerning this process, however, must go to a court specialist who summed up a view which many officers were expressing in different ways.

> Experience tells me when things don't ring true, don't hang together. You can ask some questions twice and get different answers. Sometimes I allow it, because it's harmless, but I'll point it out later. I used to have the Raffles of this area on my caseload – a very skilled burglar. For 2 or 3 years I didn't do anything to stop him going to prison because the time wasn't right. The PO's skill is knowing when a client is ready for change, and he was ready last time I interviewed him, and was starting to say, 'I'm getting too old for this game, losing my touch.' I like 'con' men – but I'm better at it than most of them. I enjoy the battle of wits. You need to understand the process but not use it. It's like the karate expert who never gets into a fight.

So perhaps it is not only important for probation officers to recognise their own capacity to 'con', but to go further and to learn how to do it better than their clients. Does this suggest a training course incorporating sales techniques of some kind, or indeed further scope for drawing upon policing methods? What would almost certainly be more relevant in the view of these officers would be the opportunity to concentrate upon ways of identifying when clients are ready to change. Certainly there is little to be said for an assessment process which cannot do this or frequently gets it wrong, since it has enormous implications for the appropriateness of particular court sentences and for the allocation of probation service wo/manpower and resources.

3   Putting it on paper – the tricks of the trade

The skills and knowledge used in the process of client assessment culminate, for the most part, in a written document, whether compiled for internal or external purposes, which inevitably exposes not only an officer's ability to operate in the two sections described above, but also an ability to intelligibly transfer those processes to another medium for the consumption of particular audiences. Probation officers are often quite critical of the quality of each other's reports, and sentencers have been known to criticise not only content but standards of English in court reports. Certainly the officers in this survey appeared to speak with some strength of feeling on the matter, and indicated in different ways that their ability to write reports, particularly for outside bodies such as courts and the Parole Board, was a matter of considerable professional pride – not least, perhaps, because it constituted 'the shop window' of the probation service.

Of equal and complementary importance, it seemed, were a good command of the English language (incorporating grammar, punctuation, spelling and a wide vocabulary) and clarity, conciseness, and the ability to summarise. One officer said, 'I go for clarity and simplicity, avoiding jargon and avoiding being too clever. Some officers do write bad English and still get to the nub but, unfortunately, the bench may never get to that nub if they're put off by the bad English. My first senior was a real stickler for the English language. I remember he stopped me writing "the majority of his time" and made me change it to "the major proportion of his time"!' Another officer agreed, 'Accuracy in the written word is crucial. I'm of the firm opinion that in-service training is needed on written and spoken English, because so many people just can't do it. Maybe we need a peripatetic report writer to "ghost" POs' reports into English!'

A prison probation officer elaborated, 'Structure and clarity, couching things in straightforward language. I never dictate reports. You can spot those who've done it because their reports are badly constructed. You need to lay it out clearly, covering all the relevant areas in logical order, with an introduction, middle and conclusion, just as people should have learned to write essays on their training courses. Things like grammar, spelling, structure – it seems there's just not enough concentration on this in training.' Finally a probation centre specialist outlined in his own practice, 'Simple English; short sentences; clear, familiar concepts; brevity; simplifying complexity.' He cited a senior colleague, who confirmed the opinion of a number of those interviewed, that English literature as well as language should be taught on courses to show how complex ideas and images can be communicated simply, because 'the reader has a low tolerance of massive wads of information.' It would appear, therefore, that content aside, the primary skill of written assessment, as seen by these probation officers, was the ability to write good English with the components which the officers above suggested. This, it seemed, was a prerequisite for gaining the necessary credibility from outside bodies and thus serving the interests of clients and courts alike.

Following closely behind the skill of writing good English was that of the particular method and style with which the information was put across. Many officers first emphasised the importance of being clear in their own minds what they were assessing, why they were assessing it, and for whom. As one officer said, 'It's building up a logical picture, and remembering why you're writing it, rather than putting everything but the kitchen sink in it.' It would then be expressed, as another officer outlined, by one's chosen method of 'selecting and filling in all the relevant categories of feeling and information, and interpreting them at the end. Training for this needs to be on two levels – how you organise, interpret, and conclude information (the structure) and how you select your theory of what goes into that structure.'

In respect of style some officers stressed the importance of particular models of writing such as, 'Use lively language'; 'Make it interesting'; 'Make sentences go upwards instead of downwards so that the tone is positive and uplifting'; 'Be punchy and to the point'; 'Make it such good reading that the reader is compelled to read it all the way through'; 'Quote the clients – sometimes their own phrases say it all.' Many officers referred to the need to avoid social work jargon in this process – one mentioning that she had not realised how much jargon she used until she'd recently been required to write a report in Welsh, and had had to think much more carefully than usual about how she expressed herself. A few officers were also concerned to avoid the use of words which labelled people for life. One gave an example of a set of case conference notes which assessed 'a child with temper tantrums which, comparing them with the temper tantrums of my own child, seemed quite reasonable along the spectrum. But the expression became re-interpreted at the conference as "hysteria" and the child was referred to a child psychiatrist for help. Such words, which can start as speculation, become writ as tablets of stone, and so you do have to be very careful to keep your language moderate.'

A positive way of keeping assessments lively and interesting, it was suggested, was to,

> give a good pen picture – bring the client to life on paper. Show the reader the real person rather than just their behaviour or the fact that they're a drug user. That is part of our professional skill. The layperson would just take the media view of a DSS defrauder as a scrounger, whereas we see the personal difficulties and sometimes hopelessness which has led to that offence. It doesn't mean we excuse them, but unless we can bring them and their realities to life for the court, the questions of 'Why?' and 'How can we stop them doing it again?' will never be answered. I suppose it's a way of putting across your commitment to helping the client as well.

So resisting the stereotypes and portraying individual uniqueness is the skill here, and this again implies being able to use words differently and appropriately in each assessment, so that the essence of each offender is revealed on the page and that, for example, no two young male unemployed car thieves sound completely alike.

Being able to communicate the right messages about the person being portrayed was also seen as a skill which, again, was about using the right words. Opinion differed here, however, as to whether the communicating of messages was an honest, straightforward process, or whether it was more a matter of finding 'nice ways of calling people a liar', 'writing between the lines', or 'using shorthand.' An example given of this was, 'He maintains he has been drug-free for four weeks.' The word 'maintains' was often used, the officer suggested, to indicate that, 'You're representing what he's told you and you don't like to call him a bloody liar, just in case you're wrong, but the court gets the message that you have your doubts.' These variations probably indicate the difficulty of balancing the interests of courts and clients, and the different ways in which officers deal with it, some being more confident of their role and thus sure of their ground than others. Two officers spoke in this context of the skill of 'steering a middle course between court and client', and 'reaching a realistic conclusion from both their points of view.' They felt that in learning the overall task of court report writing, they were very ill-equipped by their training to attain this 'balancing' skill and indeed retained uncertainty about it after years of experience.

Other skills mentioned were those of abstraction and deduction (described by one officer as, 'penning my thoughts, arguing with myself, giving it time, testing things out, and coming back to it'); the ability to distinguish opinion from fact ('It avoids you being crucified by solicitor, judge, or client'); and 'covering your back', by 'being realistic and objective and putting down the worst possible scenario as well as the best.' One of the officers who had earlier spoken about probation officers 'conning' clients as well as vice versa said, 'We shy away from criticism in reports, and that devalues the assessment. In your heart you know when someone is ready to change, but still we glibly talk about alternatives to prison when we know there's no chance. Sometimes we collude when people are on social security and have houses like palaces, or are banned from driving, but come to the office in a car.' This is reminiscent of part of the section on communication in which it was suggested that a necessary skill was self-awareness and clarity about one's own value system. In this case, it is clearly important for officers to be conscious of how they assess criminal acts themselves before they can attempt written objectivity in assessing the perpetrators of such acts.

Bodies of knowledge which were seen as being regularly needed in the written assessment process included those of the range of sentencing disposals; the 'tariff' system; terms of reference and expectations of courts and local review committees; and knowledge of psychology and sociology (particularly in criminological terms of local areas and their contributions to patterns of offending). The latter was mentioned frequently both in relation to court and parole reports and in the writing of initial and subsequent assessments for current cases, so that it would be possible, as one person said, 'to set goals, explaining that as a result of changes you and he are going to make in *a* and *b* in his family and *c* in his social life and *d* in his housing, and *e* in his employment pattern, in twelve months time he won't have reoffended.'

It is useful perhaps at this point to mention the written skills cited by some of those involved in more specialised assessment processes. A civil work specialist, for example, spoke of having 'evolved a system with a style in which, having listened to people, I briefly sum up their situation in writing, relate their views without comment, then add my own views and make a recommendation. What I'm doing, in effect, is describing a piece of interaction which demonstrates whether or not a child is happy and well-cared for. It's investigative writing – almost journalistic really.' A hostel specialist pointed to the fact that, 'People in the hostel may be high risk offenders and that is the emphasis for the court when giving background problem analysis and a suggested contract for work. We have to portray an honest optimism to the court, acknowledging it is going to be difficult, but highlighting the potential for at least small changes.'

Finally a prison probation officer (one of whose colleagues had pointed to the need for referring to remorse or lack of it, and the chances of the client getting through a parole licence) spoke strongly of the difficulty of doing 3-yearly lifer reviews to assess behaviour, risk and suitability for a lower category prison. 'You have no training for this. You're asked within weeks of coming here to say "Is this man dangerous?" and it's an enormous responsibility. Frequently we're the only people who take this seriously. I've known chaplains write reports on a 5-minute interview. To be able to do this properly we need full knowledge of the lifer system and the skills to work with disturbed, dangerous and violent clients and modify their offending behaviour within the institution.' These three quotes indicate the very specific concerns and emphases of assessment-writing for these specialists, which begin to suggest that whilst basic assessment skills may not differ greatly from generic work, skill refinements particular to the setting of the specialism are either clearly present or needed, as are some bodies of knowledge which would not be regularly required by fieldwork staff.

4 Example and conclusion

In an endeavour to highlight the viable applicability of some of the skill and knowledge areas outlined by the respondents in this section, in conjunction with some of the communication qualities referred to earlier, an example of live practice, observed by the researcher and discussed with the practitioner, will now be briefly profiled.

Mr X interviewed a young male probationer, Ben, for around half an hour, for the specific purpose of making a final assessment, based on his overall contact with Ben, as to whether he could be recommended to the court for an early discharge to his order. Following some informal discussion and the establishing of eye contact, Mr X began by stating this as the purpose of the interview, and there was some discussion of the reasons for Ben missing some office appointments.

Mr X then reminded Ben of the plans he had made for himself for 1988, contained in a mutually agreed written contract, a method which he used with all his clients, and which he now had in front of him. The plans involved staying out of trouble, saving some money, and making something of himself. Ben responded to the first point by telling Mr X of a recent conversation with a policeman who had stopped him for an informal chat and suggested that now he was maturing he was more likely to stay out of trouble. He also referred to the kinds of friends he was keeping company with. In respect of the second point he had saved £100, and fielded some probing questions from Mr X as to where the money had come from. Of the third, he spoke of his regular visits to the job centre, and his preference for an interesting, permanent job rather than a scheme. He told Mr X that he had been asked to go to a 'Restart' interview and listened to Mr X's advice about how to conduct himself during it.

Concluding the interview, Mr X asked Ben if he thought he was likely to reoffend in the next 12 months. Ben could not think of any reason why he should. Mr X then asked if Ben thought he still needed to be on probation. Ben did not. Mr X told Ben that this accorded with his view, and that he would therefore apply for an early discharge of the probation order. He explained that the court might prefer it to be substituted with a constitutional discharge, and asked Ben to sign the necessary papers so that they would be ready if needed. Ben did so and asked how long the process would take. Mr X explained that it depended on various court procedures, that Ben could be there if he wished, but was not obliged to be. In the meantime, Mr X made it clear to Ben that he need not report, but must continue to uphold the other requirements of the probation order.

In discussing this interview afterwards Mr X considered that Ben's answers to his questions today (which were slanted towards finding out how genuine were his intentions to work to the goals he'd set himself) were not in themselves sufficient to convince him. However, his assessment that discharge should go ahead was based on a continuing series of conversations which suggested that Ben was working to change his life-style, despite the fact that he did not always keep appointments. 'His explanation of his approach to decision-making gives me the impression he's doing things in the right way. My practice experience leads me to the view that he's not "conning" me, but if he is, the next 12 months aren't going to be any different. If he isn't, the order will have served its purpose and he won't have reoffended.' Mr X also mentioned the skills of representing his assessment of Ben's situation to the court – 'skills of mediation and advocacy' – and his own knowledge of the court process, discharge procedures, the employment situation, and sociological issues such as peer group influences. Qualities observed by the researcher and agreed by Mr X were warmth ('Well I'd hardly treat him as "case number 235 Johnson, come in now, your order's up!" '); honesty (about the procedures involved in discharge rather than keep the client in the dark); relaxation (Mr X sat for some of the time with his leg over the arm of his chair); friendliness (balancing the personal and the professional); and being organised (having an agenda, feeling in control of what was happening).

Summing up this section, then, the skills which have been identified and illustrated as being generally necessary for client assessment are as follows:

Interviewing and information-gathering (incorporating previously identified communication skills such as listening and timing); interpretation; analysis;

practice wisdom; ability to challenge; ability to identify readiness for change; good English usage; the provision of structure; clarity, conciseness, summarisation, flow; using appropriate methods and styles for the achievement of purpose (notably by 'bringing the client to life' on paper); the effective communication of messages; abstraction and deduction; the ability to differentiate between opinion and fact; and balancing the interests of court and client.

The broad bodies of knowledge identified, some of which were earlier described as also being necessary for communication, were:

psychology; sociology; criminology; relevant legislation; sentencing disposals and tariff; court, prison, and parole procedures; means of fact verification; and self-knowledge (particularly in terms of a practitioner's own value system).

A variety of skills and knowledge needed by specialist officers have also begun to be identified in this section, and will be dealt with in more detail towards the end of this report. Implicit in the assessment process generally, however, have also been the presence of a number of qualities to which officers have referred or reiterated, such as honesty, warmth, intuition (based on life and work experience), risk-taking, and acceptance. This serves to remind us that the three factors are as inextricably linked in assessment as they are in communication. We have begun to see also that the process of assessment sometimes requires, for its success, the injection of social work intervention. Concluding the part of the survey which relates to skills, knowledge and qualities with clients, it is to this area of probation officers' work which the investigation will now turn.

IV Modes of intervention with clients

1 Clarity of purpose

Of the sixty two probation officers interviewed, fifty six said that they felt clear about the overall purpose of their intervention with clients, and that they, therefore, had specific goals in mind as they worked with them. Three officers did not feel clear, and a further three felt clear at times and hazy at others. Of the former group, one probation centre specialist said that sometimes he found himself doing group exercises and had lost track of the purpose of them. Two of the vacillating group pointed to some confusion and depression in their practice because of the difficulty of achieving anything with clients on young offender licences, drug addicts, those with chronic debts or bad housing conditions. Both, however, acknowledged that they still aimed to reduce offending behaviour and to provide alternatives to custody.

As respondents outlined the respective purposes of their intervention it became apparent that the most frequent of these revolved round the prevention of further offending. Some officers spoke in more modest terms of objectives which they would aim for in the course of this process, such as serving the court; advising, assisting and befriending clients; and helping clients to make alternative choices, and to identify their own potential. One officer described the usual pattern of her practice. 'I go to each visit thinking "Why am I going?" and "How am I going to ask the questions which will give me the information I want?" Often I do this instinctively, but I can usually work out why afterwards.'

Three officers commented that it was often easier to be clearer about purpose during crisis intervention than subsequently. One of them said, 'I start off with clarity but sometimes lose track along the way, especially with cases which are crisis-blown, and it's difficult to maintain continuity of intervention. The tail starts to wag the dog if you're not careful.' Another suggested that probation officers were far more skilled at crisis-intervention – 'making sense out of chaos' – than at sustaining long-term purpose. 'There are other people like volunteers and priests who are better placed to do that.' However, there were a number of unequivocal answers, such as that from an officer who said: 'Yes. It's one of the most important parts of the job – saying to a client, "This is why I'm here; this is why you're here." ' Several officers from one area had found themselves helped, and better channelled towards purpose by the use of a system of record-keeping, originating from the Greater Manchester Service, which focused upon the aims and objectives to be established with clients.

Three answers, which moved to some extent beyond the aim of preventing recidivism, centred around the mediation role of the service. One officer's aim was 'to achieve a degree of reconciliation between the client and the community.' For another it was 'to move around appropriately on the care/ control continuum.' A third expressed the view that 'Your purposes for the agency and the client don't always equate, so you have to work with the two. Part of our role is being a "go-between" between agency and client. You have to know your agency well, and to be able to assess your client's true needs. There is a skill in all this.' Again we are reminded, in these officers' assessment of purpose, of the skill of balancing and holding societal tensions, which perhaps begin to touch upon an overall philosophy of working with offenders.

Finally, one of the most telling sets of answers to this question came from the specialists in the sample who, with only one or two exceptions, firmly expressed the view that being in a specialism gave them a sharper sense of purpose than they had ever experienced in the field. Purpose, for them, might be partly laid down by the courts, as with the law relating to the tasks of civil work specialists, partly by the nature of prison, hostel or court-based systems, or by the restrictions on liberty which community service and probation centres in particular provide. One drugs specialist whose purpose was 'assisting the client, with other agencies, to achieve what s/he wants – presumably in the context of rehabilitation and drug-free life-style', commented: 'My specialism helps to make purpose clear, and I'm very much in favour of specialisms for this reason.' The need for such clarity of purpose has been mentioned by respondents with regularity through the previous sections of this chapter, and the majority of answers to the first question in this particular section also indicate its presence as a prerequisite for intervening appropriately in the lives of clients.

2 The skills and knowledge of intervention

Although there emerged a wide variety of responses to this subject, some officers did begin by expressing their difficulty with and in some cases resistance to the notion that what they did with clients could be in any way reduced to labels. Here, one officer sums up this view.

> There's fancy names for all those – I'm not going to fall into it. We generally do what seems right at the time – inform, provide, facilitate, educate. Communicating, adapting, understanding, being interested, eliciting unstated needs. We work instinctively and we can't put labels on it at the time. Befriending is a skill – if people come in angry, we calm them down, if lethargic, we enthuse. The skill comes in assessing people quickly and correctly – seeing their limitations and potential, knowing where to send them for their needs.

For another officer, however, something approaching the reverse view was the case.

> The main skill is in bringing theory and practice together. Every PO *does* have a clear theoretical perspective, even though they don't acknowledge it. You have a view of offending, of sociological and other influences, and how your clients fit into this. A general consensus about this often emerges in teams but it differs across areas. Part of the perspective is how you use authority. People do go through a period of painful adjustment when they find the world isn't as they thought. The danger after ten years is that you can stop thinking – I know I go onto automatic pilot some days. Values need to be in the perspective too. Someone from outside, not trained for this job, would not operate from such a broad theoretical base.

Certainly, an implication of these differing views is that if theory and practice do, as they should, inform each other, then there may be a need in training courses for probation officers to be taught to think and articulate what theories, methods, or disciplines they are drawing upon at any given time – a process likely to improve the confidence levels which, as we have heard, are a much-needed component of competent practice.

Nevertheless, there was no shortage of ideas about the skill and knowledge which officers in this survey drew upon and, so that the problem of 'labels' can be to some extent reduced, illustrated examples of some of the answers will continue to be given. Top of the list was casework skills, followed very closely by group work skills. Respondents were only placed in the 'casework' category if they used that word themselves, though it clearly has taken on a much wider meaning today than its psycho-dynamic origins might have allowed for. Although people mostly referred to it in the context of one-to-one work, the phrase, 'family casework' was also used, and this, in turn, was sometimes seen as family therapy (also a popular answer), 'in its broadest sense.' Some of the ways in which casework was described were 'enabling, befriending, making a relationship'; 'a view of respect and care for people'; 'self-determination of the client'; 'making a personal relationship which is of the essence'; and 'looking at the whole person.' Someone else, who said that casework is not as Freudian as it used to be, quoted a free-lance consultant to the probation service, Michael Willson, who had expressed the view that 'Casework is like wiping your backside. Nobody ever sees you do it.' Another said, 'Most of the time, it's talking about the normal things in their lives with your antennae up like a Dalek.'

It seems inevitable that the mystique of casework should continue to be enhanced by connotations of invisibility and science-fiction! Two officers however, referred to casework as 'the essential ingredient of the job', one of whom expressed the views of many other officers as she continued,

> But there are a lot of other methods which enhance one-to-one work, like group work, literacy, alcohol education. But I personally hope we never get to a point where people don't have one-to-one relationships with clients, because that's the baseline and the other methods complement it. For example, I have a young lad who trots in each week to have coffee. Sometimes he talks, sometimes he doesn't. He'd fail on a group scheme. All these packages can programme people to fail. You can't just label clients as alcohol or drug problems – they're people.

Overall, then, despite long-standing rumblings about the failure and thus erosion of casework methods, these officers were continuing to view them as their most fundamental tool of intervention with their clients. But perhaps they had widened and redefined the term, so that it had come to be seen as an essential starting-point but not an end in itself; and as a simple relationship-making process which incorporated respect for the individual, rather than the somewhat obscure and esoteric practice of bygone years when, as one officer confided, 'I never knew quite what it was, or even whether I was doing it. I used to be convinced all my colleagues were doing it terribly skilfully, but after a few years I found they thought I was too! I've laughed about it with some of them since, because what we were all doing was good stuff. It just shows how labels can disable you. Thank goodness myths like that are much less these days, because people are much more open about their practice.'

The move to openness is, perhaps, partly reflected in the increasing prevalence of group work, as a mode of client intervention, where co-working with colleagues is usually the order of the day. Clearly, there is a high concentration of this work in probation centres and package schemes, but it was also quite frequently mentioned by fieldworkers. The variety of such groups mentioned appears endless, and ranged from the manifestly popular Priestley/McGuire (1985) 'offending behaviour' groups, to social skills, violence and aggression, and activity-based groups. Here, two probation centre specialists (both of whom felt that they had obtained their group work skills 'on the hoof' rather than via qualifying or in-service training) talk of the nature of the skills they use.

Officer M

> The skills involved in running groups are: communication; the ability to control and assess people; to choose the right level of contact and engagement; to select appropriate methods of work; to consciously model particular behaviour to clients; to be flexible and adaptable enough to make differential relationships. You have to be able to work with conflict and confrontation – not to de-fuse it, but to ride it out and work it, whilst maintaining your professional role and identity, and not being seduced into being one of the group. Your other skills are behaviour modification, task-centred work, administrative and organisational skills, and negotiating the politics of the criminal justice system.

Officer N

> The skills here are: presenting the task, managing the group and engaging it in the task; assessing individual members' input and the consequences of that for the rest of the group – so you know if you have to engage in damage limitation; demonstrating openness about what you're doing. With a younger group you might look at the effects of custody on their parents; with an older one at the effects on their spouses and children. You have to marry this with their own assessment situation and, if you're poles apart, try to work out why. I've learned organisational skills like planning, operating, debriefing in group work. I did a day centre course seven years ago [Officer N has only been in this specialism for three months] but mainly I'm picking it up as I go along. I think most of these skills are transferable from the field – it's just that they're more concentrated here.

Many of these skills do indeed appear to be transferable since they were often referred to by fieldworkers and other specialists. Most of the probation centre workers, however, like Officer M mentioned the ability to challenge, confront, and work with conflict, as being quite crucial in groupwork. Some felt their colleagues in the field could choose to avoid this, whereas their interaction with clients was 'non-stop, high profile stuff, with no hiding-place.' Several commented that when they returned to the field they would be better probation officers for having learned to work with conflict. It was, therefore, the necessary concentration upon this skill in the specialism that had equipped them with an expertise which they did not have before.

A knowledge of all facets of drug and alcohol addiction was the third most frequently mentioned factor in this section with the obvious rationale that both, particularly the former, in these officers' experience, appear to be on the increase. This was one of several key contexts in which the need for a comprehensive knowledge of local (and sometimes national) resources, and of those which the service itself and other agencies had to offer, was also regularly mentioned. Tied in with resources was the importance of liaison and negotiation skills with agencies such as the DSS, social services, electricity boards, and so on. In relation to this a drugs specialist officer described the process as, 'working together with other agencies to achieve goals; finding a balance in terms of who can do what, and not dumping things on them; understanding other agencies' philosophies, concerns and their interpretations of things like confidentiality.' Ability in this area often also involved a knowledge of welfare rights, and the skill of brokerage. The final factor referred to with a degree of frequency was that of life experience such as 'bringing up children, being a grandparent, using whatever I've got,' and, from one officer who drew on her past experience as a teacher, 'not just what I want to teach/tell clients, but rather what they need to learn/work on/change. It's meaningless otherwise.'

Skills in other social work methods were mentioned in small numbers. These included counselling (grief/loss counselling being referred to particularly in prison work, due to loss of freedom, family etc.); cognitive therapy; assertion therapy; (used particularly by female POs with women in hostels and prisons 'to give them models for strong women'); transactional analysis; a systems approach; crisis intervention; behaviour modification; and relaxation therapy. Two other skills which have appeared as threads so far in this survey – those of balance and mediation – were also referred to by several officers, as were five other bodies of knowledge which have also been cited previously: self-knowledge; child abuse guidelines; mental health; psychology; and sociology (an example of this being 'awareness of the social norms of the area such as traditional family functioning models where, as happens here, the mother becomes the lynchpin, and the father barely functions at all').

Finally the overall skill of organising and managing their work referred to earlier by the two probation centre specialists, was mentioned by a number of officers as a prerequisite for the effective use of their other skills. A community service specialist, for instance, likened this skill to one he had possessed as a ship's captain before he joined the probation service; whilst an officer from a generic team spoke of his need for management by objectives, and his team's practice of setting clear priorities for each case and reviewing it on a quarterly basis. His view was that, 'There's been a movement from an esoteric stance in social work and probation, to *managing* what you do. There's an acceptance that some traditional beliefs are open to question, and a move from *knowing* things to *understanding* them, what you're doing and why, and whether it's having any effect.'

If this view is accurate, it perhaps goes some way towards explaining the 'new' version of casework as something which is less obscure, more simple, and more easily understood than that which went before. It is becoming apparent, both in the nature of generic practice and in specialisms with high-risk offenders, that work which focuses on offending behaviour, conflict, drug and alcohol addiction as examples, is now very much at the sharp end of the spectrum of community-based disposals. Some officers have said very clearly that they are not helped in this task by labels to which mystique is attached, but that they do feel their own life experience is valid when dealing with the life experiences of others; and that they are assisted by skills, strategies and bodies of knowledge which help them to understand the nature of their work, and to deal with the problems and paradoxes it throws up.

3 How probation time is spent, and the qualities needed to sustain the process

Whilst probation officers are employing their skills and knowledge in intervention processes, what is their perception of how this occupies them for most of their working hours? The officers in this survey were asked what kinds of things they found themselves doing most of the time with their clients and, further to this, what kinds of personal qualities were needed to sustain them as they did this work.

There was some evident concern to simplify some of the labels of social work methods which people had given earlier, such as casework, counselling, or group work. A majority of the sample reduced such expressions to 'talking and listening'. Listening, however, as we have heard before was not as simple as it sounded. For example, there was 'listening to what people are saying, not what they say', and 'listening in a way which allows people to be heard.' Talking, however, was done according to one officer, differentially – based on an assessment of their needs at the time.

> I had a young lad on probation for two years. At first he came once a week, and later once a fortnight, but I couldn't get him to reduce it to once a month. The only thing he would talk about was football. At the end of the order I said, 'This has been a bloody waste of time, hasn't it?' He said, 'What do you mean? It's been great. You've kept me out of trouble.' I told him, 'You've kept yourself out of trouble.' But he said, 'No. Being on probation, coming here every week, has kept me out of trouble.' I was just holding him, just talking with him, but it worked. I think you can be overtrained for this job.

However, a number of other officers also spoke of the value of just giving people time to talk or to do whatever seemed important. They felt that much of *their* time was spent basically being available to their clients, and as one respondent put it, being with people through the exciting bits and through the boring bits. Giving practical help constituted a major part of people's time too, as it was sometimes suggested that other deeper and more personal problems could not be tackled before basic needs such as housing, fuel, and food had been attended to. This meant that liaison, often in the form of mediation between clients and other agencies, was a skill frequently being employed.

The process of confidence-building also seemed to occupy the time of a number of officers, who referred to it variously as 'affirming,' 'confirming,' 'encouraging,' and 'aiming for people to develop control over their own lives.' One officer described it as, 'Trying to improve clients' perceptions of themselves, and making them more aware of their own abilities, so improving their self-esteem, quality of life, and thereby to prevent offending.' This goal could sometimes be achieved by the talking/listening process, and sometimes by engaging clients in a shared activity.

Finally came the preoccupations of some of the specialists. For probation centre workers it was 'challenging and confronting', and for civil workers 'conciliation'. For most community service officers it was 'managing' in some form or other (although for the one who considered she had a social work brief, it was 'being a good friend'). For prison probation officers it was 'alleviating anxiety' and 'loss counselling'. Again, these responses demonstrate something of the concentrated nature of skills which specialists have to perform.

Many of the qualities which probation officers felt they needed to sustain them as they spent their time in some of the above ways have been outlined and reiterated in previous sections – such as honesty, warmth, and acceptance. This section will briefly discuss a few of the more popular ones which have not hitherto received much attention, and the contexts in which people put them forward.

Top of the list came resilience, patience, honesty, and a sense of humour. 'You're a paid, professional communicator,' said one officer, 'and you have to have enormous resilience not to get completely flooded by all the communicating.' A community service specialist described it as 'an ability to absorb punishment, to keep going, not to give up. I've learned that when offenders are 18 or 19, they're not going to give up crime but, if you stick with them, you know most of them will change eventually. But I get less resilient as I get older, and that's why I find specialisms easier to cope with, because they're more focused.' This confirms the view expressed in the first part of this section by many of the specialists, who found focus and purpose more clearly defined than in the field; and the speaker is indicating in addition that specialist work is, on the whole, shorter-term with quicker through-put, tangible results, and less of the waiting around for people to change than is needed in the field. Perhaps there are two kinds of resilience for probation officers: that which is needed to sustain relatively short bursts of interaction involving direct conflict and challenge; and that which is needed to sustain long periods of supervision during which there is little or no evidence of change. The latter also requires, as one officer put it, 'an incredible amount of patience when you're dealing with high-risk damaged offenders, because you know that any real change almost never happens overnight. At the same time, you need a lot of patience with the organisation too. Here they are wanting

152

figures for this and instant results for that, and you know that you're just hanging in there with your client, because that's what you joined the service to do and that's what matters.' A throughcare specialist also spoke of the need for 'incredible patience; sticking with it; seeing it through – and in *my* specialism, this means seeing people through interminable periods of time.'

A sense of humour was high on the list, as we also saw in connection with qualities for communication. But it was also viewed as a sustaining quality because, in one officer's words, 'It's no good taking yourself too seriously in this job – you have to recognise your own faults and shortcomings. You have to be able to laugh with people, and this leads you to be able to cry with them too. Our seriousness becomes restrictive for ourselves and our clients.' Humour also helped people retain what one person described as 'terrific personal optimism, which you have to have because of the high likelihood of failure in your clients. You have to be able to look beyond that to a brighter horizon at some unknown point in the future.' Many officers were sustained in this kind of belief by the personal philosophies they had developed, whether these were religious or humanistic in nature.

Tolerance was also a much-needed quality, whether of 'irritation, anger, abuse from clients,' or 'the frustrations of trying to do a particular job when you're up against an immovable object like the prison system.' Adaptability and flexibility helped here. Two prison probation officers spoke respectively of, 'being a Jack-of-all trades; avoiding bureaucracy; being the dustbin – taking whatever is thrown at you,' and

> dealing with change every five minutes in a completely alien world. You need to be very flexible for this – sometimes very tough, at other times yielding, at other times manipulative. Working in this system is like peeling away at the layers of the onion. As you get nearer the centre, you think, 'Good God, is that what it's all about?' For example, the system colludes with 'nonce-bashing' by giving 'nonce-bashers' good jobs, and 'nonces' bad ones. It's really shocking; how do you equip POs for that?

A level of curiosity was also needed for the job of working and communicating with people. 'The ludicrousness that is human nature does entertain you,' commented one officer. But to retain one's own sanity in a world where instability and difficulty was the norm, many people felt their own emotional security was crucial, and one officer said he did not know how he would do the job 'without the bolthole and the security of a happy married and family life'. Others referred to the importance of being able to 'switch off' from the job when they went home. 'You need a built-in micro-switch,' averred one officer. 'You take things on board at a personal level and you need to switch off at the end of the day. You have to balance being caring and thoughtful with protecting yourself, or the time comes when *you* become a victim or a pseudo-client. It's like having a bag of coins to give away – you have to keep one back for yourself.' One officer felt very strongly that she and her colleagues needed a good degree of both physical and mental health to sustain consistently working in stressful situations, and that if these were the requisite qualities for servicing clients, then the organisation should also service its workers by providing them with health checks and their own counselling service when needed.

In summary, then, we have seen that clarity of purpose in client intervention is both needed and experienced by most officers, with those in specialisms feeling that the focus for them is particularly clear. There has been some resistance to labels expressed and a redefining and simplifying of some of the more familiar ones. Nevertheless, officers continue to make use of a wide range of social work methods, theories, and bodies of knowledge in their intervention with clients. Specialists find existing skills considerably enhanced by their concentration and sometimes learn previously untried skills which they feel they can usefully transfer to the field. Much of probation officers' time is essentially spent doing things like talking, listening, confidence building, and giving practical help – the latter often as a prerequisite for effective communicating. Communication, then, was right at the heart of the skills needed for intervention, and to sustain this sometimes stressful, often overtly unproductive process, were needed personal qualities of resilience, patience, honesty, humour, tolerance, curiosity, and finally an ability to switch off from it all.

The first three sections of this report have concentrated upon the skills, knowledge, and qualities needed in the fundamental processes of communicating, assessing, and intervening with clients. As some of the officers have sometimes hinted, these processes, although still relatively 'invisible' and autonomous, are inseparable from the organisational requirements of the probation service as an agency, and it is to the skills, knowledge, and qualities needed to function as a member and as a professional representative of that agency that the focus now turns.

V   Functioning as a probation professional

1   The nature and importance of inter-professional relationships

Although a small number of respondents made the point that it was technically possible to function as a probation officer, more or less in isolation from colleague and other agencies, none of them took the view that to do so was in any way desirable. Good professional relationships both within and across agencies undoubtedly, they considered, strengthened the quality of their overall service delivery. Although the use of the word 'important' in the question to some extent pre-empted the nature of the responses (Appendix 4.2, Q. 12), the less structured probing into the meaning of individual answers relative to personal experiences, subsequently confirmed their authenticity. Following a range of answers defined by the respondents themselves, one said that good professional relationships were 'quite important'; five that they were 'important'; thirty three that they were 'very important'; and nineteen that they were 'extremely important'. (The latter term was sometimes expressed as, 'vital, essential, crucial, everything, or amazingly important') Four respondents did not offer a closed-ended answer to this question, but their subsequent comments indicated that they too regarded the ability to make good professional relationships as a matter of some consequence in their day-to-day work.

Some examples of the answers given to this question are listed below.

Apart from contact with the client, it's the most important thing of all.

You have to rely on colleagues in court and elsewhere to communicate essential information to you.

It's absolutely vital, particularly in joint-working or co-working settings like civil work – that way your work reaches a higher standard. It's possible to function without them, but you have far less resources to draw on.

If you've got the professional relationships right, you can make the team move – a bad team can have an agenda but go nowhere.

Being pragmatic, it's who you know and how well you know them that gets you what you want – doing a little horsetrading from time to time.

A united team with colleagues who communicate, laugh together, and work together, provides a better service.

This office used to be one big happy family. For the first time in 22 years I find I'm not happy in a probation office, and it all comes down to professional relationships.

These quotations begin to highlight issues such as unavoidable reliance on colleagues, improving standards of team and service delivery, exchanging favours, and the need for good communication. When respondents were asked to outline the skills involved in making and sustaining professional relationships, it was perhaps, then, hardly surprising that the two most frequent answers centred around communication skills and reliability which, as we have seen, is more of a quality than a skill.

Many officers considered that all the communication skills they had described as being needed with clients – such as listening, holding onto purpose, balancing the personal and the professional – were equally necessary with colleagues. However it was stressed that they took on a different format between people who shared the same or similar roles to that employed between worker and client. It was important to communicate empathy, to show that officers were tolerant of and sensitive to the dynamics within their own agency, and to the functions, concerns and pressures of other agencies. Again they had to be willing and able to *really* listen. As one officer put it, 'Relationships are a two-way process, including with your senior and ACPO. You can sit around and wait, and find it doesn't happen. Myths can build up so easily, even with the office across the road, and so you *have* to keep communicating. You also have to keep colleagues informed, and that way you get their support for your activities and projects. And you must take full responsibility for communication with other agencies, particularly social services whose days, I always feel, are much more packed and less structured than mine.'

Keeping people informed, taking responsibility for each other, being accountable to each other, were all seen as ways of demonstrating reliability and consistency, qualities which had also been cited as being important to show towards clients, partly in order to influence by example. Being 'honest, straight-forward and up-front' were also qualities referred to by many of the officers, as again had been the case in respect of clients. With colleagues, however, it was particularly important to be able to 'share strengths and weaknesses; put your own skills out into the open or you don't develop. It's not easy and it's quite threatening, but it avoids entrenchment and isolation.' As another officer suggested, 'You have to be aware that you don't have the total sum of skills and knowledge needed for the job, and so it makes sense and you must have a willingness to seek help from colleagues and other agencies.' Many officers spoke of the initial anxiety but ultimate reward and satisfaction of co-working on cases, whether with another probation colleague, or a professional from another agency. One example was given of a probation officer with experience in marital counselling doing joint interviews with a social worker with expertise in child abuse work, to effectively unearth the dynamics of a 'problem family' who were on the statutory books of both agencies. Invariably, people felt they had given a better service by joining forces and putting their practice on the line, than they would have done by working at the problem single-handedly.

Maintaining mutual respect and credibility was viewed as a necessary component of establishing a basis for inter-professional relationships. This was particularly important in relation to courts as we shall see in more detail in the next section, and a part of attaining one's own credibility was the ability to be assertive when appropriate, as well as accepting of the other point of view. Timing and balancing, again, seemed to be of the essence here. The skill of negotiating also came into play, and this involved, 'give and take; building up personal credits; doing them a favour; ensuring you only make fair demands on people'. Building up professional respect with other agencies, according to these officers, often seemed to depend on making personal relationships first. Some of them felt that there was a little hypocrisy in this process, and that it existed because the probation service hadn't really worked hard enough at establishing its own image and rationale with the public so that they had to start at square one in each negotiating process, until they had built up a network of contacts. Perhaps the acquisition of agency presentation as a skill was something for their managers to take a serious look at.

Being mutually supportive, sharing time, talking over difficult cases and feelings about them, were cited as a mixture of skills and qualities which

156

officers needed to offer each other. This implied the ability to organise time so that people could free themselves for colleague discussion and the willingness to share expertise, feelings of anxiety, and to listen to what other people had to say both to them and about themselves. It involved skills of assessment – 'knowing what others need from you and providing it' – and it involved 'communicating the enthusiasm of the job'. It was important, in the view of many officers, to know and be able to articulate their objectives and beliefs in the job and to understand those of others, so that teams, in particular, could work to common aims. The process of support and sharing facilitated this purpose. One officer had observed that, 'most probation officers are fairly gregarious, which gives them a natural ability to get on with other professionals. Some younger POs aren't like that to begin with, but it is something you acquire over time.' Is gregariousness, then, an inevitable end-product of the probation socialisation process?

Other ingredients of good professional relationships mentioned by these respondents included, 'doing your fair share of the work'; 'having a sense of humour – if you don't have humour, nobody wants to know you really,' and 'trying to maintain an objectivity and a distance from office politics – otherwise all your energy goes into the undercurrents, not into the clients, and your time is dissipated.' Members of five of the specialist groups, however, had specific points to make in respect of the skills and qualities needed in their own particular settings.

A community service specialist working in a rural area said,

> You *are* the probation service in an area like this. You are Mr or Mrs Probation, and you *have* to build up a good network of relationships. I've done it here in CS by shifting the emphasis from buildings to people and linking offenders with people. They don't work in gardens where there are buildings any more – they do gardening for old people. It means building personal relationships, but striking a balance in that and avoiding over-familiarity. There's a skill here in knowing when to be pushy and when to stay quiet. I take judges round the CS projects too, linking them with what's going on.

Clearly, this officer felt the over-riding need was one of good public relations in the CS field, and was concentrating his skills of presentation and communication in that very specific area.

An officer working on a probation 'package' scheme also felt that, 'You have to keep the PR work going,' but in addition, 'in your group set-up you rely greatly on your colleagues and we work a lot with colleagues in other agencies. The skills don't differ much from skills with clients except that your preconceptions are different, and you don't have as much patience with colleagues. Your own behaviour and your reliability are the skills really. I spent nearly a year working with a colleague in whom none of the rest of us had confidence, and it was awful. It's a myth that you can plough your own furrow in this job.' The suggestion that one expected more of, and had less patience with, one's colleagues than one's clients was reiterated by several officers, and was particularly the case with those working in high-profile group settings. Again, reliability was a critical yardstick of good professional behaviour in such situations.

Here a probation centre specialist reiterates the transferability of skills with clients to those with colleagues, and the reliance upon colleagues in group settings. 'It's like with clients – reading your colleagues and where they're at. Tolerating them. Having a sense of humour – laughing together. Honesty – because you rely on your colleagues in the group. If the group senses a divide, they'll cut straight through it.' Another specialist in the same field emphasised the need for 'continuous communication and open sharing'.

A deputy warden from a probation hostel confirmed the last two speakers' views that the necessary skills were similar to those needed with clients. 'The skill is much the same as with the residents here and applies particularly with the non-social work trained staff, who have to be assured of discretion and confidence too. I perform a balancing act between the two.' Again the skill of balancing, meeting the needs of two sets of interest groups, comes to the fore, this time in a residential setting.

One prison probation officer pointed to the need for group solidarity when working in a total institution. 'A team in the prison has to be agreed about its approach and present a united front. For example, we have made the decision not to be welfare officers and to be pro-active, so we must all stick by that. We need to back each other up and our senior needs to represent us appropriately and retain status on our behalf. We have to share with each other, be open, share the stress, and the friendship too.' Here was an example, then, of a group of colleagues who felt, as a number of fieldworkers had done, that their best chance of effectiveness was with good teamwork. Working together within a total institution clearly reflected in microcosm the validity of their beliefs in the importance of this skill.

Two other prison probation officers referred to the need to make relationships with prison staff as well as prisoners. 'You have to be able to make your own relationships with prison staff. It's back to communication skills. Each PO has to prove themselves individually with prison staff,' commented one. Another said, 'You need tact, continuity, patience, and to keep plodding. With prison officers, it's a long time before you get anything back. But they do offload too, particularly when they see me getting through to the more difficult individuals. It's important to appreciate that it's difficult for everyone working in a total institution.'

All these specialists, then, pointed in different ways to the need for communication skills in professional relationships, most suggesting that these skills were very similar to those they used with clients, but perhaps with a slightly different emphasis relating to role-awareness. Being able to rely on and share with each other was crucial. Balance was a necessary skill for one, public relations skills for another, and the very particular skill of establishing personal credibility with prison staff, largely via communication processes with them and with prisoners, was clearly an intrinsic part of working effectively in an institution. Tolerance, honesty, humour were qualities emphasised, and perhaps, indeed, it might be inferred that gregariousness was an overall quality which all these specialists needed to be able to survive professionally in extremely exposed working environments. Again, it seems, we observe in the specialisms a concentration of skills and qualities which officers have transferred from the field, and which many believe they will transfer back again in an improved and refined state. Let us conclude with a quotation from a throughcare specialist working in a generic team on the subject of communication skills in professional relationships.

'It's grasping nettles; conciliating; enabling; acknowledging individual effort and strength; working with the positives; exorcising the negatives. Without all that there's a whole layer of stuff to get through which gets in the way of working with clients. It's absolutely vital.'

2   Courtwork: taking the gravel out of life's vaseline

Whether or not, like five of these respondents, probation officers specialise in courtwork, all of them are unavoidably involved in the court process, perhaps only avoiding direct contact with it if they are working in an institution. All the probation service's statutory criminal and civil work emanates from the courts and much of its voluntary work, such as through-care and matrimonial conciliation is likely also to have its origins in court. Except where specialist court teams do it all, most fieldworkers are required to perform regular magistrates and crown court duties and all those engaged in the preparation of court reports are likely to be present when some of them are presented to the court, particularly for current clients or with contentious cases where custody is a possibility.

All probation officers, at some time, and most sooner rather than later, therefore, have to acquire the skills and knowledge needed to operate in the court setting. As mentioned in the section on assessment skills, tasks such as court report preparation, which are done for external bodies, are generally seen as a kind of showcase for the probation service: the service provided by probation officers in court, and the way in which they represent their agency's function and philosophy, is also something which is there for all to see. Possibly for that very reason, it is an issue which officers in this study discussed with considerable animation.

The respondents were almost unanimous in their view that before probation officers could begin to operate in the court setting, they needed a fundamental body of knowledge about the following:

Court functions and procedures (for example, the arrest and charge procedures that led to court appearances, and committal proceedings); the varied roles of court personnel; basic law (such as the Bail Act, the 1968 Theft Act, the rules of evidence, family law); the sentencing tariff;

159

the meaning of individual disposals and when they can be appropriately and legally used; and the law and court procedure in relation to probation service-administered disposals (such as how to take out a warrant, how to apply for an early discharge of a probation order, how to breach someone).

All this knowledge constituted a 'bottom line' requirement for most of these officers, and for the most part, only those who had operated in the court specialisms felt reasonably confident of possessing it. Many said that it had taken them years of experience to accumulate the knowledge they did have, and a number commented that their training had not equipped them for it nor, from their observation of students on placement, did it appear to do so any better today. 'Some people don't breach' said one officer, 'almost because they don't know how to do it.' It was observed earlier in the report that confidence derives in large measure from knowledge and perhaps it was not, therefore, surprising that some of these officers commented upon the lack of confidence of the probation service generally in its task and role in court, though to be able to demonstrate such confidence was thought by many to be vital.

Confidence in court, in the view of a majority of officers, came also from a clear knowledge of the service's statutory functions and duties, of the purpose, expectations and limitations of its role (for example, assisting and advising sentencers rather than doing the sentencing itself), and the ability to speak articulately in public, often at a moment's notice. Several people felt that probation officers needed training in effective public speaking, and that they needed to acquire the skill of handling their own authority and their audience in court, to reduce their fear of its theatrical setting, and to make the system work better for their particular purposes. In effect, to be the person who can, through sentencing advice, offer 'a package which represents everyone's needs and covers everything' is, as one officer suggested, 'a very powerful position to be in,' and one which probation officers, it was felt, often do not know how to exploit to the full.

The major skill of court work, however, was undoubtedly seen, as one officer put it, as 'the ability to be a wo/man for all seasons'. This amounted to 'the skill of steering the middle course – knowing the expectations and concerns of magistrates and judges, communicating that you understand that they have to have regard for society's interests, but retaining your independence, not getting sucked in, not colluding, whilst being prepared to stick your neck out for the client, but being open and honest about the risks.' It was saying, 'Yes, I respect your view, but this is what my role is.' It was the skill of mediation, balance, being the bridge. As a specialist court officer put it, 'Your central role is to be a bridge between all the different factions in the court. It takes the gravel out of life's vaseline. If you can, for example, explain a client's problems to the police and the difficulty of the police's job to clients, you get people to shift their positions. It's the same in court, because this is the central skill throughout the job. An offender is out of step with society. If you can build the bridge that helps him step *with* society, you've fulfilled your role.'

The skill of bridge-building, mediating, balancing, holding the tension, as probation officers have variously described it in the survey is perhaps performed and played out at its clearest and most unambiguous in the court setting. Several of the prison probation officers, however, referred to the similarity between their role as mediator in court and mediator in the prison, between the inmate and the system or between the inmate and the outside world. If it is central as so many of these officers appear to be saying then indeed it must be a core skill if not, perhaps, *the* core skill needed by the probation service. Most of these respondents emphasised that experience of the job had helped them improve their skills as a mediator. 'I was very much on the client's side to start with,' said one. 'You have to work through both sides and experience them in order to reach a middle point. I couldn't have done that at the beginning, but I do think that training could go much further to help students with this than it does at present.' Whilst there can be little doubt of the validity of experience in helping officers to know how to erect and tread the bridge of mediation, it seems likely that the last speaker's view is also correct, and that training for example via role play, effective public speaking, and situation analysis could perhaps offer greater prominence than hitherto in equipping students to perform such a skill at least adequately at the point of qualification.

Another piece of knowledge which touched closely on the skill of mediation, was that of the agency policy and its ethos. It was also important to have the ability to represent these two factors in court. An example of needing to know agency policy was given by a probation centre specialist. 'The magistrates might tell you they'll only make a probation centre condition in an order if the probation service is prepared to bring them back to court after more than one absence. You need to be able to stand up and say that your county's policy is to breach after more than *two* absences. So you need to *know* it – and have the courage to *say* it.' Knowledge and representation of agency ethos seems, in theory, more problematic because one does not exist in official terms. These officers, however, appeared to experience little difficulty in saying what, for them, constituted the probation service ethos. Their views did not differ greatly, and are probably best summed up in the words of two of them. 'We're trying to represent civility, and owning our offenders as a society,' said one. 'Representing the moral ethos of the probation service, which is still based on traditional social work values. That means placing worth and value on people who offend, helping them to avoid it in future, whilst understanding that they have to make their own decisions, and need to have people and systems treat them with concern,' suggested the other.

Communication skills again came into play in the probation officers' court role. The skill of interpreting court events on paper for the benefit of colleagues was seen as crucial. It was considered necessary by most officers to be able to relate verbally well and differentially to all court personnel, from police, to solicitors, magistrates, court ushers, and back to one's own colleagues. As in the last section, it also seemed necessary to make some personal relationships in this area, as one officer said, 'so you can cut corners, and they'll listen to your advice because they know you.' Again, some of them felt concerned that the service hadn't established its professional purpose and credibility in court sufficiently to be treated with respect in its own right. 'Dogsbody' and 'poor relation' were expressions used more than once to describe the way in which probation officers are often treated in court. Those who worked in small courts, however, referred to a very different process wherein the court personnel, including the probation officers, came to know each other well and would often have coffee or lunch together. Again they felt it important to avoid system-collusion and insensitivity to the client, but also thought that in this way their role in and their advice to the court came to be understood and respected. One such officer commented, 'In ten years, I had less than ten people go into custody. That was because I knew the magistrates and court officials, and they had confidence in me.' So one way or another it seems that effective communication with court personnel leads to a better deal for the clients of the probation service.

Being pro-active in court was often mentioned as something which was desirable but did not happen as often as it might, because people felt uncertain and diffident about interposing inappropriately in court proceedings. This again highlighted the need for a good knowledge of court procedure, confidence in one's role, and an ability to speak articulately. An example was given of 'a solicitor spouting away about getting a client into a bail hostel, and you knowing there weren't any places so standing up immediately and saying that you needed longer than a week's remand for a report.' Another officer thought the probation service should be pro-active in educating magistrates and judges. 'If I go and tell the judge about the conversation I've had with the distressed wife of the man he's just sentenced to ten years, then s/he begins to get some idea of the nature of my job that isn't otherwise visible,' pointed out an ex-crown court liaison officer. Being pro-active was also about identifying and helping clients in need or stress before, during, and after their court appearances, even if the service was not statutorily responsible for them – much as the police court missionaries used to do. Where the role was more reactive, such as when interviewing clients in cells after sentence, one officer made a plea for greater sensitivity. 'It takes commitment to the court setting. Unless you see and feel the emotion of the man who has just got 7 years, you don't know what it's all about.'

In addition to the quality of sensitivity were mentioned qualities of tact and diplomacy, efficiency ('Being well-prepared with necessary information at your finger tips, having read the day's reports and anticipated questions about them. Also being able to work within the demands of a tight time schedule. You need roller-skates sometimes!') and calmness ('Managing your own anxiety and stress which you absorb from the client and the pressures from the court'). A number of officers also considered physical self-presentation important in terms of smart dress and neat, professional appearance. This was felt to demonstrate courtesy and respect, not only to the court, but to the client also.

In conclusion, let us listen to the very distinctive court experiences of two specialists – one from civil work, and one from community service.

Civil work specialist

In the civil court, I need the ability to think on my feet, and a willingness to get involved. For example, in a decree nisi hearing, one parent has to appear in court with a statement of arrangements for the children – this is a section 41. One day the judge will give me a file of one of these and say, 'Here, let me know what you make of that', and another day he'll say, 'I can do this, or that, or make such an order, can't I?' I have had to learn a lot from Bromley's *Family Law* [1987], and I do now feel I have a specialist knowledge that mainstream POs don't have. It gives you recognition as a problem-solver in domestic disputes, particularly by solicitors.

Community service specialist

In the prosecuting role, you have to be familiar with court proceedings and the law relating to community service. You have to learn to communicate with solicitors on a more direct, adversarial level, rather than follow the natural PO tendency to work *with* them. Also, most POs are dealing in theories, ideas, possibilities, but as prosecutor you have to be able to present facts. To help me perform the role, I base my persona on a fictional lawyer called Sylvester Hardcastle of Anglo-Italian origin, who was adopted by an entrepreneurial Yorkshire family who needed a lawyer to keep the family business going. There's a whole story about his identity, and it's quite a joke between me and my senior, but it all helps to present things in a credible manner.

These two quotations demonstrate, in turn, a body of knowledge which mainstream officers mostly do not have, and the skill of prosecuting – playing a role, operating adversarially, presenting facts rather than ideas – most of which mainstream officers are again not accustomed to, though they do have to present a mixture of facts and ideas in their court reports. It poses the question as to whether all probation officers should be taught these specialist skills and knowledge, whether they should at least be given training in them prior to their secondment to the specialisation, or whether they should, as both these officers had done, merely be left to pick them up as they went along.

It is clear that the probation service and its work is very much exposed in the court setting, and that if it desires to make an impact, it must know and present professionally its purpose and ethos. The officers in the survey have spoken with some feeling about the need for a body of knowledge relating to court processes and personnel, relevant law, sentencing and the tariff. The overriding skill for them is that of mediating – being able to steer a middle course between court and client – and none of them suggested that this was an easy task. On the contrary, these respondents took the view that those being trained for it should be helped to understand and manage both the internal and overt conflict it is liable to produce. However, as a senior judge had, reportedly, said to one of the respondents as she left her specialist post in the crown court, 'We have had our differences – and I have appreciated those.'

3   The skill of managing a workload

In the course of a working week, probation officers have to keep appointments with clients, respond to casual callers and phone calls, keep records, write reports, attend court, team meetings, and so on. Do they consider that they can function effectively as professionals without possessing the skill of good workload management? Briefly, 42 of the 62 interviewed, believed this skill was necessary. Twenty believed it was not necessary, but of that number, ten believed it was professionally desirable. Here are the views of some of those who considered the skill to be important.

> Without it, ultimately people get in a mess, feel guilty and anxious, can't cope, sometimes become ill, and generally do a disservice to their clients.

> It's definitely a skill and you're not totally effective unless you're on top of it, including prioritization and recording.

> If you're not in control, you're not being responsible, and some of your clients get a lot of attention, whilst others get too little. The cost to those people and you yourself is too great.

> You have to be organised because you never clear your desk in this job at the best of times.

> I plan two or three weeks ahead – I've learned to leave gaps in my diary now. If you've arranged your day, and people come to the office unexpectedly, you have to deal with that so as not to let down people you've made arrangements with previously. It's a responsibility to all your clients, not just the one you're seeing at the time.

Those who differed from such views did so for some of the reasons which appear below:

> Some people operate best in a perpetual state of crisis. Maybe some people who are self-evidently good workload managers are not good POs.

> If a client needs me it's a priority. The good organisers probably put the clients second.

Organising your records doesn't mean good quality of work.

Good administrators can be bad caseworkers.

We don't help POs by requiring reams of records which get lost in a drawer somewhere.

I knew a PO who never wrote a file in his bloody life. He burned his files before he left, but his clients still talk about him fifteen years on!

There is clearly a certain extremity between these two sets of views, and an implication that good workload managers may not be good at working with clients. However, a number of respondents talked of the necessity of again retaining a balance between client contact and workload management, and several mentioned instances of soul-less administration freaks, or brilliant but totally disorganised caseworkers, who were the exceptions that proved the rule. Some officers commented that workload organisation was a skill they had not been trained for and felt they would have benefited greatly from. On the whole, as the figures show, they saw it as a core skill which, balanced properly with client contact, underpinned the overall quality of service offered primarily to their clients, but also by implication to their colleagues and to the courts.

4   Operating within the limits of the agency framework

Interlinked with the skills, knowledge, and qualities needed to do the job of a probation officer are the values and attitudes which inform and affect professional performance. Probation officers have a long tradition of autonomous practice, and a history of successfully resisting the addition to their duties of tasks which they found morally unpalatable, such as the 72 hour detention order for young adult offenders mooted in the Younger Report (1974).

Nevertheless, they have also absorbed into their practice penal measures such as probation order conditions which they initially regarded as unacceptable. Now that they see the writing on the wall for measures such as tracking and tagging, will they actively resist their imposition, will they reluctantly accept them, or will they utilise their own particular skill of absorbing the task but making the method of implementing it their own so that it remains within the bounds of moral acceptability?

Thirty eight of these officers said that they accepted the limitations of the agency framework, though a few had great difficulty in doing so; several said they regularly pushed at the boundaries; and most recognised a high level of discretion and autonomy which they had within the framework. A few found the structure helpful, 'a guide and a protection'. One respondent was unsure how to answer and three said that they did not accept the limitations. Two of these were from the same rural area, though located in different offices. One put it like this. 'No. The more the probation service tries to focus, the more some people drop through the net. Our area policy is not to do court reports on first time offenders. Well, I believe some of them need help before it's too late, so I do them. We're also supposed only to write positives in reports, and I think it's dishonest, and so is not mentioning the possibility of custody but the service does contain my dissent.' The other said, 'No. I've been called a maverick and someone who paddles my own canoe. So autonomy in this town is alive and well! I don't see anyone from headquarters from one month to the next. The senior in the next town once told our ACPO that there was a new by-pass round that town and this one, and to make sure he used it. I don't think he's been here since!' Although they viewed themselves as unaccepting of the limitations both officers were, as the first suggested, being somehow contained within the service, largely by virtue of the autonomy and flexibility which was open to them within the framework.

However, the officers were then required to be a little more specific about their actions and responses if the limitations became unacceptable. They were asked to talk about how far along that road they would go and, though a few gave specific responses to that question, most did not, and were prompted by the suggestion of electronic tagging as an example of where principle and pragmatism might clash. Of this group, twenty three gave a qualified acceptance of the idea of the probation service being involved in tagging, and eight an unqualified acceptance. Six officers did not know what they would do, and twenty officers said they would have to resign (one preferring to be sacked). Most of these shared the view of one officer who asked, 'When does the alternative to custody become as degrading as custody?' Another said, 'Your own integrity would stop you doing it, though you'd continue negotiating as far as possible.'

A further comment was, 'It goes against the ethos and spirit of the probation service. It's the same reason I don't want to be a prison officer or a policeman.' One chief probation officer had apparently told his staff that the area would not agree to involve itself in tagging. Finally, an officer who was against the idea explained how such things sometimes came about. 'People should stay aware of what's creeping in under the back door and raise their voice before it happens. You have a moral duty to do this. Things like report centres, which aren't doing social work, open the door to things like tagging.'

The qualified acceptors of the idea had a variety of comments to make. A number of them said the idea would have to be agreed with their union before they would be involved in it, and a regular response was, 'I'd try anything to save people from going to prison,' though a lot of people would want the offenders concerned to consent to being tagged, and it was recognised particularly by prison specialists, that many offenders would themselves prefer tagging to imprisonment. One prison probation officer commented, 'I don't like the idea of tagging, but from where I see it, there are young people in the prison who should not be there. If they asked me to take a whole load of youngsters down the High Street in balls and chains for an hour a week, just to get them out, I'd do it. I don't believe in tagging because it doesn't fit with the probation service ethos. But, if we don't look at ourselves and take on other things, we could lose out badly – and I don't like to think who else would do it. At least we'd do it humanely.'

Another view was that tagging was acceptable if it was used only as an alternative to custody and not in addition to it, 'Otherwise it's wide open to abuse'. Several officers felt that 'Acceptance is gradualist. You come to accept things without realising, like probation conditions and CSO, which everyone thought ten years ago would turn probation officers into screws on wheels.' Other more pragmatic individuals pointed out that they had other roles as spouses and parents and needed to support families, so could not resign even if they disagreed with tagging. One suggested, 'It would be alright as long as it was another specialism which I could dodge.' Another joked in the same vein, 'I'd say I wasn't on the telephone!' One officer, however, thought that, 'We do tag our clients in very subtle ways today. If you work a patch system, do evening work, call into the local pubs, you're tagging and tracking broadly already.' Finally came a fairly unequivocal answer, 'I didn't come into this game to save welfare, freedom and democracy – I learnt that on my first day in the job. You might as well work in a shoeshop.'

It seems reasonably apparent from these responses that most officers are unhappy about the idea of becoming involved in tagging, feeling that it is a disposal which is incompatible with the traditional social work ethos of the service. About a third of them maintain that their response would be to resign, and small numbers are either uncertain or willing to take such a measure on board unreservedly. Slightly over a third would, for a variety of reasons, be willing to take tagging on board, with various conditions such as Union agreement, offender consent, or sole use as an alternative to custody. A few would agree to its presence in the service provided they did not have to operate it. The overall sense of these responses was that if tagging could be made humane by the probation service, then they'd take a serious look at it. In this kind of discussion, the officers demonstrated a considerable degree of self-knowledge, awareness of their own values and what they saw as the service ethos and a knowledge of penal issues and how new measures come to be absorbed into the system. Their autonomous traditions mean that they will not simply accept whatever is thrown at them, but will either act to signify it is unacceptable, or use their skills of negotiation and innovation to stamp their own 'humane face' upon the mark of new disposals and requirements which come their way.

5   Professional performance in relation to management practice

Probation officers in all areas have to perform as professionals in relation to a hierarchical structure, stretching from their team senior, to the more remote groupings of assistant and deputy chiefs and chief probation officers. Are there any skills and knowledge which they need to utilise in their role of main grade workers who are answerable to line management, and how does this line management actually affect the quality of their professional performance?

In answer to the latter question, thirty probation officers said they were unaffected by management practice; fifteen felt undermined; and thirteen felt strengthened; four were uncertain.

The majority 'unaffected' group were characterised by answers such as these:

> Most of the time we ignore them.

> In this job I can get on and do my own thing.

> I'd like to think my performance would be strengthened, which it would be by greater emphasis on leadership instead of management in seniority. It's a situation produced by bureaucracy.

> I don't know what they're doing, so I don't know what would happen if they went away. We never see them.

> I told the CPO recently that he was operating a giant child's post office set, where management sit around and pass each other postal orders and stamp them. It doesn't affect anyone else in the service – we all operate like satellites.

The last group clearly felt autonomy was alive and well for them but, interestingly, so did many of the smaller groups who felt strengthened by management practice. The usefulness of various procedures, structures and good practice guidelines were referred to, but within that, as one officer suggested, 'We're not imposed upon, and there's a great deal of flexibility. Students notice the difference after social services placements.' One officer said, 'I feel quite free to take them on if I think they're getting it wrong – and I hope they would listen.' Another agreed, 'It's up to you what you make of what's on offer. I feel free to go and see the ACPO for a chat. If they know me as a person, they'll support me.'

The fifteen who considered themselves undermined, however, clearly felt very differently about their experiences. One ex-senior had resigned his position, 'because of lack of support from management'. Another referred to a process she called 'management by alienation'. There was a great deal of dissatisfaction and unhappiness in two areas about officers being moved around with little or no choice in the matter. For example, 'County policy has been very disruptive. The production process of management, the initiation of day centres and the like is *all*. The client and the PO seem to get lost in all this', commented another ex-senior. It did not help that, 'HQ is distant, and this reflects in senior management, so a lot of PO energy is dissipated in dissatisfaction.' Sometimes, immediate seniors got a better press than their superiors, but there were also criticisms. 'One of the reasons I find it difficult to say what my skills are is that my SPO has never sat down and discussed them with me.' Or 'My SPO is devious and dishonest, and it affects me badly.' A prison probation officer was frustrated that his SPO and ACPO 'would not fight the battle that's needed to establish our role in this institution,' and an ex-court specialist made a similar point in relation to the need for top level liaison in that setting. Several people actually felt undermined because county policy stopped them mentioning custody in reports, and this 'makes us look silly in the crown court'.

Others considered that management was unwise to leave the main grade out of decision-making processes so frequently. 'It's a shame that bright main graders aren't appreciated and listened to,' said one, and, 'They make a big mistake to treat experienced POs like there are in this county as children,' said another. Clearly this group felt undervalued and overlooked and their experience of management practice was, if anything, serving to side-track their energies and dissolve their skills.

As in the last section relating to agency limitations, people appeared to search for strategies via which they could carry on doing what they wanted anyway within certain boundaries, despite management practice, because its remote nature meant that it did not really touch them. Others would use basic communication skills to ensure that management came to know them as people. Direct confrontation, from this viewpoint, was preferable to the building up of myths. Those who had been directly and adversely affected by management practice, however, by for example being moved unwillingly, were disaffected and suffering from low morale. Those who felt, on the other hand, valued, supported, encouraged, and even held to account were very possibly functioning more effectively than those who did not.

In conclusion, then, this section on functioning as a probation professional has shown firmly the importance of maintaining good internal and trans-agency professional relationships, and the need for good communication and public speaking skills, and qualities of honesty, tolerance and sensitivity. It has demonstrated the necessity of acquiring a fundamental body of knowledge about court work, and the skill of mediation, steering a middle course, which appears to have applicability across most duties of the service. Knowing oneself and one's values, knowing and representing the 'probation service ethos' have also emerged as being of extreme importance. The skill of workload organisation, and balancing it with client contact was a factor which underpinned the overall quality of service delivery. Finally, it appeared, there was a skill in relating to line management. If it did not closely affect performance it could be ignored, or it could be communicated with, but either way the strategy produced the autonomy which the officers desired. Perhaps the situation also left behind it an, as yet, unanswered question about the skills and knowledge which managers need for their own effective performance in servicing probation staff.

VI Differential skills in probation

The question this chapter has set out to address in a variety of ways is what skills, knowledge, and qualities probation officers need for practice, and whether any of those elements differ from those needed by other professions. The notion of 'difference' will be addressed in three ways: how probation officers' practice differs amongst themselves in terms of personal style; how specialists differ from the mainstream; and what probation officers see as the essential ingredient of their profession which does not apply to any other.

1 Differences of personal style

Eleven of the sixty two probation officers did not believe that their style differed significantly from that of others in the profession – although a few made the reasonable point that they did not always see what other people were doing. Three people felt that they were clearer and therefore more structured about their work and its purpose than others. One of those, a probation centre specialist, described her work as 'confronting, challenging, high-profile, more exciting, stimulating, dramatic in terms of impact – and the clients say so too!' A prison specialist was clear that he wanted to stop people offending, and to focus on 'the stress, or anger, or whatever, that impedes this'. A civil work specialist said, 'I bring more structure to the work because I think about what I do and I have very high standards for practice.' We have seen earlier that many specialists consider their work to be more sharply focused than the mainstream, and perhaps it is, therefore, no coincidence that the three officers who answered in this way were also specialists. Another group of six people, again all specialists with one exception, viewed their practice as 'more creative, imaginative and innovative' than that of others. Their practice involved initiating and running a variety of groups, activities, and sports for clients, and generally being open to new approaches to the work. They were drawn from the specialisms of civil work, community service, probation centres, and throughcare, which indicates that, whilst firmly focused, there is also scope for innovation and experimentation in these fields.

Several officers thought that they were 'more available' than their colleagues and some of these together with others, that they were 'more informal with clients,' relying less on the probation officer's role than on, 'my own personality and emotional commitment. Dryness and blandness are not my style.' One said, 'Eccentricity is my style. I portray Jean Roberts [pseudonym] unafraid!' A third respondent was more graphic. 'I'm more outgoing, use my personality more – I put a lot of "me" into it. CQSW courses, in striving for professionalism, seem to be turning out clones. I miss the old characters and extroverts in the service. We don't do enough work at developing personalities. NAPO conferences used to reflect a wide range of personalities, but it's now very sterile – there's no debate and things go through on the nod. Having different viewpoints helps you develop your own. You're not allowed to be different any more.'

Another respondent, from a different viewpoint, considered that 'I intellectualise more. Feelings are less of a currency with me than for other people.' One thought he was more realistic than others 'because I've grown up in a client

170

group culture,' and a second that he was 'more belligerent and direct with the clients'. Another who also saw himself as direct with clients and colleagues explained what he meant. 'Then they know what to expect. I treat clients with dignity and courtesy and expect them to treat me the same. I try to tell the truth, and I'm honest if I don't know something. I expect them to be truthful too. I'll say to someone, "I don't really buy it that you had to drink a bottle of vodka this morning because the housing man hasn't been. What reason was it last week and what will it be next week?" '

Four officers, three of whom were specialists, were conscious that their dress and style distinguished them as being 'more authoritarian,' or 'hard' as one put it. There was experience amongst them of national service and the priesthood, so that they felt more at ease with authority than they believed their colleagues to be, and also more at ease in specialisms because of the clarity of their structure. One felt that 'one of the big attractions of this job is that there's room for all types, and you have the freedom to exercise your own style.' Four officers talked of their own styles with clients being 'quieter' than their colleagues, and a tendency 'to listen more'. Two of these linked this process to holding clients to account, and giving them more responsibility for working out what was wrong in their lives and changing it.

A number of officers took the view that they were much more involved with their clients than some of their colleagues and two of them said that they afforded a lower priority to paperwork as a result. One very experienced officer described his style as being 'like the old police court missionaries. My happiest years were when I worked from early morning till late at night. I stopped doing that when I decided to adopt professional attitudes and in some ways the reverse happened.' Others spoke of 'very high personal commitment to offenders,' and one explained, 'If my caseload's active, that's because *I'm* active, and not because I'm unlucky, as some of my colleagues say.' Another commented, 'Sometimes I overstep conventional boundaries for the client's benefit, but my age and experience allow me to do that and make it work.' In illustration of this kind of style, another officer said, 'I push the boat out in the befriending role, and go further than the service expects. I once had someone on remand awaiting sentence. I wanted him assessed for alcohol treatment and I wanted to take him there. So I had him released into my personal custody. I'm unconventional. But management has given me positive feedback for my work in keeping people out of custody.'

Finally, there were a number of respondents who felt that their style was individual because of the methods they predominantly used, such as family therapy work or transactional analysis. As one officer put it, 'I've used TA both in the field and in the probation centre setting as a way of interpreting things for myself. I'm quite free to do it if I choose. No-one stops me. No-one even knows!' In the words of a previous speaker in relation to both his personal style and his non-acceptance of agency limitations, 'I'm an independent maverick!'

The responses to this section, varied as they are in nature from similarity of style to clarity of purpose, creativity, eccentricity, informality, authoritarian, structured, committed, unconventional, and idiosyncratic, probably highlight one major feature of probation practice. The probation service has managed to recruit a wide range of individuals and personalities who develop their own styles of working in ways which are most comfortable for them, whether that be in a specialist or mainstream setting. Most of them, judging by their comments and illustrations, feel perfectly free to do this, in some cases receiving management support and in others acting without management knowledge because of the relative invisibility of the work they do with clients. Despite the concerns of one speaker about the production of clones, there seems little doubt from this evidence that autonomy thrives in the probation service, and that the desire to embrace and manage this quite central feature of their practice is a combination of skill and quality which distinguishes probation officers from the bureaucratic and prescriptive officialdom which characterises many other occupations, including, increasingly it may be argued, that of local authority social work.

2   Differences between the specialisms and the mainstream

It has often been suggested in recent years that there are now so many specialisms in the probation service that working in the mainstream with a generic, predominantly community-based caseload, has in itself become a specialism. Although there was, in the planning of this survey, an intention to ensure that all the major specialisms would be at least minimally represented, it was a matter of some surprise that the random selection process of itself produced so many specialists. In the event, over half the sample (37) turned out to be full-time specialists, with the addition of two whose workload was around two thirds specialised. If it is the case that specialists are now beginning to predominate in the probation service, largely as a result of criminal justice initiatives, and given the likelihood of new responsibilities for the service in the near future, it seems indeed not unlikely that the straight supervision of offenders in the community will also become a specialism if it has not done so already. In the meantime, however, this part of the survey sought to develop the issue which has received some attention earlier, of whether specialists possess or develop additional skills, knowledge, and qualities to those of the mainstream, or whether they merely transfer and concentrate those which they had already acquired from the field. It is from these thirty seven respondents (who are drawn from throughcare, probation centres and packages, prisons, civil work, court work, community service, drugs and hostels) that we shall now seek enlightenment.

(i) Prison Probation officers (N=8)   These officers came from a wide variety of institutions, from remand centres to long-term prisons, from male to female, from young offender institutions to adult prisons – and therefore their

experiences and predominating skills were also varied, but those which were broadly mentioned by several will be discussed here. On the whole, these officers spent more time with their clients in prison, and had more access to them because they were 'sitting ducks'. One officer, who specialised in group work with sex offenders on Rule 43 (jointly led with a colleague), also saw his clients more frequently and for longer periods of time than he had done outside. He had developed a system of direct reparation, usually between offenders and their children, by way of apology. This involved liaison with several interested agencies and, whilst there would probably be less scope for it outside for practical reasons, it was a specialised skill which was theoretically transferable. Working with a greater range of social groupings than was usual on a district team 'patch', meant having to be particularly adaptable in terms of verbal and linguistic communication skills. The ability to sustain working with a wholly voluntary caseload was also cited, as was engaging with particular groups of prisoner, such as Rule 43 or lifers, and the knowledge one gained of the nature of sex offending, violence, aggression, and the long-term effects of imprisonment in the process. Negotiation skills were needed not only with clients but with prison personnel as one officer suggested. 'We are negotiating, balancing, being the middle wo/man between the client and the institution, or the client and outside agencies, or the client and her/his family.' Knowledge of the workings of the prison and parole systems were seen as crucial for developing these skills, and one officer also felt it was necessary to know about appeal procedures, and the acts and their sections under which people were sent to prison.

Most of these officers considered their skills and knowledge to be transferable to and in some cases from the field, but they definitely felt they had concentrated and refined the skills and knowledge they mentioned, and some of them indicated that they would have appreciated some focused training for the specialism before they had gone into it.

(ii) Civil work specialists (N=6)   The skills of conciliation and joint working were highest on the agenda here and, whilst some people had learned them in the mainstream, all felt that they would take a higher level of such skills back into the field, and a greater knowledge of the dynamics which operated within families. They had had to refine their administrative and organisational skills to meet court deadlines, obtain information from county registries and so on, and had developed 'more exact and differential communication skills with lawyers and a variety of court staff and other agencies.' Knowledge of civil court procedure, family law, and judgmental precedent, were also deemed necessary by this group, as we have seen earlier in the section on functioning as a professional. Again these skills and pieces of knowledge are transferable to and from the field, but on the whole it is unlikely that non-civil work specialists would need more than a nodding acquaintance with family law or with precedents, nor indeed that they would be called upon to advise judges upon legal procedures as we heard earlier was the experience of one officer.

173

(iii) Community service officers (N=5)   These officers mostly felt that they were more orientated to practical, observable achievements, and to the 'highly organised structure and framework of CS,' rather than to social work intervention skills. However, we have heard earlier on in the chapter that one officer did use social work methods in her community service role, and was extremely committed to the process – a situation which again reinforces the view that there is plenty of room for autonomy and diversity of approach in the probation service even in highly focused specialisms. These officers, like the civil workers, felt that they had to develop their administrative skills in this job. There was particular scope for acquiring the skill of entrepreneurship, as indeed there is in the field, but in CS it is a positive requirement of the specialism. The ability to prosecute, as we also saw earlier, is a skill which, so far, is unique to community service, and therefore something which clearly sets it apart from the mainstream. The skill lies in playing the prosecutor's role rather than that of mediator, and in dealing predominantly with facts as opposed to concepts and ideas. It seemed that most of these probation officers had had to acquire their skills of prosecuting and entrepreneurship as they went along, and most also said that they would have valued some specific training for the specialism.

(iv) Probation centres and packages (N=5)   This report has referred previously to some of the skills which officers in this specialism consider they possess and these five officers reiterated some of these in answering this question. They had knowledge and skills in group work; could run offence focused programmes, often in the style documented by Priestley and McGuire (1985); had to be short-term, task and goal orientated; willing and able to work with conflict and to challenge people; able to set clear and consistent limits and willing to take people back to court if they breached those. In summary, 'We spend seven hours a day with clients, with no hiding place, staying alongside them, working through their range of emotions, exposing ourselves.' All of them thought their skills were transferable to the field and indeed one existing and one ex-specialist interviewed elsewhere had said they would be/had become better probation officers as a result of working with clear limits, and also with challenge and conflict. However, it was pointed out that the degree of comfort which individual probation officers would feel in this mode of working would vary considerably and that, therefore, whilst the skills might be transferable, it was more likely to be the personal qualities (which would centre around being at ease and relaxed in potentially threatening group situations) which constituted the crucial element in the specialism. Clearly, if it were the case, this would have implications for the way in which people were selected for probation centre work.

(v) Court work specialists (N=5)   Some of these officers were wholly court-based, whilst others specialised in court liaison from an external team base. Much of what they said about the specialist skills and knowledge needed for

court work is contained in an earlier section of the chapter which treats court work as a generic task since most probation officers have to do it. However, it is worth highlighting the specialists' specific responses to this question. They also had had to refine their skills in short-term crisis work, to communicate and liaise effectively with court personnel; to know and articulately present information and sentencing options to the court; to think on their feet; to represent the service without getting sucked into the system; to 'make clients' experiences of court as helpful as possible'; and to 'hold the balance between court and client'. These skills in their generic sense were also transferable, but combined with the knowledge needed of court procedure, and the qualities centering around integrity and confidence, they produced a network of essential factors which it was unlikely would have to be reproduced quite in that fashion elsewhere in the service. One officer felt very strongly that all these elements of court work needed to be very much better taught on training courses. His former training as a salesman had, he said, equipped him much better for the job than his probation training. 'Students and new POs' he suggested, 'see courts as the enemy – but crime is the enemy. Proper training would help them get that in proportion.'

Another officer, a crown court specialist, felt that the experience of that specialism had given him 'a greater understanding of the process and needs of courts'. As a result he was of the firm opinion that probation officers needed to 'capitalise on the power they have in court. For years the service has had an opportunity to grasp this power and what we do is just fritter it away as a resource. Both in management and individual PO terms, it's a low priority. I talk to everyone in court – the press, witnesses, jurors – there's so much to be learned. So I'm used as a resource and a source of information.' So if probation officers have skills, knowledge and the right qualities in court, then they also have power, according to this respondent. Seen in that way, effective training becomes very important indeed.

vi) Throughcare specialists (N=4)   Because these officers spent a significant proportion of their time negotiating with or visiting custodial establishments, most of the skills and knowledge they mentioned are similar to those mentioned by the prison probation officers. In addition, however, they referred to bodies of knowledge which become more pressing when dealing with prisoners on release, including local accommodation resources; welfare rights knowledge; a knowledge of mental health issues; and signs of drug and alcohol abuse. On the whole, they had again picked these up through experience, but two did say they would have been helped by training in bereavement/loss counselling, and one by an overall preparation for engaging in the variety of issues which throughcare covers.

(vii) Hostel specialists (N=2)   Because one was based in and one outside the hostel the experiences of these two officers, both female, differed in focus. The liaison officer who was attached to a female hostel had found that

negotiation skills and the quality of assertiveness were of the essence in her work – for example ensuring that other probation services did not dump their responsibilities for their clients onto her. 'I insist on at least £20 from the referring area, because often people don't have a change of underwear. I'd never had to set those kind of limits before.' In her particular situation there were also skills relating to working with a female clientele, equal opportunities, and teaching them to be assertive. Such skills would again be transferable but would only be likely to receive such concentration and refinement in a specialised residential setting. Working with a high turnover of bailees also meant that her assessment skills were more frequently required than most, and she needed a high level of liaison and communication with the residential workers in the hostel, and a good understanding of their roles and their concerns.

The residential officer agreed with the need for the latter skill, but because she was in effect the senior in that setting, and did all the formal supervision of staff, she pointed to the need for qualities of confidence, self-possession, and an ability to contain one's own anger and frustration. Self-knowledge was important – to acknowledge one's feelings and then cover them up, drawing on inner depth and strength, because 'you have no colleagues to let off steam to.' Nevertheless, residential colleagues had to be serviced, and reassured sometimes at the expense of her own leisure time. 'The other night, I had to take a knife off someone. It took 2 or 3 hours. Then I had to have him arrested. Then I had to calm the staff down too.' This illustrates the complexity and danger of working at the sharp end with offenders – not just supervising them for half an hour a week but being with them daily. Again the skills may be transferable, but again, as with probation centre work, it appears to take particular personal qualities, perhaps in this case that of courage, in addition to those of assertiveness and confidence already mentioned, for officers to put themselves and their skills on the line in a residential setting with offenders.

(viii)Drug specialists (N=1) This officer's major qualities in respect of working with drug addicts were acceptance, empathy and consistency, and having demonstrated these to clients, he then needed to set boundaries with people and challenge them where necessary. Where he differed from mainstream officers working with addicts was in 'the professionalism and skill you use in learning to hold back from drug users' problems instead of getting very caught up and involved as many colleagues do. Experience also helps you to assess the nature of the rehabilitation available, and to match clients to it. It often comes from a process of intuition – but that's based on knowledge and experience.' Because this officer and his colleague were the pioneers of this specialist role in their own area, and were aiming ultimately to establish a community drugs team, they were, like the CS officers, also in the role of entrepreneur, 'facilitating the future, and innovating'. Their skills and knowledge were certainly transferable to work with addicts in the mainstream, but again this officer's comments indicate the particular expertise which

comes with specialism, and the extent to which it constitutes a vital resource for his colleagues to draw upon.

Summary   It is clear that most of the skills and knowledge which officers in specialisms have acquired can be equally utilised in the field, and possibly this reflects the 'Jack-of-all-trades' nature of the probation officer in the diverse range of tasks which s/he is called upon to perform today. However, it may well be the case that the corollary of 'master of none' also applies to this situation, in which event the concentrated and refined expertise in specialised areas which these probation officers develop must be of immense value as a resource and as an eminently desirable quality for transfer to the mainstream or to yet further specialisms. Nevertheless, it also appears that there is a small number of skills and bodies of knowledge, such as the ability to prosecute, and in-depth knowledge of family law which remain, at present, indigenous to their particular specialist fields. Whether, however, the skills, knowledge and qualities, and their particular combinations are or are not transferable to other settings, it does appear that most officers in specialisms, with a few exceptions, felt initially ill-equipped to take on their new tasks, and thought that they would have benefited from considerably more training than they had ever received on the skills and knowledge in question. Experience was crucial and, for most of them, had taught them all they knew, but that experience, it seemed, could have been facilitated and supplemented by aspects of training (such as, for example, a course in loss counselling for prison specialists) which furnished them with the wherewithal to sustain versions of probation practice which, more often than not, constituted the sharp end of criminal and civil justice.

3   The essential ingredients of probation work

When asked to name one essential ingredient of being a probation officer which did not apply to any other job, including other branches of social work, only four of the sample considered that there was no such ingredient. One of the four was of the opinion that all skills, knowledge, and qualities used in probation were transferable within the sphere of social work, whilst a second qualified her answer with the rider that 'a separate probation service is still a necessity.' Although it was acknowledged that social services departments in most areas still have responsibility for juvenile offenders, and that a small number of voluntary agencies such as NACRO also worked with offenders, the responses of most other officers indicated their view that only they, as probation officers, were permanently located at the centre of the varying dynamics in operation between society, the court as its representative, and the entire age range and spectrum of offenders. Whilst civil work specialists were not primarily engaged in work with offenders, their role and location between courts and their clientele was seen as broadly similar to that of their colleagues. The responses to this question fell into three main groupings which covered essential qualities, essential skills, and an essential philosophy. Let us now look at the first category of qualities.

Several officers pointed to the need for a sense of realism which is required for operating in an 'in-between' role within the constraints of a criminal justice system, the strength of which lies predominantly in its theatrical and conservative traditions. Qualities of patience, tolerance, and staying power were used frequently in the context of 'sustaining working with the frustration, unreliability, and failure of offenders, the people everyone else would like to forget, through two-year probation orders, and often even longer periods of time, rather than the once or twice they might be seen by most other agencies.' This quality of patience had hope as its inevitable stable-mate, a belief that people all had the capacity for change. A typical response was from an officer who said, 'I'm prepared to work for ten years with someone, seeing them through prison and everything else, if I feel we're slowly getting there.' Another suggested, 'We are the only people who stick with them, retain hope that they will change, and have the courage to stay with sometimes quite difficult clients through their criminal careers, containing their aggression and disturbed behaviour in the community.' Courage was, indeed, a quality which the respondents often chose to underplay, despite the fact that like the deputy warden in the last section, some of them had, during the interviews, made reference to cases where they had been knowingly at risk of physical threat from clients.

Liking offenders was important, thought one officer, since her view was, 'In every PO, there's a closet offender,' and, as another officer commented, 'Offenders carry for us all the deviant bits of ourselves we don't want to own up to, just like the rest of society. If we don't accept them, who will?' Acceptance, as we have seen throughout this report, was another essential quality for probation officers. 'Everyone else in the criminal justice system moralises. We don't impose ourselves and society in the same way. Acceptance is the nub of success with offenders,' said one. 'Acceptance of the human worth of offenders, seeing them as people too, when they're treated by the rest of society as the lowest of the low,' said another. 'Being willing to give them time, showing tolerance of "man's darker side", and offering help, saying they're worth listening to,' confirmed a third. Finally, several officers also thought it essential that they displayed complete integrity to both court and client during the course of their intermediary role between the two.

As the first part of this section demonstrated, probation officers in this study had a wide variety of styles of working about which, for the most part they felt quite uninhibited – a sign, it was suggested, that autonomy in probation continues to prosper. Several officers mentioned it as a distinguishing feature of probation practice, and it was reiterated here that the management of autonomy (otherwise referred to as 'independence' and 'freedom') was an essential skill needed to function effectively in the probation service. It became clear, however, that the major distinguishing skill for a high proportion of the sample was that of 'holding the balance between court and client,' a view which confirms the increasingly insistent thread of responses which has appeared in different forms throughout the interview schedule. Below are some of the ways in which these officers described this skill.

'It's about maintaining a personal and professional equilibrium, holding the balance and tension between numerous forces, but essentially those which in some way represent either the court or the client. In most jobs you only have one possible road to go down, but in ours you have so many choices and you have to pick the right one to keep things in balance,' was the way one officer graphically described it. Another pointed out, 'You have to be able to recognise, hold onto, and work with the numerous paradoxes the criminal justice system throws up.' A third suggested, 'It's the skill of gaining the trust of courts and clients, and being part of both. Respecting both too.' Two further officers described it as 'a juggling act,' and 'the Janus quality'. A final version was, 'The skill of mediation, bridging the gap. Constantly attempting to reassess and reconcile the offender with different forces in the criminal justice system and society, and explaining one to the other. It involves arbitrating and defining limits for both the offender and the court, and the ability and commitment to function in the diversity and uncertainty of that system.' Many of these officers emphasised the difficulty of attaining a skill which had to be so finely tuned, and commented that by and large the court skills and knowledge they needed to give them confidence, and an awareness of the network of issues surrounding the skill of holding the balance, had simply been lacking in their training. Experience had, to a large extent, made up for this, it appeared, but concern was still expressed about the lack of such skills and knowledge in newly qualified probation officers.

Finally came a number of responses which continued the theme of the probation ethos or philosophy, which has again to some extent permeated the pages of this report. Nine of them appear below:

> Believing in the self-realisation and maximising of potential of offenders – and believing it's worth challenging them till they get there.

> It's a willingness to come back for more – always leaving the door open, however shitty they are to you.

> I have a personal dedication to working with offenders in the community, because sending them to prison is no answer.

> No-one is irretrievable. I believe you should never turn your back on another human being, no matter what they've done.

> I see us as the last post – the net at the bottom after people have fallen through all the other agency nets.

> We're standing alongside the malefactor, not letting them go down and be forgotten.

It's caring for the underdog. My first SPO said to me, 'We've got to love them, warts and all.'

Loving the unlovable, but without forgetting the victim. It's the reconciliation role again.

It's about sitting on a flea-filled couch, drinking tea from a chipped, dirty cup, and still conducting a sensitive conversation with an offender. I call it the Dunkirk spirit!

These statements of belief about offering help, care, and recognition to those whom the rest of society has rejected are indicative of the qualities of patience, tolerance, integrity, and liking of offenders which were listed earlier in response to this question. In order to 'retrieve' the law-breaker for society, the probation officer needs to engage with the law-maker, to see what levels of understanding and compromise can be negotiated. Thus, attaining and holding the right balance between the two becomes of the essence. Accordingly it becomes apparent that a particular blend of skills, knowledge, and qualities, attached to a basic philosophy of probation, constitute what has emerged as perhaps the most central ingredient of probation practice.

In addition we have seen in this section that probation officers, who employ a variety of personal styles, need the skill of autonomy management, probably in this very area of balance-holding; and also that specialists possess and acquire a wide range of skills, knowledge, and qualities, often subtly interlinked, most of which are independently, but perhaps not always collectively transferable to and or from the field, and a small number which appear exclusive to the specialisms. As a result, we see the extent to which the notion of 'difference' has meaning, and probably considerable currency in the probation service. Probation officers differ from each other in style; specialisms require different combinations of skills, knowledge and qualities; and the central ingredients of being a probation officer hinge upon the willingness and ability to engage autonomously in the conflicting dynamics of a mediating role which, with luck, good management and differential forms of communication, will end in a lot of doors being left open for large numbers of offenders and other clients for incalculable lengths of time. It would appear, then, that the quality of the central ingredients relies to a large extent upon diversity, and that it is, perchance, in its very diversity that the essential strength of the probation service lies.

VII Conclusion

Each of the foregoing sections offers a broad summary of the skills, knowledge and qualities which the 62 probation officers in this survey believed to be necessary for day-to-day practice. This concluding section picks up some of the continuing threads of those summaries, and is supplemented by Appendix 4.1

which describes a piece of observed probation practice highlighting some of the skills, knowledge and qualities identified in each of the five sections.

The first area of the interview schedule, communication skills, where timing, listening, balance, and a sense of purpose were all of the essence, appeared to permeate all the other sections, regularly being mentioned as the starting point for good probation work. Apart from a clearer role-awareness, those skills were widely regarded as being the same with colleagues as they were with clients. The qualities of honesty and warmth and the knowledge of human behaviour needed for effective communication were also seen as being crucial across all areas of the job.

Balancing the personal and professional, and care and control, was also a skill cited in communication, and holding the balance between the law-maker and the law-breaker was viewed as a major skill in pre-sentence assessment work, as it was in different settings throughout the respective sections. Interviewing skills, interpretation, analysis, structure, purpose and especially good command of the English language were regarded as necessary for the assessment process and committing the information it produced to paper. Knowledge of psychology again was regarded as important, with the additions of sociology, criminology, and indeed of self-knowledge; but it was knowledge of the law, sentencing, and court procedures and personnel which were seen as vital by experienced officers for themselves and for newly qualified officers who were often thought to be ill-versed in this area of work.

As in communication and assessment, clarity of purpose was perceived as a necessary skill for modes of intervention with clients, and those in specialisms considered that purpose to be more sharply defined for them than for their colleagues in the field. Although a wide range of social work methods were in use, notably casework and group work, they were not seen as mutually exclusive, and there was a clear desire to demystify and simplify traditionally complex, if familiar terms like casework, often because these experienced officers felt that their need for expertise ten years before had been replaced by life experience and practice wisdom which gave them the confidence to engage in redefinition. Specialists had learned some new skills, most of which were transferable to the field, and had refined existing ones. At the heart of the process of intervention lay communication skills again – talking, listening, confidence building – and offering practical help. Qualities needed to sustain these activities were resilience, patience, humour, honesty, tolerance, and the ability to switch off at the end of the day.

The skills of making and sustaining good internal and trans-agency professional relationships, largely ones of communication, involved honesty, tolerance and sensitivity in a similar way to the parallel process with clients. The art of public speaking emerged as being particularly important in court, as did that of steering a middle course between court and client. An enormous body of knowledge in relation to court work was seen as vital, as was a knowledge of self, personal values, and probation service ethos – viewed in terms of standing with and retrieving the offender for society. The skill of

181

workload organisation and balancing this with client contact was important, as were differential methods of relating to line management and negotiating autonomy. Dissatisfaction and disaffection in respect of lack of consultation with the main grade in matters such as job mobility left unanswered questions about the skills, knowledge and qualities needed by managers for the effective supervision and servicing of probation staff.

Differential styles and skills were revealed between individual officers, between specialists and the mainstream, and between probation and other professions. Those in specialisms demonstrated the need for particular combinations of skills, knowledge and qualities for success in their fields, and indeed the way in which the three factors interacted had emerged as an important issue throughout. The philosophy of retrieving the law-breaker for society meant that the probation officer had to engage with the law-maker to attain understanding and compromise. This was the centrality of the skill of mediation, holding the balance between court and client, for which the skill of autonomy management was also needed, as it was in most areas of probation activity. Whilst the existence of structure and boundary awareness were important, the wide-ranging nature of autonomy and balance, the two essential ingredients of being a probation officer, pointed to the potential strength which lay in the diversity of the approaches to working with clients, courts, and the communities they represent.

The experiences and views elicited from the respondents in this chapter combine to form a picture of current probation practice, and the skills, knowledge and qualities employed therein. Set alongside the three previous chapters, they contain important implications for all interested parties. In particular there is an overall view that, whilst there is no substitute for experience, training does not satisfactorily equip people for the job in key areas such as court work, workload management, and the central skill of mediating, or holding balances and tensions. There is a significant residue of implication also for the managers of the service about the way in which they consult, supervise, support, value and professionally develop their experienced staff. In-service training may be an important facility in addressing some of the above issues, but unless the essential skills, knowledge and qualities receive proper attention in basic training, then it may well be the case that probation officers will join the service less well-equipped than they should be for performing the important and demanding role of supervising the clients of the criminal and civil courts in the late twentieth century.

Appendix 4.1:
Some notes on the observation of a piece of probation practice

As mentioned in the opening section of this report, two main grade officers from different teams in the West Yorkshire Probation Service were 'shadowed' by the researcher for a day each as they went about their daily work. Notes were made by the researcher about their use of skills, knowledge and qualities in the course of each piece of work, and discussions about their practice took place with them afterwards. A piece of practice of one of the officers was described in the section on assessment skills. Here is a brief resumé of another piece of work conducted by the other officer, which describes her practice in relation to the supervision of a man in his mid-thirties, on life licence for the murder of a close relative. It runs the gamut of skills, knowledge and qualities needed in the areas covered by this survey – communication, assessment, intervention, agency professionalism, and differential skills.

Officer Z had had to keep the life licencee, Jim, waiting for half an hour while she dealt with another client who had arrived unexpectedly. She had had to weigh up respective client needs, her own priorities, and the tolerance of Jim, who had travelled a long way, in order to do this. She began by acknowledging that he would have things to say to her, but establishing that her own agenda had to come first, as he had been claiming social security from an address she had not known about. Jim indicated that he had given her this address, following admonition from her about other untruths he had told her, but Mrs Z did not accept this, saying she would have written it down because, as he knew, she had to be very particular about such matters. She then went on to clarify his position in relation to DSS arrears which would affect his application for council housing in the area to which he had now moved.

Mrs Z explained to Jim that she had sent a report to the Home Office about an instance of violence towards his co-habitee, and problems of heavy drinking from them both – factors which had given rise to his previous offence. The Home Office had expressed concern as to whether he would be provoked to

183

reoffend, and had asked her view as to whether they should send him a warning letter. She had indicated this was not necessary as he was not breaching his licence in any way. Mrs Z then explained exactly what she had said to her senior and to Jim's new supervisory area about the transfer of his supervision, so that he would understand the terms of it. Jim accepted these explanations. It emerged in his interaction with Mrs Z that he had told her senior that she was rather like a schoolma'm, but very patient and fair. He understood, also, why she had to assume this role in relation to him and his licence.

Some discussion ensued about the relationship between Jim and his young co-habitee, who was expecting a baby, and he felt that things were now going well between them. Mrs Z then asked if there was anything else he wanted to raise and, as he did not, told Jim she would miss seeing him and asked him to let her know when the baby arrived.

Immediately after the interview ended, Mrs Z's senior came in to see what had taken place. It was necessary for there to be strict accountability to him in respect of life licence supervision and, in subsequent discussion, Mrs Z also outlined her own strictness in relation to a piece of work which had to be at the controlling end of the care/control continuum. She considered herself fully supported by her assistant chief and the regular supervision discussion held with her senior. She mentioned that she had once felt threatened by Jim when she did a home visit and there was a knife lying on the table between them. Her main thought had been to get out as soon as possible. This situation had emphasised the high risk nature of her work with Jim, and the need for some physical courage on her part. However, even where control had to be paramount, and continuous assessment of his needs and the truth of his responses taking place, she believed it both important and necessary to inject something personal, as she had done both during and particularly at the end of the interview. This was about getting the personal/professional balance right, as she tried to do differentially with all her clients. Honesty was also very important with Jim, and again with all her clients, and she considered that her own example of honesty (as in describing her contact with the Home Office) was crucial in creating trust between them. It also related to her underlying values of respecting people and believing that someone has to work and forge relationships with high-risk offenders in the community.

Two subsequent phone calls between Mrs Z and Jim's new supervisor took place in which the need for good inter-agency communication was clearly highlighted. Mrs Z felt she had to be the salesperson in the interaction, establishing common aims, objectives and approach, and again being completely honest about what the supervision of Jim entailed. On the telephone she needed an ability to sum things up clearly, to speak effectively and articulately, and to check out that her communications had been understood. These skills were emphasised again later in a phone call to the Parole Department of the Home Office to let them know the arrangements for transfer of the Licence, and the individuality and differential application of the skills shown both verbally and in voice tone when, as she explained later, she had felt called upon to reassure and 'mother' the man in the Home Office who had expressed nervousness at the possibility of having to recall the licencee.

Mrs Z felt that there were extra bodies of knowledge needed for working with life licencees – the relevant law and knowledge of mental illness which was often a feature. Skills of working with aggression and violence would also be helpful, but apparently regional training courses on life licence supervision and mentally ill offenders were over-subscribed. Other than these, a refinement of existing communication, assessment, and intervention skills were required, and a sustaining belief in the importance of staying with someone like Jim for years before change was likely; of reinforcing the positives in people; of respecting and accepting them as people, though not their criminal actions. 'No-one else but the probation officer,' suggested Mrs Z, 'deals with the whole person that is the offender.'

Appendix 4.2:
The core skills interview schedule

I am going to ask you a series of about 20 questions, which are designed to provide some idea of the skills, knowledge and qualities which experienced main grade officers use in their day-to-day practice. Some of the questions are general, and others are more specific – so to help with the specific ones, it would be useful if you could just have in your mind as we talk, a piece of work with a client, which you have done in your present post, to allow us a vehicle for discussion about the nature of probation practice.

Communication

1   What are the processes by which you made human contact with your client?

2   How do you set limits in the relationship?

3   What kind of person do you need to be to your client in order to communicate with her/him?

4   How do you know that your communication with the client is effective?

Assessment

5   What skills and knowledge do you bring into play in assessing a client's needs and situation?

6   How do you know you aren't being 'conned' when you are interviewing clients?

7   What are the tricks of the trade in communicating your assessments on paper?

Intervention

8   On the whole, are you clear about the overall purpose of your intervention with clients?

9   What skills and knowledge do you draw on when implementing your workplans with clients?

10 What kind of things do you find yourself doing most of the time with clients?

11 What personal qualities are needed to sustain this kind of work?

Agency professionalism

12 How important are good professional relationships in day-to-day probation work?

13 What is the skill involved in making and sustaining those relationships?

14 What are the skills and knowledge needed by a PO in the court setting?

15 Can POs be effective without being good workload managers?

16 Do you accept the limitations of the agency framework?

    If so –

17 How far along that road would you go ... tagging?

18 On the whole is your professional performance strengthened, undermined, or unaffected by management practice?

Differential skills

19 How would you say your work differs from that of other POs:

    (a) because of personal style?

    (b) because of your specialist function? (where applicable)

20 If you had to name one essential ingredient of being a PO that doesn't apply to any other job (including generic social work) what would it be?

N.B.   The semi-structured design of the interviews meant that the responses to these questions were not always treated as finite, but led to further questions and answers (often around the area of skills training), giving the opportunity for full exploration of the issues covered by the schedule.

5   Probation training in the early 1990s

This chapter constitutes an attempt to summarise some of the changes which have taken place in college-based probation training, since our research was conducted in 1987/88. It also looks at the evidence for such change as it is perceived at agency level. (This discussion does not address changes in placement-based teaching, which was little criticised by our respondents, though it is acknowledged that CCETSW Papers 26.3 and 30 have brought about significant developments in style, content and quality of placement teaching.) For these purposes, in November 1992, questionnaires were mailed to the thirty college bases of CQSW/Dip.SW programmes with a Home Office sponsored probation option, and to the fifty five probation areas in England and Wales. They were returned, collated and analysed between December 1992 and February 1993. Forty three probation areas replied. Thirteen of the thirty training programmes replied, less than might have been hoped, but enough to constitute an indicator of current trends. The material they provided will be outlined in the following six sections.

I   Training for the 1991 Criminal Justice Act

The 1991 Criminal Justice Act, with its 'just deserts' model outlined in the introduction, is the major development in penal policy to have emerged since the authors reported on the relevance of probation training to practice in the late 1980s. Chapter 1 of this book (Tables 1.4–1.6) has shown that probation law, principles of sentencing, criminology, penology and probation practice were all given insufficient emphasis by training courses in the view of a substantial majority of consumers. How, then, other than through conventional lectures and seminars, have probation educators shifted to implement the very specific training requirements associated with this Act? Two of the thirteen replied that they continued to teach the Act through conventional lecture/

188

seminar means. Eight drew predominantly on the probation service's own in-house format (devised by NACRO) for the training of the Act, which is practice-based and utilises prior reading, video film, quizzes, diagrams, exercises etc. Two of this number additionally used workshop and mock court formats. One drew partly on in-house and partly on its own material. Two used workshop settings in conjunction with the local probation service.

Table 5.1
Format for 1991 Criminal Justice Act training

Conventional lectures/seminars	2
Probation service in-house only	6
Probation service in-house/workshops/mock courts	2
Part in-house/part own material	1
Workshops with local probation service	2
Total	*13*

Clearly, then, there has been a strong move, in line with the service's own in-house training for its existing staff, to teach the principles of this Act in a way that is relevant to practice.

II   Anti-racist, anti-sexist and anti-discriminatory practice

In its 1991 publication 'Rules and Requirements for the Diploma in Social Work' (paper 30, paras 1.20 and 1.21) CCETSW lays out its expectation that training programmes both in 'the content of learning and the context of learning' promote and develop the preparation of students for ethnically sensitive practice, and the challenge and confrontation of institutional and other forms of racism and discrimination. In the late 1980s, some courses were offering input on race and gender issues and all, according to Coleman (1989, p. 16), 'had developed or were developing courses and workshops addressing the problems of social work in a multi-racial society and had introduced special sessions on (e.g.) working with black offenders, ethnically sensitive probation work and racism in the criminal justice system into their course sequences. Most had adopted strategies of incorporating consciousness of these matters into all their teaching. Some accepted that provision was inappropriate or inadequate (and had been criticised by students for it)'. Chapter 1 of this book (Tables 1.4, 1.6 and 1.7) certainly confirmed this latter statement to the extent that the teaching was seen as marginal or absent in over 50% of cases, and was the worst-taught of all subjects offered. The current student consumer view is not available, but training programmes provided some encouraging responses on their questionnaires.

Ten had provided some form of teaching on racism, sexism and discrimination prior to 1989. (One programme did not then exist). All but one now provided discrete generic teaching on the subject of *anti*-racist, *anti*-sexist and *anti*-discriminatory practice (albeit under a range of titles), whilst five did so additionally in the probation practice teaching. The thirteenth programme was at pains to point out that these issues were integrated throughout rather than taught separately. When asked specifically if they integrated such a teaching approach into all subjects, eleven replied that they did (or tried to), whilst two did not, largely because not all staff were agreed about it.

Table 5.2
Teaching on anti-racist, anti-sexist and anti-discriminatory practice

	Yes	No	N/A	Total
Discrete in any subject pre-1989	10	2	1	13
Discrete generic in 1992/3	12	1	-	13
Discrete probation in 1992/3	5	8	-	13
Integrated generic in 1992/3	11	2	-	13

It is apparent that almost all programmes are taking seriously the requirement to teach this subject, but perhaps surprising, given very clear statistics about racism and sexism in the criminal justice system, that discrete anti-discriminatory probation teaching is not offered in more than five cases. The two programmes which do not integrate the subject into all their teaching are possibly failing to meet CCETSW's expectation in relation to 'the context of learning' cited above. Overall, however, it would seem that with the advent of the Dip.SW there has developed a high commitment both to discrete and integrated forms of generic teaching in anti-racist, anti-sexist and anti-discriminatory practice.

III Changes in teaching content and style

(a) Teaching content

Programmes were asked to list any further new teaching inputs, beginning post 1988 and still continuing, which include probation students. Their responses are summarised in Table 5.3 below.

Table 5.3
New teaching inputs

Criminology	4
Criminal Justice	4
Penology	2
Probation law	2
Sentencing	1
Social work skills/methods in CJ system	4
Probation practice	4
Other	4

N = 13

It should be clarified that most responding programmes now include many or all of the above subjects (sometimes with alternative titles) in their curricula, though it was troubling that at least two appeared not to incorporate probation practice until the second year. Those referred to in Table 5.3 have initiated or else substantially increased teaching in the listed subjects between 1989 and 1993. As Section I above has indicated, input on most of these topics was assessed as being insufficient by the 1988 study and so it is clear that some development in the right direction has subsequently taken place. Whether this development is yet sufficient in quantity or quality is not possible to judge at this point in time. The 'Other' section refers to one course entitled 'Individual & Community Responses to Crime'; one incorporating a range of workshops on relevant topics such as addictions and sexual abuse; one on 'Self-directed studies' focusing on 'pathway' interest; and one on psychology as it related to probation issues. One programme said that it had instituted no new teaching since 1988. Several others pointed out that they had recently changed the structure of their programmes radically in line with CCETSW Paper 30 requirements (some having moved over to a modular delivery) but that whilst titles may have altered, the fundamental content had not. The amount of it, however, had increased significantly. Asked about their reasoning for innovating change, those in Table 5.3 emphasised again the need to conform to Paper 30 and to become more practice-relevant.

(b) Teaching style

Programmes were also asked to state whether their *style* of teaching had changed significantly since 1988. For example, had it become more participative or more skills-based?

Table 5.4
Teaching styles

	Yes	No	N/A	Total
Significant change since 1988	12	-	1	13

All programmes other than the new one, which was not in a position to be comparative, claimed that their teaching styles had changed significantly since 1988. Six said that the whole programme (except law, in one case) had become more participative and more skills-based. The other six said the same thing had happened, particularly in relation to probation-relevant teaching. Four cited the Paper 30 requirement of probation seminars/tutorials as a significant style change, though this is not to say that the other programmes did not employ that forum also. Additional comments added up to a general tenor of experiential learning through use of video, role play, exercises, workshops and self-directed learning.

(c)   Influence of Davies/Boswell/Wright Home Office research

As most of the developments in Section III above reflected a remedying of deficiencies highlighted in the authors' 1988 research, it was clearly of interest to us to try and identify the extent to which the research had directly influenced change. Table 5.5 outlines the results.

Table 5.5
Influence of Davies/Boswell/Wright research

	Yes	Partially	No	N/A	Total
Influenced programme content and/or style	5	1	6	1	13

Five answered that the 1988 research had influenced the changes they had made. Another said that it was 'consulted and may have had an effect'. The new programme again could not refer to actual changes made. Of the 'No' answers, one had not heard of the 1988 research and two commented that they were influenced almost wholly by the requirements of Paper 30. Asked about the changes which our research had influenced, the five who had answered in the affirmative listed areas related to criminology, criminal justice, probation policy and practice (notably PSRs and court work) and reiterated the changes in teaching style listed at the end of sub-section III(b) above.

This was not intended as a wholly narcissistic exercise! Although different in purpose, method and content, the Coleman Review and the two probation-specific Annexes in Paper 30 (themselves influenced by Davies and Coleman) offered very similar conclusions about the direction in which qualifying probation training needed to move. The evidence thus far suggests that their recommendations about teaching style and content are beginning to take effect.

IV Programme partnerships

CQSW courses have traditionally drawn upon local probation service practitioners and, to a lesser degree, managers to bring the practice context into the college-based teaching of students. In some cases this facility has been perceived as under-used and in others over relied upon. Some courses were able to benefit from joint college/probation service appointments to engender the necessary balance. Chapter 1 (p. 14) has shown that 96% of the consumer sample thought there should be more teaching input by practising probation officers, including the setting-up of joint appointments so that those teaching probation did not get out of touch with the field. The Coleman Review (p. 38) recommends this in points 3, 4 and 6 of its 'model probation course', as does CCETSW's Paper 30, Annex 3, point 5. Current programmes were thus asked if they currently had or were actively planning a joint teaching appointment with a local probation service (Table 5.6); and if so, to specify the nature of the appointment (Table 5.7).

Table 5.6
Joint appointment with local probation service

	Yes	No	Actively planning	Total
Joint appointment	11	1	1	13

Table 5.7
Nature of existing/planned joint appointment

Type	Number of programmes
One 50% college lecturer/50% field SPO	2
Two 50% college lecturers/50% field SPOs	1
One 50% college lecturer/50% field – grade unspecified	5
One 50% college lecturer/50% main grade field team PO	1
Full-time seconded post (3 years)	1
Not listed	2
(No joint appointment)	(1)
Total	*13*

Clearly there has been a concerted move towards joint appointments in line with all the recommendations. Some respondents were not specific about the probation grade occupied by their joint appointee, though many are known to be senior probation officer grade. With the exception of one, all twelve with joint appointments operated a 50/50 split in terms of time spent in the college-base and time in the service. Many functioned in the areas of training/practice teaching/placement support and co-ordination with their service hat on, so that there was a natural cross-over of the two roles. Only one was known to act as a main grade officer in a field team setting. One programme enjoyed the services of two joint SPO/lecturer appointments; and another employed a full-time probation representative seconded by three probation services for a 3 year period only, presumably so that the occupant of the post would not in time lose touch with practice issues.

Although we have no current information about the quality of teaching engendered by these appointments, it is at least reasonable to assume that the practice/skills-based ethos in probation teaching is being aspired to in the evident commitment to bringing the posts about.

V   A wholly specialist probation stream?

Ever since CCETSW assumed responsibility for the oversight of social work education in 1971, there has been a debate about the appropriateness of training probation officers via the medium of generic social work. Many, including most recently Mike Nellis (1992) have argued, if not for a completely separate 'Institute of Probation', then certainly for a distinct and wholly specialist probation stream within the existing qualification. This might have seemed the most obvious solution to the deficiencies exposed by our research and the Coleman Review, and yet none of the programme respondents in this survey had chosen to move in that direction, some of them citing, rather strangely, their sense of constraint imposed by Paper 30's guidance of a 35–40% 'minimum' of taught probation content. It was thus considered pertinent, especially in the light of subsequent developments, to invite programmes to say whether they envisaged their probation students moving into a probation only specialism (i.e. with *no* shared generic teaching) at any point during the next two years.

Table 5.8
A probation only specialism

	Yes	No	Total
Envisaged within the next 2 years?	1	12	13

As Table 5.8 shows, only one respondent felt this move likely to occur, commenting that any further increase in student numbers was likely to necessitate a move towards three distinct courses (one being probation) within a single programme. Another respondent viewed such a development as 'very sensible', but considered that 'there would be too much resistance to it especially from probation agencies'. Another programme cited its teaching as already being 70% probation-related or specific; and another pointed out that the whole of its second year was treated as an 'area of particular practice', this being another CCETSW Paper 30 provision which requires that students undertake such an area (e.g. probation) of assessed practice for at least 80 days over a period of six months in the final stage of their programme. Neither of these two latter respondents, however, appeared to envisage these developments extended to a full-time specialism in the foreseeable future.

Additional comments invited at the end of the questionnaire centred around respondents' views that the structure and content of programmes have altered radically since 1989, allowing in particular for a far greater degree of probation input and use of practising probation personnel, the latter helping to ensure practice-relevant course content. A contribution which summed these comments up was as follows:

> The probation route clearly differentiates between Home Office sponsored students and the rest, and the agency participation in its design and operation is very great.

Overall, then, it seems clear that, from the college-based viewpoint, the past five years have seen significant developments in practice-relevant course content for probation students, and that these changes are considered sufficiently adequate for further specialism to be seen as unnecessary at this stage. It now seems pertinent to follow up the college-based view by asking how the fruits of these developments are perceived at the point of qualified training delivery in the probation areas themselves.

VI The probation service perception of change in qualifying training

As the introduction to this chapter explains, questionnaires were sent to the 55 probation areas in England and Wales, asking for evidence as to the nature and effect (in terms of practice-relevance) of content and style changes (if any) that were perceived to have taken place in qualifying probation training since December 1989. Forty three areas replied, two of which expressed their inability to treat the request for this information as sufficient of a priority to be able to provide it. The data discussed in this section is, therefore, confined to that collated from the remaining 41 areas. Firstly Table 5.9 shows the responses to the question 'Do you have any evidence to suggest that probation training has changed in content and/or style since December 1989?'

Table 5.9
Training changes since December 1989

	Yes	No	Don't know	Total
Evidence for change in content and/or style	28	8	5	41

This response clearly points to strong support for the college-based view of significant changes; two thirds of the responding probation areas considered that they possessed evidence that such change had occurred. Of the 'Don't Know' category, three considered that input (including their own) into programmes had increased and developed significantly, but that it was too early to say whether such changes had manifested themselves in practice. One area which had sought specific response from its senior probation officers had not found that response sufficiently homogeneous to be able to comment.

Of the eight who considered they had no evidence for change, four were involved with college bases still running the CQSW, but from their attachment to Dip.SW planning consortia three were feeling hopeful that significant improvement and development would shortly ensue. Two further responses were impressionistic only. A final response expressed the chief probation officer's view that our 1988 study was 'flawed', largely because its lack of attention to the views of probation managers (though the latter, of course, was not its brief) and, feeling that it was too early to make objective comment, was concerned not to provide 'an anecdotal, impressionistic response which researchers might represent as hard data'. It is thus important at this point to emphasise that any response which areas have called impressionistic or subjective, or which were not accompanied by evidence, will be represented as such in this section.

Of the twenty eight areas who considered that change had taken place, one referred to their view as impressionistic and another as partially impressionistic. The remaining twenty six respondents cited their evidence as emanating from several sources, as follows: Dip.SW programme partnership processes and outcomes (11); 1st year probation officer competence (10); practice learning agency approval processes (5); practice teacher award programme consortia processes and outcomes (5); student training units/semi-specialist practice teachers (5); student/practice teacher/SPO awareness of Dip.SW emphasis upon assessment of workplace competence (4); joint college/agency appointments (2); training analysis for Home Office (1); and support to black students (1).

Table 5.10 outlines the twenty six service areas' views about the types of change which have taken place, based upon the sources of evidence given above (NB Most areas gave more than one answer).

Table 5.10
Types of change in content/style of training since December 1989

Contribution of Dip.SW programme partnerships	21
New skills/knowledge	15
Changing values/attitudes (notably anti-discriminatory practice)	10
Emphasis on clearly assessed competences	7
More active agency teaching involvement	7
Practice teacher accreditation	7
Practice learning agency approval	5
Total	72

(N = 26)

Perhaps not surprisingly, the most frequently cited change was that of services' recent involvement in Dip.SW programme partnerships, and the outcome of their contribution to curriculum planning in this forum, which had often included changes in teaching style (less formal, more participative and skills-based) as well as content. Whilst, as one respondent pointed out, 'At times this has been the most difficult work imaginable', she felt certain that 'the results have been worth it. Understandings about the imperatives facing universities and agencies have been exchanged and a communication mechanism has been set up which actually provides the means of solving problems'. These comments encompassed an overall positive view from these twenty one services about probably the most crucial influence on the pattern of qualifying training in the early years of the present decade.

Those fifteen areas who referred to the acquisition of new skills and knowledge related this in the main to training given for the implementation of the 1991 Criminal Justice Act, and to teaching in criminology, probation law and general probation practice. A minority of these areas suggested that whilst improvement had occurred, there was still some way to go; and the lack of teaching (whether college or agency-based) on the notions of case management and workload management was still seen as a problem by several. The ten areas citing changes in values and attitudes related these almost universally to students' ability in the field of anti-discriminatory practice. Two of these areas also mentioned shifts from the 'welfare' to the 'justice' philosophy, associated again with Criminal Justice Act training.

Seven areas considered that the new emphasis on clearly assessed competences, set out in CCETSW Paper 30 and its probation annexes, was a welcome improvement on previous vagaries in learning requirements. A further seven were clear that more active agency teaching involvement through programme partnerships and joint appointments had been significantly instrumental in rendering qualifying training more relevant to practice. Seven also thought that the move towards practice teacher accreditation, which requires the satisfying of fourteen competences set out in CCETSW Paper

26.3, had been significant in providing higher quality placements and more thorough and rigorous student assessment in recent times. Similarly, there were five areas who cited the need for CCETSW approval as a practice learning agency, as a spur to working towards high standard placement provision which was properly resourced, monitored and evaluated.

Finally, Table 5.11 shows the response of these twenty six areas to the question 'Is it your perception that these changes have made training more relevant to practice?'

Table 5.11
Relevance of training to practice

	Yes	No	Total
Have recent changes made it more relevant?	21	5	26

Clearly the predominance of answers (21) reflects areas' perception that the changes referred to in this section have made qualifying training more relevant to practice. All those who gave a negative response (5) were doing so through a rigorous sense of insufficient evidence at this stage, though most commented that the changes which have taken place have provided the necessary structures for such a development to come about.

Overall, then, these responses from the forty one probation areas serve to provide a sense of change and development which is very much in parallel with that received from the college bases. It would be surprising if there were complete homogeneity or total satisfaction, and there is bound to be an inherent tension in the respective emphases of each party upon their juxtaposed theoretical and practice bases. It is apparent, nevertheless, that many of the deficiencies in content outlined in our 1988 research (i.e. insufficient emphasis upon criminology, penology, principles of sentencing, probation law, probation practice, race and gender issues) have begun to be remedied by Dip.SW programme partnerships in particular; that teaching styles have changed, becoming more participative and relevant to practice; and that these improvements are starting to be experienced at qualified practice level, as evidenced by almost half (26) of the fifty five probation areas in England and Wales who also point to the changes in quality of placement provision and assessment processes. It is, of course, possible to argue for continued change and improvement, perhaps further specialism, but as many college and service responses have emphasized, the facilitating machinery is now in place for the dialogue to lead where it will. It is encouraging to see how national research findings, combined with organisational will and high level professional determination, can help provide the foundations for change which is not only long overdue but is already beginning to influence the future shape and quality of probation practice.

6 The social work boundaries of probation work

I Introduction

If one fact emerges unambiguously from the data presented and analysed in these chapters it is that probation officers and social work educators alike perceive CQSW/Dip.SW qualified probation employees as social work professionals operating within the fields of criminal and civil justice. We have seen that probation officers draw heavily upon the fundamental social work skills of communication, assessment and intervention; and that most qualifying training programmes, whilst now paying considerably enhanced attention to probation-related teaching, see no need to move conclusively away from this generic social work education base. This concluding chapter offers some mildly provocative reflections on this situation as it relates to the current climate of punishment and cost-effectiveness. It brings together some of the salient findings of the 1988 research and some modest data from recent staff leavers to ask whether the service and, by implication, those responsible for its qualifying training need either to reconceive and extend the notion of social work or to concede that it is an activity which is no longer central to probation practice.

II From rebellion to pragmatism

Despite eighty six vigorous years of 'advising, assisting and befriending' (Probation of Offenders Act 1907), there has been over the last three decades a slowly mounting sense of fragility surrounding the preservation of the social work ethos. Notable landmarks of the impingement of control and surveillance have included the introduction of parole (Criminal Justice Act 1967), the advent of Community Service (Criminal Justice Act 1972) and Schedule 11 probation order conditions (Criminal Justice Act 1982), and the 'just deserts' model of sentencing (Criminal Justice Act 1991) with its accompanying requirements for the measuring of offence seriousness, proportionality, restrictions on liberty and the new supervisory aim of protecting the public from harm. Whilst some of the earlier innovations provoked keen, often rebellious, debate about the fundamental incompatibility of the social work notion of care and the correctional concept of control (Bottoms and McWilliams 1979, Harris 1980, Walker and Beaumont 1981), more recent commentaries have taken on a more pragmatic flavour in keeping, perhaps, with prevailing political ideology. Parker, for example, suggests in relation to the 1991 Criminal Justice Act that 'pro-active probation practice can mediate and modify the way sentencers behave' (Parker 1992). In a document significantly sub-titled 'Limiting the Damage' the National Association of Probation Officers, the nearest thing to an internal radical-left voice, begins 'The 1991 Criminal Justice Act has not itself altered the essence of probation practice. That will only happen if workers in the Probation Service allow the punitive policy behind the Act and the mechanistic enforcement procedure of National Standards to control their work' (NAPO 1992). Harris himself now says of his 1979 paper (which advocates a splitting of care and control, giving responsibility for the former to the probation service and for the latter to another criminal justice service), 'The political world was not that of the 1990s and the conceptual logic of the case I argued then can, ironically, only be followed by arguing almost (though not quite) for the reverse of this. For the deprived, distressed but marginal offender love and compassion can no longer be provided by the probation service. Perhaps we need to turn the wheel full circle and reinvent the Police Court Mission to provide the necessary voluntary help and care which once such people received. The policy vacuum which exists in criminal justice is at present huge, and the probation service should be involved in filling it' (Harris 1992). For all of these commentators the new framework is a 'given', to be manipulated perhaps, but evidently not to declare war upon.

III   From pragmatism to powerlessness

What becomes of pragmatism when it is set against a climate of stringent cost-effectiveness where those who are fortunate enough to have employment (including probation officers) struggle and compromise to keep it at all costs? What happens to the preservation of the social work ethos then? In recent commentaries we have seen none of the old familiar shaking of the foundations; no attack on the threat posed by the 1991 Act upon individualised justice; no barricades against the encroaching proximity to the service's work of curfews and electronic tagging (a matter for resignation, if asked to administer it, according to 33% of our 1988 sample of experienced officers). Is this to be taken as a new, mature form of 'realism' within the profession; perhaps as a reflection of that learned powerlessness sometimes seen in the more impoverished of the service's clients; or is it the case that probation is silently capitulating to those forces which would have it both trained and operating as a straight agency of punishment? In all likelihood each of these elements applies in greater or lesser measure. We live in an era where the '60s and early '70s 'radicals' have grown up and either left for greener pastures, settled into the relative comfort of experienced practitioner autonomy, or become probation service managers.

During the 1980s and early 1990s managers have been called upon to operate a 'new' managerialism based upon efficiency, effectiveness, economy, accountability, streamlining, shared information systems, and standardisation of practice. The experienced and hitherto autonomous practitioners have had to submit, whether willingly or unwillingly, to these processes; and even those who have moved to greener pastures will, if they have remained in the public sector, have found their performance under scrutiny and their professional discretion reduced. This is not to undermine the legacy of the new managerialism which has served to sharpen aims and objectives, remove sloppy, idiosyncratic and maverick practice, and ensure that public money is spent responsibly. In the process, however, a new culture has been born which amounts to 'good resource management' and which has supplanted 'good social work' as the dominant ethos. It is thus much harder both practically and philosophically to fight for a concept which, whilst still alive, is clearly no longer as central to the probation service as it was up to the end of the 1970s. It is entirely possible that those uncompromising probation officers who once sabotaged virtually wholesale a report proposing 'custody and control', 'supervision and control' and '72-hour detention orders' (Younger Report 1974) now find themselves experiencing the same syndrome of powerlessness in the face of scarce resources and administrative indifference as do some of their clients.

Is it possible, too, that these phasic developments in the last third of the service's life have led it to a point of disillusionment, fatalism and sapped energy levels equipped only for residual bargaining with the professionally contentious strands emanating from the items on someone else's agenda? Where the probation culture was once preoccupied with defining and fighting those whom it perceived as inimical to the social work ethos, does it now content itself with refining the 'enemy's' image and marketing it for palatable staff consumption? Is the task of seizing the 'kairos', the moment of creative opportunity (Elliott 1988), now so thankless amidst a rising sense of alienation from social structures from which not even probation officers are immune, that the social work tradition is liable to unembattled shrinkage and finally to sink without trace? These are the goadings of the devil's advocate but they are the kinds of questions which hang heavily in the air for many of the country's public services, and to which the probation service should give serious thought if it wants to preserve its traditionally robust character in preparation for criminal justice developments towards the millennium. As Raine and Willson (1993) suggest, there are signs that the service, having been put in detention for ten years and made to recite 'I must give priority to economy, efficiency and effectiveness' may shortly be conditionally released from its punishment. 'Reformed and rehabilitated, the professionals must now be resettled and supported so that we can benefit from their capacity to exercise discretion in complex and uncertain circumstances'. If this analysis is correct, the service must reassemble all its energies and instincts to be ready for the challenge to come.

IV   Disaffection amongst service leavers

If the service is to be poised to play a vigorous part in the next phase of its development within criminal justice policy, it will need to take account of the effect of its new culture upon those who have lived through all the changes of the last decade and a half, listen to their views, and find a way to take them forward. If there is residual disaffection about the erosion of the social work ethos, it seems likely that this might be reflected in the views of recent service leavers. Therefore, the 41 probation areas who provided data in respect of changes in qualifying training were also asked to provide information about staff who had resigned from their services between September 1990 and December 1992. It is intended that the analysis of this material should form the basis of a separate article but, in addition to other information sought, areas were asked to give numbers of resignations (for those who were *not* moving to other probation areas), in terms of ethnic background, sex, age, grade, new post if known, and to state whether any ideological disaffection with the service had been expressed in the process of leaving.

During the period in question, 158 qualified staff (147 POs, 10 SPOs, and one ACPO) from the 41 responding areas had resigned from the probation service. This number comprised 133 who were classified as white European, 18 whose ethnic origin was unknown, and seven who were variously classified as black (2), black Caribbean (2), Afro-Caribbean (1), black British (1), and British Jewish (1). There was a slight preponderance of women (76) amongst this number, 61 men, and the sex of 21 was unspecified. Almost half (73) were between the ages of 31–40, when career moves are perhaps seen as particularly significant; 46 were between the ages of 41–50; 29 between the ages of 22–30; and 10 between 51–65, the group most likely to have superannuation and retirement benefits on their minds. The posts they had moved to (known in all but 21 cases) were extremely wide-ranging, but the occupation most frequently cited was that of local authority social worker, and this applied (occasionally entailing promotion) in 41 cases. Other people had left to become lecturers, voluntary agency social workers, to enter the Church, to travel, to emigrate, to continue their education, for personal/family reasons, or simply to seek new forms of employment. Apart from two who had gone into their own or family businesses, it was easy to see the continued links between the nature of the probation service's work and that of the specified new occupations. These links centred largely around social work/caring/counselling in fields where the professional role was perhaps less obviously ambiguous than in the probation service. In 72 cases it was unknown whether leavers had expressed ideological disaffection with the current direction of the service; in 61 cases it was known that none had been expressed; in 25 cases such disaffection was known to have been expressed. Only one area in fact made use of an exit questionnaire, though several mentioned that they were considering devising one. This area provided a copy of its questionnaire, though not of the comments of the five people in the requested category who had completed it during the relevant period. The main areas covered by the questionnaire sought leavers' comments on salary, conditions of service, working relationships, training, career prospects, organisational and management structure, reasons for leaving, and new job. Under the heading 'Reasons for leaving' main reasons, other reasons, and factors which would have encouraged people to stay, were outlined. None of the five people concerned were said to have expressed ideological disaffection in this section of the questionnaire.

Another area, however, was kind enough to send out a special questionnaire to its three leavers, in response to the authors' request for information. One leaver could not be contacted but the two other responses are reproduced in full below.

Q. On leaving the Probation Service did you feel any ideological disaffection with the Service?

Respondent A: White/British; female; aged 47; main grade PO; no new employment.

YES:

1. I left the Service in June 1991 – partly because I wanted to work part-time on job-share but this was, I was told, not feasible. (Equal opportunities?)

2. I anticipated an ever-increasing shrinkage in autonomy and the social work values which I hold.

3. I did not feel that Probation management was working *with* field officers but in opposition.

4. I sensed that Government policies would move towards increasing devaluation of our professional skills.

5. As a profession I did not feel we had a united code of ethics or practice – which would have protected and enhanced our standing in the social work professions.

6. Targetting and Performance Indicators and all the other technical jargon do not take account of the skills which can be effective and *are* subjective (for which I do not feel apology is needed) and cannot be truly measured on a computer.

7. *Quality* of work needs to be examined and not *just quantity*.

8. The Service needs to talk to each other across all levels to find common ground.

9. Officers with training need not feel a need to justify their salaries alongside unqualified ancillaries (which I was originally).

10. I envisage our great willingness to co-operate could result in the increasing use of volunteers, ancillaries, etc. Perhaps we are our own worst enemies!

Respondent B: White/British; male; aged 29; main grade PO; left to enter priesthood.

I would have to state at the outset that I would have left the Probation Service whether or not it had changed, given the nature of my new employment. However, there was an increasing sense of ideological disaffection which could be summarised in the following ways:

1. A feeling that the overall ethos of the job was changing from that for which I had been trained.

2. Ever-increasing depersonalisation of Probation clients, e.g:

    (a) change of status from 'client' to 'offender';

    (b) the diminishment of Through-Care with the implicit message that those imprisoned no longer mattered;

    (c) the idea that clients/offenders could increasingly be dealt with by 'programmes' rather than being treated as individuals.

3. Ever-increasing depersonalisation of Probation staff, e.g:

    (a) the amazing growth put into administration and administrative posts;

    (b) the distancing of senior management, popularly perceived 'behind' the administrative;

    (c) the increasingly impossible role of Senior Probation Officers;

    (d) the excessive fascination with 'Aims and Objectives' and Gilpin Black's KOAs (Key Output Areas). [Author's note: Gilpin Black Associates of Belfast have conducted Corporate Development

Programmes for many Probation Services in the UK over the last five years].

4. Home Office and Government policy which really is the starting point to all the above. A desire to see the prison population decreased with, in my opinion, a misplaced philosophy for doing so as demonstrated in the various papers culminating in the Criminal Justice Act 1991.

The citation of these two responses is not intended to create an impression of large numbers of probation staff leaving the service for the kinds of reasons outlined above, (though the other 23 for whom disaffection was reported fell into similar categories, with the addition in eight cases of low pay/promotion prospects). Indeed, the overall figure of 158 staff from 41 areas, leaving over a period of 2.3 years can certainly not be construed as unreasonably high, and one might indeed conjecture that, despite underlying philosophical change, probation staff like everyone else in the current climate, are holding on to their jobs at all costs. What is interesting, however, is that the only two people to have been directly asked this specific question have produced material which reflects the essential differences between the culture of 'good social work' and the culture of 'good resource management'. This includes concerns about equal opportunities; devaluation of professional skills; decrease of autonomy; a move away from social work values and emphasis on the person as an individual; alienation from management, administration and government; an emphasis upon quantity at the expense of quality; excessive fascination with aims and objectives; and perhaps underpinning it all the pragmatic development of penal policy related more to cost-effectiveness and short-term solutions than to the long-term valuing, befriending, and, in traditional social work fashion, staying with some of the most difficult, often damaged and intractable individuals whose response to crisis and conflict situations is to break the law. Whilst people may choose to hold onto their jobs in this climate it is possible that they are finding it increasingly difficult simultaneously to hold on to their own integrity and to a sense of organisational morale. Social work may still be surviving in their very attempt to keep it alive but, as with offending, something has to give ultimately in a conflict situation. In theory this 'something' may be the government or the organisation, but in practice it is more likely to be the individual staff member, or finally the social work ethic itself. Does the probation service corporately desire, or view it as necessary, to retrieve and perhaps rehabilitate these potential casualties of the system? Let us look more closely at the history of the changing culture and some possible ways forward.

V Purpose and philosophy

Some would argue that these issues insofar as they relate to the care/control debate have always been with the probation service in one form or another.

But the parameters of the care/control framework have narrowed over the last decade at least partly in relation to the economy/efficiency/effectiveness mandate which, it could now be argued, has turned from a necessary regulator into a pendulum swung too far. There is little doubt that during the late 1960s and 1970s the probation service, long characterised by a tradition of the one-to-one casework relationship between autonomous fieldworker and offender, suddenly faced a huge expansion in tasks, methods and hierarchical structure which caused it to lose its sense of direction, an onslaught from which it had not recovered before the far-reaching election of the Tory Government in 1979. Surprisingly, its overall purpose had never been laid down in statute nor in any other identifiable source, save for semi-pious statements such as 'The duty of the Probation Officer is to make our gaols emptier and our world better' (Whiteside, 1939). During the first half of the 1980s, Boswell pointed to the need for the service to produce an explicit statement of goals if its organisational survival was to be assured (Boswell 1982, 1985). What followed was a Statement of National Objectives and Priorities by the Home Office in 1984, and a response to this by local probation areas a year or so later. Specific goals were still, however, not laid down. Following a consultation process at the end of 1992, however, the Home Office produced a 'Statement of Purpose' for the probation service which, oddly, sets out its objectives first, its tasks second, its values third, and its goals last. There is a list of eleven goals; only the first part of the first listed goal, 'Reducing and preventing crime', is anything other than an objective or an abstract ideal. Other 'goals' for example include 'Achieving excellence in management' and 'Promoting community involvement, voluntary effort and partnership in work with offenders'. Neither of these explains to what end or goal this activity is to be directed. On the whole, confusion still reigns.

Where there is a lack of clarity about goals there will be uncertainty surrounding the objectives which stem from them, the tasks needed to meet the objectives, and the methods by which the tasks will be effectively performed. No small wonder, then, that meaningful evaluation of the service's work has proved so problematic in recent years; or that performance indicators which relate largely to quantity and throughput will seem unintegrated and therefore irrelevant to a longstanding culture implicitly aware that its heart is in helping offenders, via social work methods, to reach their legitimate human potential, and puzzled at a political ideology which holds that this can or should be measured by the number of joyriders who can be processed through a probation centre over a given period. With these factors in mind, it is unfortunate in the extreme that the service did not, long ago, when its activities were both unquestioned and smiled upon, take the opportunity to assert itself independently and to follow if not precede the British Association of Social Workers' example of drawing up a Code of Ethics (BASW 1975) as an expression of its aims and underlying philosophy. Instead, order, duties, objectives and goals (insofar as they exist coherently) have been effectively imposed upon it, using the language of official rhetoric to redefine and sideline its social work parameters. Financial constraints leave managers with little choice but to work, or be seen to work, to these parameters; yet May (1991) has demonstrated the implementation gap that can ensue between managers and 'the front line service', and the desire of the front line to hold onto its fast-eroding autonomy within this kind of conflict. The current situation has all the ingredients of potential organisational disequilibrium which Boswell (1985), drawing upon organisational theorists March and Simon (1958), has characterised elsewhere as an imbalance of inducements (aspects of participation desired by the organisation's participants – in this case, the caring role) and contributions (aspects of participation that are inputs to the organisation's production function, but that generally have negative utility to the participants – in this case the controlling role). If equilibrium is to have any chance of being maintained then the contributions need either to be reduced or some of them to be reconstrued as inducements. To put it another way, some of the controlling function needs to be replaced by more opportunity to assume the caring function. Alternatively a section of the controlling function needs to be reconstructed as part of the social work brief.

VI   The continued relevance of social work in probation

Social work is a term which has always been notoriously difficult to define. Davies (1985) notes that it is a professional activity which can 'usually be characterised as operating in response to human needs'. These needs, Davies goes on to point out, 'might as often be those of society as of the individual in distress', a clear reminder of the unique skill of the probation officer encapsulated in Chapter 4's title, 'Holding the Balance between Court and Client'. Equally, however, as David Faulkner, at the time Deputy Secretary at the Home Office, once famously pointed out at a criminal justice conference on probation issues, 'It is not always clear what a social work base does and does not mean' (Faulkner 1989). In the end perhaps the nearest one can get to a definition of social work in the probation service is to state that it is what probation officers say they do with their clients. Although, since our 1988 surveys were completed, probation services have moved, in line with social services departments, into the role of case and resource managers operating in a more narrowly defined field of community-based sentences, supervision of prisoners, and family court welfare work specialisms, they are still utilising all the social work skills which they themselves described in Chapter 4. For example, when preparing a pre-sentence report, a probation officer is drawing on considerable skills of assessment to determine the seriousness of the offence committed, the client's suitability for one or more community sentence, and the ways in which such a sentence can help to reduce the risk of re-offending. None of the information required for this assessment process can be gained reliably without the successful employment of communication skills as described in section II of Chapter 4 where 'the officers spoke of the

207

importance of putting them (clients) at their ease in order to create an atmosphere of trust and confidentiality in which the purpose of the PO/client contact could then be explored.' Coherent writing skills are required, as is an ability to liaise appropriately with all other criminal justice professionals involved, and to 'hold the balance' between court and client. An understanding of the causes of crime and of the methods most likely to reduce its committal by a particular individual is also a necessary concluding ingredient of the report. It may prove to be the case that a straight two year probation order with regular one-to-one counselling is going to be the most effective means of helping someone with a long history of relationship loss, who fears group situations, to avoid 'comfort' stealing from the local department store. Social work methods and the traditional valuing of the individual are still at work here, and would form part of the sentence proposal, though their scope has decreased because the offence now has to be 'serious enough' to merit a community sentence which itself should correspond to the seriousness by the degree of 'restriction on liberty' it offers (Criminal Justice Act 1991, Section 3). Probation areas' own resource-conscious targetting procedures also mean that first and probably second offenders are likely to be excluded from probation order proposals. Assessment skills which take all these factors into account are thus all-important in the new sentencing climate.

At the same time we have seen in Chapter 3 that specialism is fast becoming the norm in the probation service, and by the time they have served five years most officers will have entered a specialist field. Some of them were quite happy to point out that specialisms such as Community Service, hostel work, and the newer probation order conditions have already diluted social work traditions and pushed the discipline of social work to its furthermost boundaries. The clear implication for this growing scenario is that there is the opportunity for those who are comfortable at the controlling end of the care/control continuum to move there, leaving the familiar balance-holding ground to those who prefer to be free to employ traditional social work methods of intervention as appropriate.

VII   Reconceiving social work on the care/control continuum

Perhaps, then, there is a way forward which entails categorising the main tasks of the service on, say, a 10 point scale along the care/control continuum, not along the lines of a sentencing tariff, but in terms of the likely predominance of the care/control ingredients in each task. Thus, Community Service which has no social work intervention brief, might rate at point 10 on the scale; straight one-to-one probation supervision at point 1; and court work, the classic setting for the balance-holding role, somewhere in the middle. In this way, the service could spread out its personnel, taking proper account of professional development needs and interests, so that the inducement/contribution equilibrium was met through a numerical allocation rather than through the (often uneasy) struggle of each individual officer. This activity does, however, entail some bald and realistic statements about which tasks do and which tasks do not entail the high levels of non-punitive communication/ assessment/intervention talked of by our respondents in a way which helpfully extends the traditional 'helping people' understanding of the term 'social work'. Such a concession probably represents the biggest shift which the service currently needs to make if it both desires to reduce its potentially stifling ambiguity and is genuinely content to continue operating within the narrowed-down confines prescribed by the new Criminal Justice Act.

If the service is to make such a shift then clearly qualifying training must move in parallel. Should the existing machinery move to equip qualifying probation officers to deliver their variety of services in a more applied fashion? Bearing in mind the need for practice relevance, it would be possible to introduce a tri-modular system of training in which all probation students took as their foundation module applied criminology and penology. They would be introduced to the sociological and psychological causes of crime and to the system that is set up to deal with those who offend. Thus they would have their framework for operation. In the second module they would acquire a set of skills to become operational, which would centre around the broad areas of communication, assessment and intervention and the application of these to specific probation service tasks with the addition of ingredients such as rendering people accountable, and risk-management which are key factors at the controlling end of probation work but tend to be taught only peripherally. The third and final module would offer students (and perhaps experienced probation officers too) a range of choices from areas in which the probation service has frequently shown itself lacking in expertise – public relations; advertising; marketing; trade union studies; fund-raising; accountancy; information technology; and journalism. The end-product would be a body of professionals clear about its framework, competent in 'good resource management', still possibly generically taught in social work methods but with specialised training on their application, and able to engage with key sections of society in a more effective and expert fashion than is currently the case. When thinking through the implications of the research findings in 1989, such possibilities began to spring to mind, and are surely even more pertinent as the service seeks to explain and justify its activities to a general public which sometimes seems willing to throw its deviants to the lions.

VIII Conclusion

It is important to emphasise that the ideas expressed in this book are not the product of outside observers but have been almost wholly generated by serving probation officers and social work educators. They have clear notions of the tasks of contemporary probation practice and the skills, knowledge and qualities needed to practise them. Crucially they see social work as a necessary and desirable ingredient in their work and need to find a way to ensure its survival within current managerial and criminal justice frameworks. For this reason it is suggested that the service engages in an honest analysis of the 'social work' components of each of its tasks, ranks them accordingly along the care/control continuum, and sustains its organisational equilibrium by allocating staff to tasks in line with their interests and professional development needs. Our research suggested that, in a rudimentary way, this is already happening and is waiting to be built upon. Qualifying training programmes now should respond accordingly, acquainting students with additional non-social work skills required for some of these tasks, and equipping them for competent, confident engagement with key sections of society. At all costs, however, the probation service must guard against degenerating from pragmatism into powerlessness as it wrestles with the latest set of changes and uncertainties. As Handy (1992) comments, 'Change is *not* heady when it happens to you – just frightening'. Response to fear, as many offenders know, can vary from head-on challenge to paralysis. The probation service has always had a knack of finding its own characteristic niche in penal policy, but it is getting harder all the time and personal integrity and staff morale are at risk if social work disappears without trace and punitive philosophy is implicitly accepted wholesale. Strong professional leadership which keeps in touch with the essential 'helping' motivation of the majority of staff, holds purpose *and* values at the centre, provides clear policy guidelines, codes of practice and coherent systems of staff appraisal and in-service training can serve to keep probation areas interacting energetically with change. This is vital if reflective, humane professionals such as those who contributed to our research study are to sustain the service's longstanding role as the proverbial bridgebuilder between those who make the law and those who fall foul of it.

Bibliography

Boswell, G.R. (1982), *Goals in the Probation and After-Care Service,* unpublished Ph.D. Thesis, Liverpool University.

Boswell G.R. (1985), *Care, Control and Accountability in the Probation Service,* Social Work Monographs, University of East Anglia, Norwich.

Boswell G.R. (1989), 'Holding the Balance between Court and Client', Research Report 4, in *Skills, Knowledge and Qualities in Probation Practice,* Social Work Monographs, University of East Anglia, Norwich.

Bottoms, A.E. and McWilliams, W. (Summer 1979), 'A Non-Treatment Paradigm for Probation Practice', *British Journal of Social Work.*

British Association of Social Workers (1985), *Code of Ethics,* BASW.

Bromley, P.M. and Lowe, N.V. (1987), *Bromley's Family Law* (7th Edition), London, Butterworths.

Central Council for Education & Training in Social Work (1975), *Education and Training for Social Work,* Paper 10, CCETSW.

Central Council for Education & Training in Social Work (1986), *Three Years and Different Routes,* Paper 20.6, CCETSW.

Central Council for Education & Training in Social Work (1989), *Improving Standards in Practice Learning. Regulations and Guidance for the Approval of Agencies and the Accreditation and Training of Practice Teachers,* Paper 26.3, CCETSW.

Central Council for Education & Training in Social Work (1991), *Dip.SW Rules and Requirements for the Diploma in Social Work* (2nd Edition), Paper 30, CCETSW.

Coleman, D.A. (1989), *Home Office Review of Probation Training,* Home Office.

Davies, M. (1984), 'Training – What we think of it now', *Social Work Today,* Vol. 15, No. 20, 24 January.

Davies, M. (1985), *The Essential Social Worker: A Guide to Positive Practice,* London, Heinemann Educational Books (2nd Edition).

Davies, M. & Wright, A. (1989), 'Probation Training: A Consumer Perspective', Research Report 1, in *Skills, Knowledge and Qualities in Probation Practice,* Social Work Monographs, University of East Anglia, Norwich.

Davies, M. & Wright, A. (1989), 'The Changing Face of Probation', Research Report 3, in *Skills, Knowledge and Qualities in Probation Practice,* Social Work Monographs, University of East Anglia, Norwich.

Elliott, C. (1988), *Signs of our Times,* Marshall Pickering.

Handy, C. (1992), *Waiting for the Mountain to Move,* Arrow Books Ltd.

Harris, R.J. (1992), *Crime, Criminal Justice and the Probation Service,* London and New York, Tavistock/Routledge.

Home Office (1962), *Report of the Departmental Committee on the Probation Service* (The Morison Report), Cmd.1650, London, HMSO.

Home Office (1974), *Report of the Advisory Council on the Penal System, Young Adult Offenders* (The Younger Report), London, HMSO.

Home Office (1984), *Probation Service in England and Wales: Statement of National Objectives and Priorities,* London, Home Office.

Home Office (1992), *The Probation Service: Statement of Purpose*, London, Home Office.

McGuire, J. & Priestley, P. (1985), *Offending Behaviour: Skills & Stratagems for Going Straight,* London, Batsford.

March, J.G. & Simon, H.A. (1958), *Organisations*, New York, Wiley.

May, T. (1991), *Probation: Politics, Policy and Practice*, Milton Keynes, Philadelphia, Open University Press.

National Association of Probation Officers (1992), *CJA 1991 and National Standards: Limiting the Damage,* NAPO.

Nellis, M. (June 1992), 'Probation Training after 1991: The Need for Debate', *Probation Journal* Special Issue.

Nellis, M. (1992), *CCETSW, Criminal Justice and the Idea of a Probation Stream,* Birmingham University, Faculty of Commerce & Social Science, Discussion Paper Series G, No 5.

Parker, H. (June 1992), 'Saving Community Penalties: Remaking Sentencing Tariffs', *Probation Journal* Special Issue.

Raine, J.R. & Willson, M.J. (1993), *Managing Criminal Justice,* London, Harvester Wheatsheaf.

Walker, H. & Beaumont, B. (1981), *Probation Work: Critical Theory and Socialist Practice,* Oxford, Basil Blackwell.

Whiteside, J. (1939), 'The Duties of Probation Officers under the Criminal Justice Bill', *Probation Journal,* Vol. 3, No. 6.

Wright, A. & Davies, M. (1989), 'Becoming a Probation Officer', Research Report 2, in *Skills, Knowledge and Qualities in Probation Practice,* Social Work Monographs, University of East Anglia, Norwich.